Snazzy Seniors

The Fastest-Growing Population in the United States

Cheri McDaniel

Baton Rouge, LA

Copyright © 2018 by Cheri McDaniel

All rights reserved. No part of this book may be reproduced in any form without written permission from the publishers, except by reviewers and authors, who may quote brief passages in a review to be printed in a book, newspaper or magazine.

ISBN-13: 978-1-944583-20-0

Published by Laurel Rose Publishing
www.laurelrosepublishing.com
laurelrosepublishing@gmail.com

Steve Shamburger, Illustrator
steveshamburger@blogspot.com

To my parents

Ruth and Arthur McDaniel

who taught by example

HOW TO LIVE

and

HOW TO GIVE

CONTENTS

Preface

Acknowledgments

Part I. History Makers Tell Their Stories: World War I, World War II, Korea, Vietnam, and Desert Storm

Section 1. War and Marriage

1. Murray Hawkins Survives Pearl Harbor Bombing, Marries Julia Welles by Trans-Pacific Telephone……………………………....*16*

2. Dick and Ellen Fox: USOs and Live Oaks…………….…………*21*

3. Joyce Jackson Finds True Love in 10 Days, to Last for 63 Years ……………………………………………………………………*26*

4. Woman Stands behind Her Important Man: Mary and Duke Faulkner……………………………………………………………*29*

5. Parker and Edna St. Amant: Love at First Sight……………..*35*

6. Pete Petersen: FBI Special Agent Makes the Big Catch………*41*

7. Determined to Serve His Country: Sidney Flynn……………..*46*

8. Lieutenant Michael Kearns, B-29 Navigator, Killed; His Wife Millie Pregnant with First Child……………………………………*50*

Section 2. Our Greatest Generation

9. Leon Standifer, Recipient of the Purple Heart and French Legion of Honor..*56*

10. Destined to Serve Their Country: Lt. Col. Philemon St. Amant Paves the Way for Col. Philemon St. Amant II......................*61*

11. Col. Philemon St. Amant II..*65*

12. Lt. Col. Ralph Stephenson's 31-Year Career: World War II, Korea, and Vietnam..*69*

13. Eighteen-Year-Old Aspiring Pilots Reunite after 73 Years....*80*

14. Capt. Jerry Black: US Army Tours Officer, Golfer, Fisherman, and Lover...*83*

15. English Royal Air Force Flying Officer Jack Bartle............*87*

16. Lt. Col. Joseph William Carmena................................*92*

17. Ageless Warriors..*95*

18. Lt. Shaun McGarry: Honoring Our Veterans....................*98*

Section 3. Military Women at St. James Place

19. Women in the World Wars......................................*103*

20. St. James Place Resident Women Who Served in the Military *104*

Part II. Socialization of Seniors

Section 1. Personal Reflections on Senior Care through the Years

21. The Guest House (Nursing Home), 1966–1971................*111*

22. The Catholic Presbyterian Apartments, 1973–1992...........*112*

Section 2. Eat, Drink, and Remarry

23. Nonagenarian Bert Knight Marries Octogenarian Doris Akers *115*

24. Walking Their Dogs: Arthur and Joyce Dickerson………...*120*

25. Families That Play Together Stay Together: Will and Margaret Roussel……………………………………………………………*123*

26. Esther Lynch, an Inspiration to All She Meets……………..*128*

Part III. The Choice Is Yours: Live Life to Its Fullest or Just Exist

Section 1. Shedding of Responsibilities: Time to Enhance Your Life

27. Live Life Well..*136*
by Janet Dewey

Section 2. How Two Generations Chose Senior Living: The Judge Jess Johnson Family

28. Ada Dowdell Johnson..*143*

29. Jess and Ada Johnson's First-Born Son, Jess Johnson Jr.....*147*

30. Jess and Ada's Younger Son, David Johnson..................*153*

Section 3. Choosing to Live Life Well: Surround Yourself with Beauty and Music

31. From Carnegie Hall to St. James Place: Gwen Bruton..........*159*

32. The Camellia Lady: Mary Jane Kahao........................*164*

33. Legendary Jazz Artist: Jimmy Jules.........................*167*

34. Singing Praises to God: Claudette Thigpen..................*172*

Section 4. Personal Enrichment

35. Renowned Artist Byron Levy and Wife Carol..................*178*

36. Louise Couvillion, a Role Model for Successful Aging........*182*

37. Marjorie Colomb: Mistress of Ceremonies and Tour Director *189*

38. Different Strokes for Different Folks: Mr. John Whitson, a Traditionalist...*192*

39. A Morning with Senior Olympians Julia Hawkins, 101, and Jack Bartle, 93..*198*

40. Julia Hawkins Breaks Two Senior Olympics World Records *203*

Part IV. Living a Life of Significance, with Purpose

Section 1. Purposeful Living

41. Soul Purpose: Seniors with Strong Reasons to Live Often Live Stronger..*209*
by Judith Graham

42. India, Moscow, USSR, and Hong Kong: AP Bureau Chief Henry Bradsher... ....*213*

43. Jack ("Pete") Sebastian Serving Others at St. James *Place*..*236*

44. Messengers for God: Jerry and Nancy Dumas...…............*240*

45. T. O. Perry, a Dedicated Community Leader...... ... ...…*246*

Section 2. Rotarian Seniors Serving Humanity

46. Mr. and Mrs. Rotary: Mike and Martha Collins...............*251*

47. 9/11: Helen Reisler, President of the Rotary Club of New York, Becomes a General..……......*258*

48. Clarence Prudhomme: Rotarian, Churchman, Molder of Youth, and Servant to Mankind.......................................*267*

49. Lucy Bowers, LSU Professor of Law: Championing Rights of

Children, Juveniles Given Life
Sentences, and Sex-Trafficking Victims.................................*272*

50. Rotarian and Humanitarian Patricia Robinson.................*281*

51. Jay Brown: Awarded the Rotary Meritorious Service Award
....*285*

Part V. Confronting Death

Section 1. Professionals Weigh In

52. Living in the Shadow of Death.......................................*294*
by Janice McDermott, M.Ed, LCSW

53. A Few Hospice Experiences..*308*
by Kathryn Grigsby, Retired CEO, Hospice of Baton Rouge

54. The Gift of Grief..*312*
by W. Nicholas Abraham, PhD, LPC

Section 2. Facing Your Own Mortality

55. Margaret Oswald, Girded for Life and Death...................*317*

56. Henry and Monica Bradsher Take Turns Confronting Mortality
....*322*

57. Sharing an Afternoon of Faith with My Friend Maria Konert
....*329*

58. Walking through the Shadow: My Personal *Journal*............*334*

59. Loving Gifts for Our Family...............................343

Part VI. Centenarians

60. 105-Year-Old Millie Saucier Wood Gladney: Doing It Millie's Way………………………………………...............346

61. "*I Remember* . . . : Life Stories by Marnie": Margaret Grier Beste, Age 102…………………………………………...356

62. Lumina "Mina" Newchurch, an Angel in Our Midst………363

63. Eldine Colligan's Love of Life…………………………...369

64. Dr. Ed Hawkins, Born July 19, 1917……………………..374

Epilogue: Dr. Ed Hawkins and Eldine Colligan Elected Mardi Gras King and Queen………………………………………...378

Recommended Reading

PREFACE

Writing this book has become more exciting as I have listened to the stories of seniors I have interviewed. Many are fellow residents at St. James Place Retirement Community in Baton Rouge, where I have lived since 2008. Perhaps their children or grandchildren have heard their stories. Unfortunately, many seniors have not written their life stories, which would, in time, benefit future generations who might be looking for a sense of connection and purpose in an uncertain world. Regardless of your age, it is never too late to begin writing your memoirs, a great therapeutic endeavor. You will be reminded of many events in our history. Through this book you have the opportunity to meet those who, in many cases, were history makers, laying the foundation for today's world. Let's not allow social media to ignore and/or simply toss out the values many of us were taught by our ancestors. Values will never go out of style!

ACKNOWLEDGMENTS

I am grateful to all the seniors at St. James Place and elsewhere who shared their stories and memories with me. They have been a constant inspiration and are the reason I wanted to write *Snazzy Seniors*. In particular, I wish to thank:

Jack Bartle
Margaret Grier Beste
Jerry Black
Lucy Bowers
Henry and Monica Bradsher
Jay Brown
Pete Poirrier
Gwen Bruton
McGarry
Joseph William "Bill" Carmena
Eldine Colligan
Morgan
Mike and Martha Collins
Newchurch
Marjorie Colomb
Oswald
Louise Couvillion
Arthur and Joyce Dickerson
Jerry and Nancy Dumas
Duke and Mary Faulkner
Sidney Flynn
Robinson
Dick and Ellen Fox
Roussel
Mildred "Millie" Wood Gladney

Bert and Doris Knight
Maria Konert
June Lank
Mary Ann Larson
Byron and Carol Levy
Esther Lynch and

Shaun and Katie

Irma Moore
William "Bill"

Lumina "Mina"

Tom and Margaret

T. O. and Linda Perry
Pete Petersen
Clarence Prudhomme
Helen Reisler
Patricia "Pat"

Will and Margaret

Josephine "Jo" Salter

Frank and Millie Hathorn
Dr. Ed Hawkins
Amant
Julia Hawkins
Ada Dowdell Johnson II
David and Anne Johnson
Jess and Peggy Johnson
Jimmy Jules
Mary Jane Kahao

Jack "Pete" Sebastian
Parker and Edna St.

Philemon St. Amant
Philemon St. Amant

Leon Standifter
Ralph Stephenson
Claudette Thigpen
John Whitson

    I am also grateful to W. Nicholas Abraham, Janet Dewey, Kathryn Grigsby, and Janice McDermott for the essays they wrote for this book. Judith Graham graciously granted my request to reprint her article "Soul Purpose" from her column "Navigating Aging," on the Kaiser Health News website. Thanks also to Richard Meek of the *Catholic Commentator* for allowing me to quote portions of his December 9, 2016, article on Mina Newchurch. I am also grateful to the *Baton Rouge Advocate* for permission to print Günter Bischof's "Guest Column" of December 29, 2016, and parts of George Morris's May 1, 2017, article, "'You Ready? Strap Yourself In': Ancient Warbird Takes Veterans Back in Time." The USA Track and Field website allowed me to reproduce their press release on Julia Hawkins from July 15, 2017.

    The award-winning illustrator David Norwood III (DIN), who for many years drew cartoons for the *Baton Rouge Advocate/State-Times,* graciously contributed numerous illustrations and also designed the symbolic front cover, Walking Toward Eternity.

    Finally, I wish to thank Michelle Dewey, Amber Bryant Campagna, and Patricia "Pat" Robinson, who gave generously of their time and computer skills in putting this book together.

Part I

History Makers Tell Their Stories: World War I, World War II, Korea, Vietnam, and Desert Storm

Section 1

War and Marriage

The history of our world has been framed by wars, and rumors of wars continue. Wars bring a sense of urgency, a heightened sense of wanting to join the fight to preserve our freedom and way of life.

Most of our oldest seniors are the offspring of soldiers returning from World War I. They in turn, in many cases during World War II, signed up while still in high school, too young to be drafted. At the same time, as revealed in many of their stories, they sought a mate to care for them, to write letters every day—a desire for connection and the fuel of which dreams are made, to begin a brighter future together, once the war ends. . . .

Psychologists are still trying to understand why so many of these young marriages, most before the age of 21, have lasted for so many years, versus the continuing rise of divorces since that time. A priest I talked with recently attributed the divorces to the fact that millennials have not faced the problems and difficult times their parents did, and so, when problems arise in a marriage, easily say, "I didn't buy into this."

Now professionals admit they have no way to predict how the trend of today's late marriages after age 30, and even later births of children, will play out in society.

MURRAY HAWKINS SURVIVES PEARL HARBOR BOMBING, MARRIES JULIA WELLES BY TRANS-PACIFIC TELEPHONE

Murray Hawkins, Julia's college boyfriend, had received a BS in chemistry and an MS in physics from Louisiana State University (LSU). The tides of war were looming and Murray, along with perhaps thirty others from across the United States with master's degrees in physics, were hired and sent from Washington, DC, to work for the US Navy in the Pacific, demagnetizing naval ships.

He was in Pearl Harbor during the surprise bombing, in all the chaos; it would be an agonizing week before it was known that Murray survived. He was to be commissioned into the Navy as ensign in twelve months, at which time he would qualify for leave to return to the States and marry Julia. Wartime took precedence, and he was advised that once commissioned, he would be sent to follow and demagnetize the US fleet.

Once Murray was commissioned and ready to be shipped out, he asked Julia to marry him, though oceans apart. Considering the uncertainty of wartime, they decided not to wait to pledge their love in marriage. Their wedding vows were transmitted by Trans-Pacific telephone on November 29, 1942. A year would pass before the newlyweds saw each other.

Murray was sent to Washington State, and Julia met him there. They had three long-awaited months together while Murray awaited an assignment to a ship still under construction. They were separated another year, as Murray was sent back to the South Pacific. He was reassigned as a lieutenant to head a warfare test station in the Solomon Islands, where he was joined by Julia. The war ended later that year.

World War II Ends

Murray and Julia returned to Baton Rouge, where Murray was employed by Ethyl Corporation for about a year before he began teaching petroleum engineering at his alma mater, LSU. They lived in campus housing for three years. During vacations and days off, Murray and Julia built their home. They moved in with their two sons, Lad and Warren, and the family grew with the birth of their two daughters, Margaret and Julia ("Jugie").

The beautiful gardens they developed and lovingly cared for continue to be a joy for Julia and her family, guests, and passersby. All of their close-knit family loved the outdoors. They kept bikes strapped to the side of their car, to teach their four children the love of cycling. They also hiked, fished, swam, and golfed.

Murray later became head of the Department of Petroleum Engineering at LSU. After his retirement at age 60, in 1977, LSU renamed the department as the Craft and Hawkins Department of Petroleum Engineering. Murray died in 2012 at age 95, and Julia continues to live surrounded by many family mementos.

Retracing Julia's Steps

Born in Lake Geneva, Wisconsin, a suburb of Chicago, Julia began pioneering at an early age. Her parents, Julius and Margaret Welles, and her mother's sister and husband, Dorothy and George Goodman and their son Jimmy, came by boat from Chicago, down the mighty Mississippi River to Morgan City, Louisiana. George became the editor of the *Enterprise* newspaper and later served as president of the Louisiana Press Association in Ponchatoula.

The two families planned to open a shell-dredging business, to supply shells for road building. A hurricane ended that business and they moved to Ponchatoula, where they opened a summer resort on the scenic Tangipahoa River.

As the resort was mainly occupied in the summer months, Julia's enterprising parents moved to Baton Rouge, where her mother ran a large household. In addition to son John and nephew Jimmy, a couple of the boys' friends also enrolled at LSU boarded with them. Julia entered Baton Rouge High, and her younger sister Mickey was an elementary student. After Julia graduated from high school in 1934, she earned a BS in education from LSU and taught for three or four years.

Writing Her Life Story

Julia began writing her life story when she was 60 and continued until she was 80, providing copies to all her family members. She was inspired to trace and write about her family from its early roots in England, when they came to the New World in 1620 on a ship named *The Handmaiden*.

At the time, Julia felt that by staying active and involved, she would live to age 80, and that would be a good place to stop! She said so many interesting things continued to happen that she kept writing. . . .

Celebrating Julia's 100th Birthday

Julia's 100th birthday was celebrated with over two hundred family members and friends at LSU's Lod Cook Alumni Center, on a brilliant, sunshiny day, February 14, 2016. It was a Valentine celebration of her actual February 10 birth date. In true LSU spirit, Mike the Tiger mascot paid a special visit to congratulate and dance with Julia. The lively music played by a New Orleans jazz orchestra continued to lure Julia, with the flush of a debutante, onto the dance floor for just one more dance with her grandson.

When her 101st birthday rolled around this year, plus the Senior Olympics competition, there was much more to add to her journal.

Julia continues to work in her garden and care for the prize bonsai she has lovingly trimmed for many years. She has the luxury of having her evening meal and breakfast prepared by a companion, who spends each night. One of Julia's grandchildren had a picture of Murray's face transferred to a pillow cover, which Julia sleeps with in memory of her beloved husband. His body, as well as hers, will be donated to the LSU Medical School in New Orleans.

Julia's nearest child, also named Julia, lives in Lafayette. Gregarious Julia maintains a bevy of neighborhood friends. She is a member of St. James Episcopal Church, the Bonsai Society, and a book club. No moss is growing under Julia Hawkins's feet!

For more of Julia's continuing adventures, don't miss her

other story later in this book: "A Morning with Senior Olympians Julia Hawkins, 101, and Jack Bartle, 93."

Takeaways

A successful marriage requires falling in love many times, always with the same person.
 —Mignon McLaughlin

Your sacred space is where you can find yourself over and over again.
 —Joseph Campbell

The privilege of a lifetime is being who you are.
 —Joseph Campbell

DICK AND ELLEN FOX:
USOs AND LIVE OAKS

St. James Place's 52-acre campus is anchored by the Duplantier live oak, circa 1776. It was registered in the Live Oak Society in 1983 when St. James Place was built. When the Foxes moved to St. James in 2007, they chose their second-floor apartment adjacent to the historic oak. The home Ellen's family built, and where she lived until marriage, had a registered live oak named Holly Garden. When Standard Oil, now Exxon, enlarged its refinery site by purchasing the two adjacent streets and homes, the Smiths' historic live oak was carefully protected, while the houses were demolished.

The historic Duplantier live oak outside their window, their many friends, and the amenities of St. James Place have added joy to the Foxes' lives, while likely contributing to their longevity. Dick is now 95 and Ellen is 90. "We could not be happier living in our own home," Ellen praises life at St. James Place.

Their only child, Kathleen, is married to Dale Redman, a retired CPA, and lives nearby. Kathleen taught at Trinity Episcopal School for a number of years.

Dick and Ellen have three grandsons and six great-grandchildren—two boys and four girls.

Their Early Years

Ellen Smith, an only child, was born at the original Our Lady of the Lake Hospital, situated across the lake from the Louisiana State Capitol. Her father was employed by Standard Oil Company. Ellen graduated from Baton Rouge High and entered LSU in 1943, majoring in home economics.

Dick Fox was born in Whistler, Ohio. His father was a farmer and cattleman. Dick is the youngest of three boys and three girls.

Baton Rouge's Role in World War II

It was 1942. Baton Rouge's Harding Field was a base for the Army Air Force, training pilots to fly without radar. Community members, eager to do their part in wartime, established a local USO on North Boulevard, with a dance floor and jukebox to help entertain the servicemen. At the larger American Legion Hall on Florida Street, volunteers periodically invited groups of LSU female students to entertain and dance with servicemen. Most of Baton Rouge's school and community dances were held there.

The First United Methodist Church, located at the corner of North and East Boulevards, played an important role in the lives of the airmen. A book celebrating the church's 175th anniversary, published in 2015, shares a verified poignant and symbolic story. Pilots flying without radar in the night skies surrounding Baton Rouge used the lighted cross on the church tower to find their way home.

An unsubstantiated story is also circulated periodically, of startled auto passengers seeing daredevil pilots (in training) fly under the upper steel arch of the US 190 highway bridge over the Mississippi River.

Ellen's mother was a volunteer chaperone in the Military Maids, a grass-roots organization providing entertainment and relaxation for the servicemen. She, as did others, often called the chaplain at Harding Airfield to invite a specified number of men to come to their home for a meal.

A Chance Meeting Lives on 75 Years Later

Fifteen-year-old Ellen, feeling older than her years, would go to dances her parents chaperoned and sometimes was allowed to dance. At the 1942 Thanksgiving dance, a never-to-be-forgotten day, Ellen met Dick Fox, who asked her to dance. Their five-year age difference evaporated; the young couple was smitten from that day forward, a love evident seventy-five years later when they are seen together at St. James Place.

Dick was drafted in the Army Air Corps immediately after high school graduation and was sent to Baton Rouge. The day before Ellen graduated from high school in 1943, eleven grades at that time, Dick was sent on maneuvers in Tennessee. Ellen visited him that summer.

Ellen wrote letters daily, and there were phone calls. However, they did not see each other from late 1943 until January 1946.

Youth obviously matured earlier, after growing up in the Great Depression. If not, they were forced into maturity as they donned uniforms to fight in World War II. Their early marriages, consummated before age 20 in many cases, resulted in a high percentage of successful marriages that withstand the passing of time. Ellen and Dick's 70-year marriage is such a love story.

World War II Ends, Homeward Bound!

It was fall 1945 when Dick and thousands of other soldiers were released from their respective branches of service. They filled multitudes of ships to cross the Atlantic to New York, where they would travel home by train. Only one captain defied orders not to risk crossing the stormy Atlantic Ocean, determined to get his valiant solders home for Christmas. Dick was on this lone ship crossing the dangerous ocean that day. After arriving in New York, he traveled by train and arrived at his Ohio home on Christmas Day. Next he boarded another train, with plans in place to be met by Ellen's parents in Hammond en route to Baton Rouge to see his future bride. Ellen had chosen to welcome him in Baton Rouge. Unfortunately, Dick slept through the stop and disembarked in Ponchatoula, and took a cab to Baton Rouge.

The reunited couple took a romantic trip to Lake Pontchartrain shortly thereafter, where Dick proposed marriage and placed an engagement ring on her finger. It was January 1946. They were married that May at Ellen's church, First Presbyterian Church on North Boulevard.

GI Bill: College and Living Expenses, $90 a Month

Dick enrolled at LSU. The birth of daughter Kathleen further stretched the monthly stipend of $90.

After graduation, he worked as an accountant for Standard Oil Company and retired with thirty-five years of service. This gave them time with their grand- and great-grandchildren. The Foxes were avid travelers, across the United States and on cruises to the Caribbean.

Takeaways

Never give a sword to a man who can't dance.
        —Muhammad Ali Jinnah

Opportunity dances with those already on the dance floor.
        —H. Jackson Brown Jr.

If you really fulfill the royal law according to the scripture, "You shall love your neighbor as yourself," you are doing well.
        —James 2:8

Read more about the Foxes:

"Expressions of Love in All Forms across the Capital City, Just in Time for Valentine's Day," by Kayla Randall, *Baton Rouge 225 Magazine,* February 1, 2017.

JOYCE JACKSON FINDS TRUE LOVE IN 10 DAYS, TO LAST FOR 63 YEARS

Joyce's hometown was Miami, Florida. It was wartime, and there were uniformed Navy men everywhere! At the beach with her sister Zelda and one of her sister's boyfriends, she met another sailor, Leicester Landon, who was enrolled in the Navy's sub-chasing school. The foursome went to dinner that night. Joyce continued seeing Leicester for ten days, at which time he received orders to leave for New York. Joyce said she knew he was the one when he asked her to become his fiancée.

Fortunately, Joyce's family had had opportunities to meet their future son-in-law. While in New York, awaiting orders to leave for the South Pacific, Leicester purchased a set of rings and sent them to Joyce's father, asking him to put the engagement ring on her finger.

They did not see each other for about a year. Leicester's brother, stationed in France with the Army, was killed in action. Leicester was sent to Folsom, Louisiana, with his brother's body for burial. Joyce came by train from Miami to New Orleans, to attend the funeral in Folsom.

It was an impromptu decision to marry while at Leicester's family ranch home in Folsom. Joyce traveled to Los Angeles to be with Leicester while awaiting his orders to return to the South Pacific.

Tragedy Hits after Release from Navy

Ten days after Leicester was released from the Navy, the couple was in Folsom with their fourteen-month-old son, Lewis. Their car was packed, and all the relatives were telling each other goodbye. No one had noticed the car door was ajar, and that Lewis had slipped out. He had wandered to a small creek below and drowned.

Leicester Becomes a Veterinarian

Leicester enrolled in the University of Georgia with plans to become a veterinarian. The couple used the GI Bill for support, supplemented by Joyce's employment at the university as office manager. Their second son, Lester, and a daughter, Victoria, were born while they lived in Georgia.

Leicester's love of animals while growing up on the Folsom farm, coupled with his love of family, prompted him to begin his veterinary practice in nearby Covington. This is where their last child, Lawrence, was born.

They moved to St. James Place in 2001, and Leicester died in 2008. Joyce has two grandsons and one great-grandson.

Takeaways

Live life to the fullest, and focus on the positive.
    —Matt Cameron

We must be willing to let go of the life we planned so as to accept the one that is waiting for us.
    —Joseph Campbell

Life is 10 percent what happens to you and 90 percent how you react to it.
    —Charles R. Swindoll

WOMAN STANDS BEHIND HER IMPORTANT MAN: MARY AND DUKE FAULKNER

You readers—and perhaps Duke for just a moment—will wonder where I got that title. Read on and you will follow Duke's amazing career around the world. You will see that by Mary's quiet strength, her *standing behind her important man*, she made this possible. . . . They are truly a team, married for seventy years. Duke has now taken the lead with a gentle hand to protect Mary as she walks with, thus far, untreatable vertigo.

I am sure many said they were too young. Mary and Duke were both attending high school in Beech Grove, Arkansas, when they started dating. Duke was seventeen, and Mary Ida Hammond was only fifteen. They married the following year, shortly after she graduated.

Mary's father was the postmaster of Beech Grove. Her sister was born when Mary was thirteen. Duke had two sisters, but was raised as an only child by a single mom.

Duke Serves in Korean War

After they married, the Faulkners moved to St. Louis to work at menial jobs until Duke was of age to be drafted in 1952. He served almost two years of active duty in Korea.

Upon his return, Duke attended Arkansas State University in Jonesboro, using his GI Bill, coupled with Mary's income as an office clerk. He graduated in three years with a BS in agricultural engineering and went on to receive his master's degree in agricultural engineering from LSU. He joined the LSU faculty in 1959 and was stationed at the Crowley Rice Experimental Station.

Mary and Duke welcomed their first son, Bryan, in 1961. Brett was born in 1963.

Mary, *the Woman* . . .

Not only had Mary helped fund Duke's college education, but she had birthed two sons. In the early 1960s, how many women would move to India with a one-year-old and a three-year-old? Duke was given a one-year assignment to India as a rice-processing consultant for the government, sponsored by the Ford Foundation. Now you understand Mary's *standing behind her man*, seldom easy, and continuing during his remarkable career which carried him back and forth across the world for thirty years until he retired at age 62.

A week after they arrived in India, baby Brett, their one-year-old son, was seriously ill. Mary went into the chapel at the Catholic hospital to pray. A small gray-haired woman took Mary into her arms and asked what was wrong. When she heard about the sick infant, she said, "He will be okay, everything will be all right." When Mary returned to her baby, his condition had improved, and he regained his health.

Not only was Brett healed, but Mary received perhaps a once-in-a-lifetime assurance of her depth of Christian faith as a Methodist.

Let's fast forward for a moment with this wonderful family. Brett is a retired police officer, living in Eunice, Louisiana, and Bryan works at a Christian academy in Baton Rouge. The Faulkners have three grandchildren and eight great-grandchildren.

Tiger Ransacks Villages, Killing Twelve Natives

Surely the news of the young American consultants had spread; who except the fearless young Americans could kill a man-eating tiger who had invaded a remote village, killing and eating twelve villagers? Surely the Americans would come to their rescue....

You guessed right, none other than Duke Faulkner, mounted on an elephant alongside the other consultant and led by an elephant driver, ride into the jungle, tiger hunting.

Duke had left behind a distressed Mary, with their young sons. They had no idea that this trek would take ten long days, much less what the outcome would be....

Back to this exciting journey. Their first encounter with wildlife bigger than themselves was a 450-pound boar. Duke handily shot the boar, which the villagers hung in a tree for a future celebration, hopefully of the killed tiger. A villager they met along the way pulled up his clothes to reveal a healed scar reaching from his foot to his buttocks. Imagine his encounter with this wild boar, over three times his weight; he was obviously fortunate to be alive. Another notch on Duke's belt! Once they neared where the tiger had been last seen, the villagers made a seat of vines in a tree for the two elephant riders. To lure the tiger, they tied out baby buffalo calves, which soon proved successful. Once the tiger was in sight, Duke's consultant partner shot and killed it.

Okay guys, no wild imagining here, I saw the proof! Duke showed me a photo of the tiger, backdropped by Duke, his fellow consultant with gun in hand, and the elephant driver; and oh yes, there was roasted boar that night, celebrating the killing of the man-eating tiger. The Americans had risen higher in esteem in India!

Hopefully Duke and I have convinced Mary that many villagers' lives were saved, thanks to the elephant-riding consultants. She fretted that animal rights' advocates might object. Surely human life takes precedence.

For ten years, Duke would return to India for a month each year, for rice farming consulting, under the auspices of the United Nations. To say that Mary kept the home fires burning is an understatement, as we perhaps remember what raising two sons can entail.

Duke's Expertise Spreads, Consults in 108 Countries

His expertise not limited to tiger hunting, Duke was an American ambassador, improving the growth of a major food source—rice. Think of how many more people do not go to bed hungry thanks to Duke Faulkner, our friend and fellow St. James Place resident since 2007.

His consultations, sponsored by the World Bank International and the Food and Agriculture arm of the United Nations, kept Duke traveling during his thirty-year career to such places as Burma, Egypt, Sierra Leone, and Liberia. Duke continued, after retiring at age 62, to volunteer to find solutions to agricultural problems in far-flung countries, such as Hungary and Nicaragua. I would love to see a world map highlighting the 108 countries Duke has worked in.

Mary, First Female Elected to Office in Acadia Parish

Mary was elected to the Acadia Parish School Board in 1976, a first for women at that time. Interesting that a woman could birth the children that attended such schools, yet not be considered to help make policies to aid their education. Or perhaps women had been reticent to run until spunky Mary became a role model. She was unopposed for a second term, which ended in 1984, the year Duke and Mary moved from Crowley to Baton Rouge.

Mary and Duke joined First United Methodist Church in Baton Rouge. Duke, as former director of the LSU Rice Research Station, has been honored as an outstanding alumnus of LSU and an honorary consultant with the World Bank and the United Nations. He is also an honorary member of the Louisiana Senate and House of Representatives.

St. James Place Residents

Mary and Duke moved to St. James Place in 2007. Duke has served on the building and grounds committee, organized Evening with the Experts speakers, and is an honorary member of the St. James Place Foundation Board.

Takeaways

Success is not the key to happiness. Happiness is the key to success. If you love what you are doing, you will be successful.
    —Albert Schweitzer

Integrity is the essence of everything successful.

—Buckminster Fuller

Successful people have a social responsibility to make the world a better place and not just take from it.
—Carrie Underwood

Postscript: **Mary Faulkner's Memorial Service, October 1, 2017**

The Duplantier Auditorium and hallway at St. James Place were filled with family, residents, and off-campus friends, celebrating Mary's life. Reverend Brady Whitton, senior pastor at First United Methodist Church, gave the eulogy, framed by beautiful renditions of hymns by the pianist.

Memories of Mary and Duke's love remain, holding hands as they walked about campus.

PARKER AND EDNA ST. AMANT: LOVE AT FIRST SIGHT

Can we truly believe in love at first sight? William Shakespeare, in *Twelfth Night,* proclaimed, "Whoever loves, loves at first sight." Romantic utterance, yes, but that isn't enough for me to believe it to be true. It is Parker and Edna's story that verifies that premise.

I know it did happen, and is still happening, after seventy years of marriage, as it is quietly exhibited, without words, evident to all who are privileged to know Parker and Edna. It is a well-known fact, however, that Edna is always quick to say, "And we're still madly in love."

You can tell I feel such first and lasting love is unexplainable, except for perhaps a few who have experienced it. Fewer still are willing to share such intimacy.

After reading Steve Jobs's testimony, I surmise that he likely was propelled by the love, peace, and tranquility of his personal life. He wrote, "As with all matters of the heart, you will know when you find it. And like any great relationship, it gets better and better as the years roll on." In the wedding ceremony, it is stated that *two are becoming one,* and this is theoretically true. However, as the years roll by, *two are seen as being one.*

Parker completed two 30-month periods of stateside service in the Army Air Corps as a bombardier, but the war ended before he was sent overseas. He came home and obtained a job with the Standard Oil Company of Louisiana, which granted him educational leave to enroll at LSU, using the GI Bill. Parker was also ready to settle down and raise a family. Accomplishing this, however, would require a wife, so he decided to start looking. Too much time had gone by, and he was eager to get started.

Parker Lost No Time Spotting His Girl!

It was September 1946, the beginning of the LSU fall semester. Standing outside the freshman Spanish classroom door, Parker saw a "good-looking chick" approaching, carrying a tennis racket over her shoulder. As she entered the door, he turned and went in immediately after her. Fate was in his favor, or perhaps it was the luckiest of the luck, as seating was alphabetical. This meant sitting next to Parker St. Amant was Edna Genevieve Torres, the "good-looking chick" (and she still is at age 89). She is the only child of an American mother, Ellie Converse, and a native-born Guatemalan father, Joaquin Torres, who had met at LSU when he was studying to become a sugar chemist.

When Edna was five years old, her father had died. She and her mother had moved to St. Francisville, her mother's hometown. Her mother remarried in 1932, and Edna eventually gained a half-sister, six-year-old Robin Robb.

Edna's stepfather, Elmo Robb, owned a drugstore a few blocks from their home in Baton Rouge, and both Edna and Parker worked part-time in the store while attending LSU. One night in November, they were dancing at David's Night Club as the band was playing the unforgettable song "Stardust." Wanting this moment to last forever, Parker blurted out the words, "Will you marry me?" Seeing Edna's mouth drop open in surprise, followed by a few seconds of silence, Parker, not wanting to close any doors, quickly told her to think about it. On their next date, he anxiously asked if she had thought about it. Edna said, "Yes," and, "Yes, I will marry you!"

Edna's stepfather and mother gave the young couple their blessing, and her stepfather went to work converting their backyard garage into an apartment, ready for the newlyweds after their December 21, 1946, wedding, in her family home.

Their mothers knew each other, as both had worked for the same merchandising store years before. Parker's father, Chester P. St. Amant, wanted to be a writer and a poet, but he had to take a job with Standard Oil in order to support his family of four, including Parker's older brother, C. P. St. Amant Jr.

Aside: Huey Long versus Chester P. St. Amant

In the early 1930s, Parker's father was the leader of a group of Standard Oil employees working to having Governor Huey Long impeached. This eventually raised Huey's temper to the boiling point. Two men came to the St. Amants' small Southdowns house and told the maid that if Chester P. St. Amant did not leave the state within the week, he would be killed.

Standard Oil transferred Chester to the Memphis, Tennessee, sales office, and the family lived there until Huey was assassinated on September 10, 1935, in the Louisiana State Capitol. Many believe it was an inside job, and that Huey had been assassinated by his own bodyguard, rather than by Dr. Carl Weiss.

Louisiana is known for its colorful politics. I reveal much of that era in a chapter titled "Only in Louisiana," in my book *He Lays the Stones for Our Steps*. But back to Parker and Edna's story.

Education Continues; First Son Born

Edna dropped out of LSU in her junior year to give birth to their first son, Robert Parker. Their other son, Dale Keith, was born two years later. The couple purchased a home shortly after Parker received his BS degree in accounting and returned to work at Standard Oil.

Parker was on the cutting edge of computers. He had planned on a career in accounting, but when Standard Oil bought its first business computer, he changed his thinking.

He had worked with the old electronic accounting machines for over a year and was very interested in the idea of having a real computer to work on. When the IBM 705 was installed and operational, he really became hooked. After seven years of training, operating, and eventually programming the 705, he decided he would make data processing his career route rather than accounting. He found an opening with All American Assurance Company in Lafayette as vice president in charge of data processing.

The family moved to Lafayette, where Parker was pleased to learn that All American was using the same type of computer as Standard Oil, just a smaller model. All American operated a service bureau in addition to processing the company's own work. Parker managed that division from 1963 to 1967. When All

American was sold to Republic Life in Baton Rouge in 1967, Parker and a coworker purchased the service bureau. They successfully operated their company, Datamatic, Inc., until mid-1980. Parker then went to work for their best customer, SLEMCO, the south Louisiana electric cooperative, as manager of data processing. He retired in 1990 at the age of 65.

Retirement: Golf, Cruises, and Dancing; Moving to St. James Place

Playing golf was Parker and Edna's favorite pastime, interspersed with Caribbean cruises, and a lot of dancing and playing bridge. They both loved to dance, and they rarely missed an opportunity to satisfy this craving. After Parker's retirement, they had more time for their family of two sons, six grandchildren, and nine great-grandchildren.

They moved to St. James Place Assisted Living when Parker was 90 and Edna was 87. Their family had planned a special 70th wedding anniversary on December 21, 2016. Unfortunately, Edna had a virus, and it became very low-key.

The most important thing to them is that they still have each other, continuing their long love affair. Parker also leads a Bible study group with memory-care residents.

Takeaways

In marriage and during love and caring you forgive. It is an ongoing sacrament.
—Bill Moore

Choose to encourage rather than criticize.
—Rick Warren

Grow old with me! The best is yet to be, the last of life, for which the first was made. Our times are in His hand.
  —Robert Browning

Postscript: **Parker St. Amant's Funeral, May 20, 2017**

Parker St. Amant's life and death were celebrated in a beautiful service at the Episcopal Church of the Ascension in Lafayette on May 20, 2017. The service was followed with the playing of "Taps" and a flag ceremony in the courtyard, in honor of Parker's service in World War II.

A reception followed for the large gathering of family and friends. Several long tables were filled with family pictures. While I was watching the family video alongside grandson Dr. Brandon Scott St. Amant, I saw Parker dancing the low, bowlegged alligator dance. Brandon remarked, "Parker continued this dance until age 90. They were true party animals!"

St. James Place furnished a bus to carry residents to encircle Edna, assuring her of our continuing love and support, while she continues living in their St. James Place apartment, filled with memories of her *love at first sight* husband.

PETE PETERSEN:
FBI SPECIAL AGENT MAKES THE BIG CATCH

Pete Petersen was an FBI special agent *par excellence,* given assignments other agents had not successfully completed to obtain convictions. Perhaps his most recognized investigation eventually led to the conviction of Jimmy Hoffa, head of the corrupt International Teamsters Union.

Pete grew up with two sisters and one brother in Sioux City, Iowa, the son of a building contractor, who knew all the trades and often completed the entire project himself.

Pete has an excellent voice and sang "The Star-Spangled Banner" at his high school graduation. He said his mother knew he was coming home when she heard him whistling as he came up the hill, after leaving the skating rink before midnight.

He enlisted in the Navy while still in high school and began his two years of service the day after graduation. After Pete was discharged from the Navy, he was employed by the FBI in the Identification Division in March 1948. To become an agent, applicants were required to earn a degree in either accounting or law. Pete earned his degree in accounting at Benjamin Franklin University in Washington, DC.

Pete Meets and Marries Margie

During that first year in Washington, on a double date, he met Marjorie ("Margie") Evans Bradshaw, and they were married thirteen months later.

Margie worked for the Department of the Interior. One of her duties was to deliver the payroll to various government agencies, including the White House. She became closely associated with the entire Truman family. Bess and Margaret Truman treated Margie as though she was their daughter.

After the birth of their first child, Margie worked for the Army Air Force Motion Picture Industry, where she selected movies to send to military bases within the US and overseas.

Margie did not want Pete to be transferred to different locations, as the Bureau required of their agents. In 1951 they had a son, and she became pregnant with their first daughter in 1953.

After her third pregnancy, and a call for Pete from the Bureau, she finally agreed, enabling him to become a special agent. His first assignment was a two-year stint in Newark, New Jersey, followed by a two-year assignment in Hattiesburg, Mississippi.

Back Door to Jimmy Hoffa Conviction: Edward Grady Partin

From Hattiesburg the FBI transferred Pete to its New Orleans division, assigning him to the Baton Rouge resident agency. Part of his first assignment was to investigate Grady Partin, the thirty-year head of the Baton Rouge chapter of the Teamsters Union. Partin was a close associate of Jimmy Hoffa, president of the International Brotherhood of Teamsters from 1958 to 1971. The FBI had reason to believe Partin and Hoffa were stealing from the Teamsters' pension fund. Therefore, Partin was the potential route toward the conviction of Hoffa.

Federal judge E. Gordon West presided at Partin's pretrial hearings in Baton Rouge. The investigation of Partin developed a 28-count indictment, charging obstruction of justice and embezzlement of pension funds. The indictment could net Partin over seventy-five years in a federal penitentiary.

As Partin, who knew Pete on a first-name basis, walked out of the federal courtroom after an attempt to get his case dismissed, he told Pete, "Mr. Pete, I have been getting by with shit all my life, but I don't know how I am going to get out of this." Pete replied, "Well, I don't know how, but wait a minute, maybe there is a way, but I can't discuss it with you. You need to talk to your attorney." Of course, Pete knew that Partin's testimony would nail Jimmy Hoffa, who was of prime interest to US attorney general Bobby Kennedy.

It was reported that at Hoffa's trial, he said, "My God, there's Partin," when he saw his former colleague enter the courtroom. Hoffa knew the handwriting was on the wall.

Retirement at Fifty Years

At that time the retirement age for FBI agents was set at 50; perhaps longevity on the job was endangered by the corruption they investigated. In any case, after Pete retired officially at age 51, he continued working as a background investigator for the FBI. He eventually decided to hang up his hat at age 65.

Pete and Margie enjoyed their retirement years at their Baton Rouge home in Villa Del Rey. They did considerable traveling, including Mediterranean and European cruises, and made the Inside Passage of Alaska.

A New Life for Pete, Blessed by the Flood

Margie was Pete's soulmate; she had been there for him through sixty-four years of marriage. When she died in 2013, Pete was devastated.

His daughters tried to convince him to move to a retirement community. But it was easier for Pete to stay put in their home, filled with reminders of her.

Perhaps Pete received a blessing when his home flooded, with so many others in Baton Rouge, in August 2016. After moving to St. James Place, he now has an opportunity to rebuild his life and to heal from the isolation of living alone, dwelling on the pain of his past loss.

Takeaways

I am forever changed. . . . You will not be forgotten.
    —Author unknown

Love yourself. It is important to stay positive because beauty comes from the inside out.
    —Jenn Proske

To love is the greatest gift in the world. Most people just exist.
    —Oscar Wilde

DETERMINED TO SERVE HIS COUNTRY: SIDNEY FLYNN

Sid's story is one of honor and patriotism. Some young men reportedly fled to Canada to avoid the draft. Sid only spoke of being an adventurous youth of 18, which I have seen in many I have interviewed—idealistic, wanting to serve our country and join the fight.

He was inspired by young uniformed servicemen, from several Army bases who filled the sidewalks of his Alexandria hometown. The service population in the surrounding areas ballooned at times to 400,000, according to Wikipedia:

Louisiana Maneuvers

"The Louisiana Maneuvers were a series of US Army exercises held around Northern and Western-Central Louisiana, including Fort Polk, Camp Claiborne, and Camp Livingston in 1940 and 1941. The exercises, which involved some 400,000 troops, were designed to evaluate US training, logistics, doctrine, and commanders."

"Many Army officers present at the maneuvers later rose to very senior roles in World War II, including Omar Bradley, Mark Clark, Dwight D. Eisenhower, Walter Krueger, Samuel E. Anderson, Lesley J. McNair, Joseph Stilwell, and George Patton."

Sid Keeps Trying

Sid could have easily avoided the draft by being upfront, revealing his undeveloped leg muscle and foot damaged by polio while a child. But he kept trying. To quote Sid, "Life is an adventure filled with opportunities to open doors to see what's on the other side."

He was one of three boys and three girls born to Frank Arthur Flynn and Mary McGowan in Alexandria. His father, a self-employed contractor struggling during the Great Depression, obtained a job with the Civilian Conservation Corps (CCC), established by President Roosevelt. The CCC provided jobs related to conservation and use of natural resources on federal lands, one of which was the Kisatchie National Forest of 604,000 acres established near Alexandria in 1930. According to Wikipedia, workers were paid $30 a month, of which $25 was sent home to the family.

In the 1930s, at age 4, Sid was stricken with polio. It severely affected one leg, leaving him with a clubfoot. Years later, he spent several summers at the Shriners Hospital in Shreveport having corrective surgeries on his foot. This treatment was provided without charge, and enabled him to lead a normal life like other young men, and eventually to fulfill his dream of serving his country in wartime. There he honed his sense of adventure, reading and play-acting in his mind the exploits of bandits and other unsavory characters in the books he read.

Sid was seventeen when he graduated from high school in 1943. He applied to the Navy but was turned down because of his physical condition. When he applied to the Army Air Force, they also rejected him upon learning that he had been rejected by another corps.

Nearing the draft age of 18, he was called to Shreveport for a medical review. In the recruitment hall, when told anyone interested in the Navy should step forward, Sid was among them.

Success at Last!

Sid said, "With the nation mobilized, I would have died if I could not have served." On his 18th birthday, he was sent for processing to Fort Humbug, on the Red River near Shreveport. He told me the story of how the Confederate army, during the Civil War, built fake cannons from logs and placed them on a hill overlooking a curve in the river, to fool the advancing Union army. Gen. John B. Magruder said, "That will not work. Your forts are only a humbug." It did work, and the name remains today.

Sid and his fellow recruits were sent to Lafayette to board a Navy train for Houston. From there they traveled by bus to Camp Wallace, a boot camp, prior to being transferred to Shoemaker, California, for schooling at a Navy hospital. This was followed by a stint at a Bethesda, Maryland, hospital to study the mosquito, transmitting malaria to servicemen in the South Pacific. Sid's superior officer released him from that study and assigned him to a medical support team for personnel serving in both Alexandria, Virginia, manufacturing torpedoes, and in Piney Point, Maryland, where they were shipped for test firing.

By this time Germany had surrendered, and the invasion of Japan was imminent. Afraid he would miss serving overseas, Sid asked for a transfer. He sailed on the USS *Harry Lee* for the Philippines—Manila and south to Luzon—picking up more troops along the way, prior to the drop of the atomic bomb. He had an opportunity to see Mt. Mayon and was amazed at the fire-bomb devastation in Yokohama.

Sid had fulfilled his desire to serve overseas. After Japan surrendered, he returned to the States and was hospitalized in Oakland, California, and in Glenwood Springs, Colorado. The vibration in the movement of the ships had affected his leg once crippled by polio.

Back to Civilian Life

Sid enrolled at Springhill College in Mobile, Alabama, in 1946. He attended college from 1946 to 1949.

That last year, as Sid and a group of friends traveled by train to the Sugar Bowl, they met and talked with two young ladies en route to New Orleans. As he put it, he "clicked" with Mary Elizabeth Fields, a hospital dietitian at the Huey P. Long Hospital in Pineville. They were married in 1951, while he was working in a wholesale hardware store in Alexandria.

In 1967, Sid moved his growing family to Lafayette, where he worked in the sales office of his father's steel-fabricating business. The family business continues today under the leadership of two of his four sons.

Adventures in Travel

During these years, and continuing after his retirement, Sid and

Mary Elizabeth enjoyed many adventures in South and Central America, Europe, and South Africa.

They had nine children, followed by fourteen grandchildren and a great-granddaughter. After Mary Elizabeth died in 2008, Sid lived alone prior to moving to St. James Place. Here he enjoys a pleasant and gregarious lifestyle, laughing at our physical challenges, all the way to the bank!

Takeaways

It's never too late in life to have a genuine adventure.
—Robert Kurson

Life is full of adventure. There's no such thing as a clear pathway.
—Guy Laliberté

Life is either a daring adventure, or nothing.
—Helen Keller

LT. MICHAEL KEARNS, B-29 NAVIGATOR, KILLED; HIS WIFE MILLIE PREGNANT WITH FIRST CHILD

This tragic accident happened in 1957, on a routine mission over France, when it was reported to the other two B-29s that Michael's plane had an oil leak. The pilot who diverted to get a closer look accidentally clipped Michael's plane. It was shortly before Millie and Michael's second wedding anniversary. Millie was five months' pregnant.

Millie had met Michael on a blind date while she was a student nurse at the Baptist Hospital in Alexandria near England Air Force Base.

Shortly after they married, Michael was transferred to Sculthorpe RAF Base in England. Millie joined him once she had completed her nursing program and passed the board to become a registered nurse.

After Michael's death, Millie returned to live with her parents in Alexandria, where son Michael was born four months later. Millie's mother cared for him while Millie finished her BS in nursing at Northwestern State University in Natchitoches.

After graduation, Millie joined the staff of the Pineville VA Hospital, across the river from Alexandria.

Howard Johnson Matchmaker; Divine Intervention

When a new Howard Johnson motel announced its grand opening, Millie, her young son, and her mother made plans to go to the restaurant. A sign on the door announced the opening was delayed until 6 p.m. as a water line had broken.

When they returned, there were only two seats left. I agree with Millie that divine intervention took over her life, as she exchanged quick glances with the good-looking young man she was seated by. She told her mother that she was returning alone at 6 p.m. the following night, just in case. . . .

Sure enough, he was there, surrounded by other coffee drinkers. When she left, he quickly followed her to her car. They introduced themselves, and as Millie said, "The rest is history!"

Frank Hathorn was a graduate of Louisiana State University, where he received his Army commission as a lieutenant through the ROTC. In three short months, they were married. Frank adored Michael, and Millie gave her blessing for his adoption. Later a beloved sister, Meredith, and a beloved brother, Steven, were born.

Frank, an Army reservist, worked in the state office of the Federal Housing Administration in Alexandria, implementing water and sewer systems in small Louisiana towns.
When their children were older, Millie resumed her nursing career at the Baptist Hospital. In her fifties, she enrolled at Webster University and received an MA in management. She was, as her mother referred to her, "a Girl Friday to the lawyer," in a law firm in Alexandria. She worked as a paralegal and legal nurse consultant.

Frank Retires to Pursue Other Interests

At age 60, Frank retired from the Army Reserve with the rank of lieutenant colonel. He also retired from his employment with the FHA, allowing him time to pursue his love of golf and to become an adept cook. He and Millie volunteered in several community outreaches and spent time with their four grandchildren.

They enjoyed traveling, including a memorable trip to Switzerland to visit Michael and his family. Michael is an international business consultant.

Music Is the Wine . . .

Frank and Millie love music and dancing. While I was interviewing them, Millie noticed a quote on my desk from Robert Fripp: "Music is the wine that fills the cup of silence." She loves gentle, quiet Frank, as we all do here at St. James Place. She says that she questioned his quietness when they first met but soon realized he was a listener. I assured her those were in short supply.

Millie is now Frank's caregiver. Knowing his love of music, I invited the Jimmy Jules Jazz Band, now referred to as the St. John Icons, to play a special concert honoring Frank. He seemed transformed as he listened intently, rather than dancing with his beloved Millie. . . .

Takeaways

Nothing is so strong as gentleness, nothing so gentle as real strength.
  —St. Francis de Sales

A gentle heart is tied with an easy thread.
  —George Herbert

There is great force hidden in a gentle command.
  —George Herbert

Section 2

Our Greatest Generation

Beginning in 1986, over a period of seventeen years, I made three or four trips yearly to the Normandy area of France, buying for our Fireside Antiques business. The French people, particularly in that area, are quick to express their gratitude and appreciation of the Americans who freed their country from the Germans. I have been privileged to be guests in their homes and have opportunities to reflect back in time. The Germans took over many homes and estates. It is amazing how the French have restored their historic picture-book cities to their former glory.

    I have walked the landing beaches and seen the bunkers, trying to get some sense of what transpired there—the horrors that took place to free the French. Lastly, I brought home memories of the sorrow buried in the Normandy American Cemetery and Memorial.

    The Normandy American Cemetery is located in Colleville-sur-Mer, Normandy, on a bluff overlooking Omaha Beach. Over 9,000 American troops, including three women, are buried there, most of them killed during the Normandy invasion. There are also troops who died in earlier operations in France.

    The Greatest Generation is the title of Tom Brokaw's 1998 book profiling those who came of age in the US during World War II. Brokaw wrote, "It is, I believe, the greatest generation any society has ever produced." He argued that these men and women fought not for fame and recognition, but because it was the "right thing to do." The book was inspired by his attendance at the 40th-anniversary celebrations of D-Day.

    Veterans of World War II are rapidly decreasing in number,

and the annual Veterans Day observances are more poignant. At St. James Place, our number of veterans, once in the eighties, is slowly declining each year as death calls. There were sixty-three on Veterans Day in 2016, and fifty-seven in 2017.

A common lament of the World War II generation is the absence today of personal responsibility. What kind of world will our future generations grow up in?
—Tom Brokaw

LEON STANDIFER, RECIPIENT OF THE PURPLE HEART AND FRENCH LEGION OF HONOR

Our St. James Place observance of Veterans Day in 2016 duly praised and honored our sixty-three veterans, serving in World War II, Korea, and the Vietnam War. There was an acknowledgment, both from the lectern and in our hearts, mourning the absence of Leon Standifer, our fellow resident, friend, and hero, who always came in full dress uniform. A veteran of World War II, he was a recipient of the Purple Heart and received the French Medal of Honor in April 2012.

    Leon was at peace and ready for death, yet valiantly clinging to life, fighting for just one more time to join his fellow veterans on November 11 in Duplantier Auditorium. Leon Standifer died November 6, 2016, He was 91.

LSU Professor of Horticulture

Dr. Standifer was a professor of horticulture at LSU. As I am an ardent gardener, I was always asking for, and getting, information from his vast storehouse of knowledge, reinforced by the ongoing research at the large acreage of the LSU AgCenter's Burden Museum & Gardens on nearby Essen Lane. Until macular degeneration prevented my driving, at Leon's invitation, I would pick buckets full of my favorites, figs and muscadines, on the museum grounds. Leon had a presence beyond his tall and stalwart frame—always approachable, open, and friendly.

Columnist for *Country Roads* Magazine

I looked forward to the monthly *Country Roads* magazine to read the column "Lawn Chair Gardeners," which the two retired LSU research professors, Drs. Leon Standifer and Ed O'Rourke Jr., had been writing since 2002, until Ed's death in 2012. Their book, *Gardening in the Humid South,* published in 2002, continues to be invaluable to multitudes of gardeners.

    Before his death, Leon had been sick for several months and, by his own admonition, was "ready to go." The last time *Country Roads'* publisher, James Fox-Smith, talked with him,

Leon said, "I had a full life and a good time, so just promise you'll write about me when I go." And so James did, in the November 2016 issue of *Country Roads*. Mickie Chubbuck, Leon's good friend for nine years, gave me a copy of that issue. On one occasion, when I stopped by Mickie's apartment, I noticed a chair piled high with newspapers that Leon had placed there during many of their visits. She lamented the loss of her special friend and confidant.

My conversations with Leon all concerned horticulture. Perhaps, when he was with buddies like Larry Mann, now deceased, and Jerry Black, they spoke briefly about their World War II experiences, perhaps as further catharsis after the horrors they endured.

On the Passing of "The Greatest Generation"

This is the title of the *Baton Rouge Advocate* article by Günter Bischof, the Marshall Plan Professor of History at UNO who also serves as a presidential counselor at the National World War II Museum in New Orleans. In this tribute to Leon Standifer, he wrote:

Leon Standifer recently passed away.
He was a veteran of World War II, decorated with the Purple Heart and much later awarded the French Legion of Honor. He had served as a professor of horticulture at LSU, and after retirement, began to deal with his wartime experiences. I was impressed by his apparent total recall of his wartime exploits and the honesty of his observations on serving in World War II.
Here was an American veteran who did not boast about his wartime heroics, but one who tried to exorcise his wartime demons and overcome the painful memories of the war that he apparently had carried with him throughout his life.
I met Standifer in the early 1990s and began to invite him to come to my World War II classes at UNO and reflect about World War II and his memories of the war (written down in two

memoirs published by LSU Press—Not in Vain: A Rifleman Remembers World War II *[1992], and* Binding Up the Wounds: An American Soldier in Occupied Germany, 1945–1946 *[1997]).* *He was never tired of reflecting on how the war changed him from a young boy from Mississippi to an adult, forced into learning the business of killing within a period of eighteen months. He had entered Europe through Omaha Beach three months after the D-Day invasion. He left 18 months later in the winter of 1945–46. His final assignment was guarding German POWs in the small town of Bad Aibling, Germany, as an occupation soldier. He came to my classes for 20 years, sharing his memories of World War II stories with hundreds of students.*

Returning home, he experienced "a feeling of depression and dread," and wrote in an unpublished memoir: "The roots of my depression were deeper: I was not the ethical, deeply religious boy that my small community of Clinton, Mississippi, had sent off to war."

Standifer provided one answer to the question "What were we fighting for?" in his message to my students: The soldiers he fought with "didn't feel or look like patriots, and they were fighting because they were too proud to run, to leave their friends to do the job alone." And he added: "They were also fighting against a purely physical need for relief from the cold, the pain, the sights and the smells."

Standifer remained a humanist and loved to quote Rudyard Kipling's timeless invocation of the warrior: "Men who were grit for the combat, me who were grit to the core." America has come to mourn the loss of "the greatest generation" of World War II soldiers. Leon Standifer was one of them, but made every effort to address the physical and mental wounds that war wreaks on young men.

Takeaways

Be brave enough to live life creatively. The creative place where

no one else has ever been.
—Alan Alda

The real man smiles in trouble, gathers strength from distress, and grows brave by reflection.
—Thomas Paine

Those who dare to fail miserably can achieve greatly.
—John F. Kennedy

DESTINED TO SERVE THEIR COUNTRY: LT. COL. PHILEMON ST. AMANT PAVES THE WAY FOR COL. PHILEMON ST. AMANT II

This is a *son-like-father* story, not only in name, but also in a mutual dedication to serve our country. The lives of both father and son were so intertwined with the military, remembering the supporting roles of their wives and children was challenging for me as a writer, and possibly at times for our military men. Obviously, sacrifices had to be made by all.
LTC Philemon A. ("Phil") St. Amant Sr. was the fifth of six children of Alfred D. St. Amant and his wife, Lucy Clifton Andrews St. Amant. At the time of his birth, the family resided in Natchitoches, Louisiana, where his father was a professor of engineering at the Louisiana State Normal School (later Northwestern State University).
When Phil was about six months old, his family returned to Baton Rouge, where he attended public schools, including Baton Rouge High School and LSU, from which he received his BA degree in 1939.

Beginning a Military Career

At LSU, Phil enrolled in the ROTC program, and soon decided on a military career. Upon graduation, he applied for entry onto active duty and was commissioned a second lieutenant of artillery. Anticipating the approaching war, the Army assigned him initially to train National Guardsmen at Camp Shelby in Hattiesburg, Mississippi. He subsequently joined 190th Field Artillery Regiment, with which he deployed to Northern Ireland for further engagement in Europe. With a proficiency in French, he was recalled to the United States to be trained as a member of the Office of Strategic Services (OSS), the forerunner of the Central Intelligence Agency (CIA).

Normandy Landing

Having returned to England following his training, he landed with Omar Bradley's First Army on Utah Beach, in Normandy, and was assigned to several OSS missions in France.

Following World War II, he served with a parachute field artillery regiment at Fort Bragg, North Carolina, until becoming a student at the US Army Counterintelligence Corps (CIC) School in Maryland, where he studied Japanese. He was then reassigned to the Army Language School in Monterey, California, where he spent a year studying Polish.

Counterintelligence Assignments

From 1949 to 1952, Phil was assigned to the army of occupation as a counterintelligence officer in Germany, and later as director of the Intelligence and Military Police School in Oberammergau. Returning from Germany, he commanded the CIC region headquartered in Kansas City for nearly four years. He was then reassigned to Fort Bragg, where he commanded an artillery battalion, and later became the intelligence officer for the Third U. S. Army Missile Command.

Retirement after Horse Artillery to Missiles

Phil retired at age 41, with more than twenty years commissioned active service that began with horse artillery and ended with missiles. He has received numerous honors for his service to our country.
Upon his return to Baton Rouge, he and his wife Corinne began a small business-consulting firm, which they operated together for over fifty years. Phil continued to go to his office each morning until he was past his 99th birthday. He and Corinne, married more than seventy-seven years, have four children, nine grandchildren, six great-grandchildren, and three great-great-grandchildren.

Takeaways

Brave men rejoice in adversity, just as brave soldiers triumph in war.
—Seneca

Mankind must put an end to war before war puts an end to mankind.
—John F. Kennedy

The supreme art of war is to subdue the enemy without fighting.
—Sun Tzu

COL. PHILEMON ST. AMANT II

Philemon St. Amant II was the oldest child of LTC Phil St. Amant and wife Corinne. He graduated from high school in Fayetteville, North Carolina, a few months before his father retired.

Appointment to West Point

Philemon II received an appointment to West Point from Senator Allen Ellender, of Houma. After graduating with a Bachelor of Science degree, he was commissioned a second lieutenant of artillery in 1963. His first assignment was with the 82nd Airborne Division Artillery at Fort Bragg, North Carolina.

Two Tours to Vietnam

In 1965, Philemon became an advisor to the Vietnamese army, first with Regional and Popular Forces, and then with a field artillery battalion in the mountains near Pleiku. In 1969, he was deployed for a second year-long tour in Vietnam, this time with the 101st Airborne Division, serving first as a fire support officer with a parachute infantry battalion, and then as the commander of a field artillery battery.

Teaching French at West Point

Philemon was sent to Paris to study the French language and literature at the Alliance Française and the University of Paris (Sorbonne), through a two-year program with Middlebury College in Vermont. After receiving his Master of Arts degree, he began a three-year tour teaching French at West Point and was then assigned as a student at the US Army Command and General Staff College at Ft. Leavenworth, Kansas.

Promoted to Lieutenant Colonel
Philemon was eventually promoted to lieutenant colonel, and commanded a 155 mm towed howitzer battalion at Fort Bragg for nearly three years. He was then as a student at the Navy War

College (Senior Course) for a year, followed by a posting to the United Nations Truce Supervision Organization in Palestine (UNTSO), as the senior US observer, and concurrently as Commander, Observer Group Lebanon. This was during the civil war in Lebanon, and at the time of the bombing attack on the US Marine barracks in Beirut.

Upon his return to the United States in 1984, he became an action officer in the J-5 (Strategic Plans and Policy) of the Office of the Joint Chiefs of Staff. In that position he worked initially with the Persian Gulf Group and subsequently was the Egypt Desk Officer, and Chief of the Middle East Group (Israel, Lebanon, Syria, Jordan, and Egypt).

Promoted to Colonel

After being promoted to colonel, he served a year as the chief of the Current Intelligence Group for the deputy chief of staff for intelligence at US Army headquarters. This was followed by a stint of over thirty months in Greece commanding a US Army Artillery Group. His final assignment was as chief of staff of the Alaskan Command, headquartered at Elmendorf Air Force Base near Anchorage, Alaska. That assignment lasted for his final three years in the Army.

Retirement in 1993, Ending over Thirty Years of Service

Colonel St. Amant retired in 1993 to return home to Baton Rouge, after more than thirty years of commissioned active service.

He and his wife Harriet had three children. The eldest, a son, served in the Army at Fort Carson, Colorado, and was subsequently a student at LSU–Shreveport, where he died in an automobile accident. Their two daughters live in Baton Rouge and Prairieville. He and Harriet have four grandchildren and three great-grandchildren.

My Observations

Perhaps, considering COL St. Amant's prestigious career, from the Vietnamese battlefield to professorship at esteemed West Point, I could have expected an overly dignified military man. Instead, I found Phil one of the most affable people I have met, filled with humor, along with an awesome knowledge and sense of history.
I asked where the small town of St. Amant, located between Baton Rouge and Gonzales, got its name. Phil said when the post office official inquired at the St. Amant general store, he said the post office would bear the name of the town of St. Amant.

Second Cousins Reunite

After our interview, I asked Phil if he knew Parker St. Amant, a neighbor of mine. I was privileged to witness the reunion of second cousins who had not seen each other since a family reunion four or five years previously. My eyes fill with tears as I witness poignant reunions, while learning more about my friends. Phil referred to his cousin Parker as the family genealogist and historian.
You will recall reading the love story of Parker and Edna St. Amant in the "War and Marriage" section.
Sadly, within several months, we attended Parker's funeral, and raising of the flag in honor of his military service, at the Episcopal Church of the Ascension in Lafayette.

Takeaways

I extend my deep gratitude to our armed forces and first responders for serving both at home and abroad against terrorism.
—Horace Mann

Doing nothing for others is the undoing of ourselves.
—Horace Mann

Not for ourselves alone are we born.
—Cicero

LT. COL. RALPH STEPHENSON'S 31-YEAR CAREER: WORLD WAR II, KOREA, AND VIETNAM

As far as I know, Ralph is the only St. James Place veteran to have served in three wars: World War II, Korea, and Vietnam. Ralph wrote about World War II, inspired by a writing group for residents. (I was inspired in the group toward publishing my first book, *He Lays the Stones for Our Steps*.)

A Veteran's Tale
(Excerpts from the Pen of Ralph Stephenson)

My boyhood in Jena, a small rural town in central Louisiana, was not anything out of the ordinary for that period. I was the oldest of four children and raised during the Great Depression by middle-class parents. My father was a bank employee who eventually became bank president. My mother was completely involved in raising and educating her children. I was always enthralled by the stories of Eddie Rickenbacker, Wiley Post, Roscoe Turner, and other aviators in the '20s and '30s. My earliest memories include barnstormers landing at the baseball field near town and their taking folks up for short rides. My father took me with him on a trip to Shreveport when I was about six or seven years old, and we visited Barksdale Air Force Base. I was fascinated (and still am) with the biplanes of that era, with the yellow wings, blue fuselage, and red and white stripes on the tail. On a visit to childhood friends in Monroe about the same time, the whole family crowded into the old touring car to visit the local airport to watch the airplanes land.

Japanese Bomb Pearl Harbor

When the Japanese attacked Pearl Harbor, the war was suddenly very real to all of us in the high-school senior class, and we became very interested in such things as deferments, draft notices, physical disabilities, and the good and bad points of each of the military services. The Navy was one of the best choices: *"You don't have to dig foxholes."* The Marines were the elite: *"They get in the first fight and the best."* The Air Corps was the most glamorous: *"You live in fame or go down in flames."* The Army always came out last: *"You spend all your time slogging through the boondocks killing snakes."* My ambition had been to fly and build airplanes, so the only choice for me was to join the Air Corps for aviation cadet training before I was drafted to serve in one of the "ground-pounding, gravel-agitating" branches of the Army, such as the infantry or artillery.

Attending LSU and ROTC

Graduating from high school in 1942, I entered LSU (1942–43) and into my first taste of military life and training. ROTC was mandatory for the first two years, as it had been for many years in the "Old War Skule." I had no problem adapting. We were all hot to go and win the war, and were all set to begin preflight school, wherever we might be assigned. It could be anywhere in the country, and most of us from Louisiana were ready to see the world, or as much of it as the Air Corps wanted us to see at the time.

At this stage of the war in Europe, the Allies were already planning to open a "second front," although it wouldn't take place for a couple of years, so I'm sure that many of my friends from basic training ended up in the Normandy invasion and the campaign across Europe and into Germany, if they lived. I have always felt very lucky to have avoided that.

Military Service

At age 19, I became a second lieutenant on January 27, 1945. While I was preparing for B-17 duties, another airplane had been developed that would need bombardiers. The Boeing B-29 Superfortress would change my life in many ways, as it did too for many others around the world. I started with orders to proceed to Buckingham Army Air Field at Fort Myers, Florida, for training as a B-29 gunner. As in all bombers, the nose section of the B-29 required a trained gunner, as well as a bombardier, and the new equipment in all the firing positions meant that we had to go to gunnery school again. I arrived at Fort Myers in the spring, after a short leave following commissioning and graduation as a bombardier.

Preparing for the Invasion of Japan

Because of the urgency to train new crews to be used in the invasion of Japan, our training schedule consisted of nine-day "weeks." We would fly or attend classes for seven days, and then be off for a day and a half, when we could leave the base to enjoy whatever local entertainment we could locate.

The Defeat of Germany

With the defeat of Germany in the spring of 1945, the pace of our training gained speed in anticipation of the expected resistance to our invasion of the Japanese home islands. War-weary soldiers from the European theater were being reassigned to units destined to be the spearhead of the forces to hit the beaches. We were preparing for the worst, with little hope for a reprieve. The base continued to train, not only the personnel in the pipeline for combat in the Far East, but also many of the permanently assigned troops who were being prepared for assignment to combat commands. MacDill Air Force Base [in Tampa, Florida] could easily send many of its housekeeping and administrative troops overseas because of the presence of hundreds of German and Italian prisoners of war from the North African campaign, who were housed in separate camps and who were used for routine jobs on the base. The Italians were generally given jobs as cooks, waiters, housekeepers, and other inside employment, while the Germans worked mostly outdoors, maintaining the buildings and grounds, including electrical and plumbing tasks. They were locked into their fenced compounds at night, but were sent to their jobs during the day by truck, and returned after completion of the workday. Even though they were rather loosely supervised, there were no serious escape attempts while we were there, most of them being glad to sit out the rest of the war in these conditions. We were told that, on more than one occasion, however, one of them would slip out for a day or two and then return voluntarily, much like a three-day pass. As one officer told us, "That barbed wire fence around our compound is mostly to keep curious people like you out, rather than keep them in."

VE Day as Germany Collapses

After the collapse of Germany gave the victory to the Allied armies, VE Day was declared on May 8, 1945, and the entire base took an unplanned short holiday of a day or two before getting back to preparing to finish the job started December 7, 1941.

Atomic Bomb Used Against Japanese in Hiroshima

Our training routine resumed, and kept us busy until the war was over. We had heard very little about the possible use of the atomic bomb against Japan, although newspapers had been full of stories for months about the theoretical power of such a weapon. We had been much more interested in tales of the Japanese secret weapons and their superior airplanes than nuclear theory. When the first one was used against Hiroshima on August 6, we all began to read about its effectiveness and how an entire city was reduced to ashes. When the second one hit Nagasaki three days later on August 9, we knew that the war was over, even though the formal surrender on the battleship *Missouri* did not take place until September 2, 1945.

Deciding to Stay in the Service

Those who were not essential to the operation of the base, or to the Army in general, were relieved of their wartime obligations and discharged in record time. In about two hours, a person could have a discharge in hand and a ticket back to his home of record. Our pilot was the only one of our crew, other than me, who didn't opt for an immediate release from the service. I still wanted to fly. I had little desire to return to Jena [Louisiana], and told my parents that I intended to stay in the service, but realized that my education had been inadequate.

I talked it over with my father, expressing a desire for an education that would point me toward a military career, perhaps at the Citadel or VMI. He thought that might be a good idea and he asked if I had ever considered West Point. I had heard of this place before, but had never thought of going there. It was a place up north that trained cadets, and was important enough that a soldier could, and often was, pulled out of his combat unit if he got an appointment to enter the academy as a cadet. I knew only that they graduated as a second lieutenant and served in the Army. When I agreed that the idea sounded fine to me, he told me to look into it, and he would do the same.

Occupation of Japan

Early in January 1946, we boarded a troopship of the General class, so called because we were named for Army generals. We officers were taken by Army trucks to Fuchu, a town a few miles west of Tokyo, and temporarily housed in large hangar-like structures that had been part of a chemical plant.

Wong, a former Japanese soldier I had made friends with, had been in town several days and had access to a jeep. He took me around many parts of Tokyo that had been affected by the war. The devastation caused by the firebombing was hard to believe, extending for miles in all directions. The only buildings in these areas that remained standing were of concrete or brick construction. Everything else was blackened ruins. The main parts of downtown Tokyo near the Imperial Palace had been spared from the bombing. It was a very sad experience, and made even more poignant by the attitude of the Japanese people. They, who had been fierce fighters in the spirit of Bushido during the war, were now quietly accepting their fate, and the presence of the erstwhile enemy on their sacred soil. Even then, it was hard for me to understand their seemingly cheerful compliance with our rules, and their quiet determination to make a better Japan for the future. During this, and two later assignments to Japan, I never heard a harsh word against our troops, even from veterans of the armed forces who were no doubt bitter about the outcome. While many of them acknowledged their role in combat, a suspiciously large number of veterans claimed to have been cutting timber or repairing roads on Hokkaido or Kyushu, but I met a taxi driver who was a proud fighter pilot who had shot down American planes, one of the few that had survived aerial combat. We could not verify his war record, of course, but treated him as a fellow soldier who had done his duty, even on the losing side.

Accepted at West Point

Due to the diligence of my father and Senator Allen Ellender, the US Army Air Force had finally caught up with me, and was in the process of cutting orders for me to fly back to the US to enroll in the prep school for entry to the Military Academy. By now, political attention to my situation had spurred the bureaucracy into action, and I was told that I would be leaving immediately. *Immediately* would make full use of its ambiguities. As a cadet at the academy, I was also a member of the Army Reserve, and was promoted to the rank of first lieutenant.

Graduation from West Point; Marriage and Family

With a lot of luck and some hard work, I managed to graduate on June 6, 1950, a date on which I pinned my new second lieutenant bars in the newly created US Air Force and was married to June McFarland, who had for three years faithfully made the trip from her home in Yonkers, New York, for a date with me. How we met, fell in love, and coped with the cadet system together is another story, but it all worked out beautifully, resulting in a full Air Force career, fifty-six years of marriage, two daughters, and two grandchildren. We must have been doing something right, and we've always been lucky. . . .

My father's sister, living in Camden, Arkansas, had heard about the crash of a B-25 into the Empire State Building in New York on the same day that I called my parents and told them about hitchhiking a ride on a B-25 from Washington to Massachusetts. Somehow, she had learned that one of the people killed in the crash was named Stephenson, and she was afraid that it was me. Both of my aunts in Arkansas and all the family there and in Jena had decided that I was now deceased. As I managed to explain to them, I had picked another B-25 and was now on the ground at Fort Devens and would go by bus to Amherst.

Bombing in Korea: "Hours of Boredom and Moments of Sheer Terror"

Let's pick up the story where Ralph left off.

After Ralph graduated from West Point in June 1950, he entered pilot training at Goodfellow Air Force Base, Texas, and received his pilot wings one year later at Vance Air Force Base in Enid, Oklahoma. He was assigned to a B-29 crew training for duty in the Far East. He deployed to Korea as copilot on nighttime bombing missions. He named the makeup of the crew: pilot, copilot, navigator, bombardier, flight engineer, radio operator, and left and right gunner, and a tail gunner. After each mission, the crew checked their aircraft for any signs of being hit by enemy fire. He flew on thirty bombing missions in the Korean War, which ended in July 1953. Ralph said, "I love flying. There were hours and hours of boredom, penetrated by moments of sheer terror." Miraculously, Ralph's crew never took on enemy fire.

In 1952, based at Yokota Air Base in Japan, he flew 45 combat missions over North Korea. He returned to Roswell, New Mexico, to the Sixth Bomb Wing, flying the 6-engine super bomber, the B-36. As a requirement for upgrading to jet bombers, he entered navigator training at James Connally Air Force Base, Texas, in 1954, pinned on navigator wings one year later, and became a jet pilot, flying the RB-47 at Little Rock Air Force Base, Arkansas, a base opened in 1955.

In 1959, the first class graduated from the new Air Force Academy, and Ralph was selected for duty as an Air Office commanding officer, supervising the training and discipline of a squadron of Air Force cadets. He taught in the Squadron Center at the Air Force Academy for three years to increase in speed by training to fly solo in Denver. In 1962, he was tapped for duty in the Far East.

Assigned to duty at Yokota Air Base for the second time, he spent three years there flying the B-57, a twin-engine jet bomber with a nuclear wartime mission. Because Japan did not allow nuclear weapons, he made monthly trips to Pleiku, South Vietnam, to stand alert with a nuclear bomb ready to go to war if that should occur.

In 1965, he was assigned to LSU as assistant professor of aerospace studies at Air Force ROTC Detachment 31, where he served for three years.

Vietnam War and After

Ralph was next ordered to serve as a C-47 pilot in Vietnam, flying classified intelligence missions in 1968–69. His plane was equipped with communications equipment and flew over some dangerous territory.

After returning from Vietnam in 1969, he was assigned to the Alternate National Military Command Center. Between 1979 and 1982, he served in Joint Chief of Staffs appointments and worked at Fort Ritchie, Maryland, completing top-secret duties near Camp David and occasionally at the Pentagon. In 1972, he was named commander of the 1369th Photo Squadron at Vandenberg Air Force Base, California, which photographed missile launches with large tracking cameras and developed the film in a movie-studio facility.

Retirement from Air Force, Becomes an Attorney and

Administrative Law Judge

After retiring from the Air Force in 1974, he attended LSU Law School and graduated in the Class of 1977. Following a period of private practice, he joined the legal section of the Department of Public Safety as a staff attorney, and served as an administrative law judge until his retirement in 1997. In those days Ralph and his wife, June McFarland, lived just behind St. James Place; they watched Phase II being built just on the other side of their backyard wall.

Even after his final retirement in 1997, Ralph stayed busy: as a family lawyer and notary public; a volunteer with LSU ROTC and the Louisiana West Point Association; cofounder of the Baton Rouge chapter of the Military Officers Association of America (the last living founder of MOAA in 2017); president, vice president, and secretary of the Air Force Association; and an active member of the Friends of the LSU Library.

Moving over the Fence to St. James Place

In 2001, he and June downsized and moved into a new apartment at St. James Place. The two of them deeply enjoyed living with so many friends, old and new, in the congenial atmosphere. June died in 2011. In 2017, Ralph downsized again into the Health and Wellness building, where he stays sharp reading and enjoying his St. James friends and fellow veterans.

To learn more about Ralph, view Baton Rouge channel 33's "Hometown Heroes":
http://www.brproud.com/news/local-news/hometown-hero-ralph-stephenson

Takeaways

So I would say God hates war, but God loves every soldier.

—Rick Warren

The first virtue in a soldier is endurance of fatigue; courage is only the second virtue.
　　　—Napoleon Bonaparte

The patriot volunteer, fighting for country and his rights, makes the most reliable soldier on earth.
　　　—Stonewall Jackson

**EIGHTEEN-YEAR-OLD ASPIRING PILOTS REUNITE
AFTER 73 YEARS**

Today I witnessed a miracle! While veteran Shaun McGarry and I were visiting with Ralph Stephenson in the Health and Wellness building, Parker and Edna St. Amant approached. They stopped by Ralph, and the two men in their wheelchairs greeted each other. As I made the introductions, I noticed that Ralph was staring at Parker. Suddenly he asked Parker if he had been stationed in Missoula, Montana, during World War II. Parker said, "Yes," and quick as a flash, Ralph looked at him and said, "We were bunkmates." Parker looked shocked and asked him, "What is your first name?" When he responded, "Ralph," Parker said, "Of course, Ralph Stephenson! What a wonderful coincidence!"

Squadron I, April 44

It was April 1944 at a US Army Air Force training center in Missoula, Montana. Ralph and Parker had roomed with two other men. How can they be so sure after seventy-three years? Parker has a book of photos of their entire squadron, titled "Take Off," with a sketch of a propeller, reminding us the old airplanes were started by hand-spinning the propeller. He pointed to each of them in their flight uniforms.

"We Are the Lucky Ones"

These words are said by most veterans of all the wars, quietly, almost like an afterthought, after sharing their excitement in serving their country, though not having all their youthful aspirations fulfilled. There is no doubt they have thought those words in times of quiet contemplation in the years after returning home to their loved ones.

Unaware Ninety-Two-Year-Old Vets Living Six Hundred Feet Apart

Neither Ralph nor Parker was aware the other was living at St. James Place. Now, after seventy-three years, they can think back to the days they were eighteen, and compare notes on the rest of their experiences during World War II.

My Observations

My eyes had filled with tears as I witnessed this reunion. Despite the horrors of war, I have seen the camaraderie of our brave soldiers. We can learn much from their spirit! I was told they talked of their experiences while receiving physical therapy side by side, until Parker's death a few months later. Ralph was sad that he was physically unable to make the trip to Lafayette for Parker's funeral.

Takeaways

When we assumed the Soldier, we did not lay aside the Citizen.
  —George Washington

To be prepared for war is one of the most effectual means of preserving peace.
  —George Washington

Integrity is the essence of everything successful.
  —Buckminster Fuller

CAPT. JERRY BLACK: US ARMY TOURS OFFICER, GOLFER, FISHERMAN, AND LOVER

I love people; Jerry loves the ladies . . . and people. I first met him at one of the weekly dinner parties I initiated shortly after I was a new arrival in 2008, for newly arriving residents. This was one of my ways to meet people and to be with a small group of friends who were regulars.

Golf, Fishing, and Football

Jerry quickly announced his four major interests: golf, fishing, football, and of course, you guessed right, women, more particularly one woman. But first things first! Jerry was anticipating many fishing trips with his Baton Rouge son, Dough. He had arrived at the right place, as south Louisiana aptly toots its horn as Fisherman's Paradise. There are multitudes of lakes, bayous, and rivers, with the Gulf of Mexico lying at its feet.

The Girl He Left Behind

Jerry asked his companion, Marge Lindsey, to move with him to Baton Rouge. They were both avid bridge players and travelers, enjoying cruises together along the Danube River and the Inside Passage of Alaska, as well as the Caribbean, with fellow residents of Arizona's Sun City West Retirement Community. Marge, being a Scottsdale girl, feared leaving that lifestyle, nor cared to learn to fish.

So much for that exotic and romantic experience, but look ahead, Jerry—there are lots of southern, and Yankee, belles, at St. James Place. . . .

When I teased Jerry about his special ladies at St. James Place, he quickly responded, "I am afraid my reputation as a ladies' man is greater than the actuality." Dare we believe him, as he is only 95 and we just had a 92-year-old take a fellow resident as his bride!

Jerry's Early Life; College and Courting Years

Jerry and his sister were born in New York of parents who had migrated from Russia. Jerry was eight when the family moved to Bridgeport, where his father managed a manufacturing plant for one of the largest lines of exclusive women's clothes, R and K Originals.

Several of Jerry's friends came to Louisiana to attend LSU. They drew a picture of the beautiful, lush landscape, a paradise with multitudes of southern belles. . . . Jerry lost no time and was on his way to LSU.

He wasted no time finding his own southern belle, Laulette Marcus, from Alexandria, Louisiana. Jerry referred to these four courting years as the best years of his life. Must have been pretty smart, as, along with his courting, he received a BS in business and a commission in LSU's ROTC in May 1943. He was sent to Fort Sill, Oklahoma, for Officer Candidate School and became a second lieutenant, receiving four days off to marry Laulette! He was not sent overseas until 1944.

Tours Officer of Navy's Mediterranean Theater

Although Jerry was Jewish, some of the most memorable trips he made, with celebrities and soldiers, were to Rome to meet Pope Pius XII. On one such visit, escorting celebrities Jinx Falkenburg and Ed Gardner, Pope Pius presented them with mother-of-pearl crucifixes. When Jerry told him he was a Jew, Pope Pius replied, "My son, I want you to keep it as a token of your visit here today."

The largest tour Jerry directed as tours officer for the Mediterranean theater was a three-day trip to Rome for 100,000 Catholic soldiers to the Vatican to attend the Consistory, where they witnessed the elevation of archbishops to cardinals.

Captain Jerry's last official duty as tours officer, in the months as World War II was winding down, was to plan five-to-seven-day trips to major European countries for the soldiers, to break the boredom and to help the men adjust emotionally before going home to resume their civilian lives in the US. This was a side of the war effort many of us did not know but that instills pride in our humanitarian country, far beyond the pales of war.

To learn more about Jerry, view Baton Rouge channel 33's "Hometown Heroes":
http://www.brproud.com/news/local-news/hometown-hero-jerry-black

Takeaways

A pretty girl is like a melody, that haunts you night and day . . .
　　—Irving Berlin

She had been proud of his decision to serve his country, her heart bursting with love and admiration the first time she saw him outfitting in his dress blues.
　　—Nicholas Sparks

It's a good idea always to do something relaxing prior to making an important decision in your life.
　　—Paulo Coelho

ENGLISH ROYAL AIR FORCE FLYING OFFICER JACK BARTLE

Reminiscences of England resonate as I play the word game Quiddler with other residents, including Jack Bartle, still a proper Englishman with a distinguished accent, despite his years in America. His knowledge of (to us) quirky English words gives Jack a distinct advantage.

I was curious to compare early memories of farm life of our grandparents. Food for the family was foremost, with the excess sold or traded for other essentials. In neither case did our grandparents, and in my case parents, have electricity or plumbing. Apparently, his grandfather had relatively small acreage to grow potatoes and raise chickens and ducks. Jack recalled rushing to get drinking water from a nearby spring before the ducks were let out of their pen. They used large vats to collect the prolific rainfall from the roof of their house for their other water needs. Rural north Louisiana homes were fortunate to have drilled water wells with a rope and pulley to draw buckets of water.

Jack's father was a fireman and rented a house for the family next to the fire station. Jack's proudest moment occurred when he was a tall, lanky teenager and the fire alarm sounded. He was the only person available to ride the firetruck, with sirens blaring, to help his father extinguish the fire.

England Joins World War I

According to Wikipedia, England had all-volunteer armies until January 1916 when the United Kingdom, for the first time in its history, introduced conscription. By the end of 1918, the British Army had reached its maximum strength of 4 million, most of whom fought against Germany in France and Belgium. Jack's father served most of the war in Palestine.

World War II: Jack Bartle's Story

Jack wanted to join England's Royal Air Force (RAF). He was an advanced student in a school for boys and graduated at age 11, but he could not join the RAF until he was 18. In 1943, he became a pilot trained by the US Navy in Michigan, with final training in England.

While waiting in the RAF for assignment in India, Jack joined his family on vacation. Walking on the seashore, he met a pretty English woman, Lillian Westrop, who would eventually become his bride. After enjoying each other's company for a week, they pledged to write.

Awaiting orders to leave for Burma, his squadron was called in from night training and told the Germans had surrendered. Shortly after they arrived in Burma to transport soldiers, the Japanese surrendered. (Word must have gotten out that Jack Bartle's squadron was ready to join the fight!)

A Chemical Engineering Degree and Marriage

After Jack was discharged from the RAF, he obtained his chemical engineering degree at the University of Leeds. (England provided the equivalent of the US GI Bill to assist veterans in obtaining a college degree.)

Once he had entered college, according to Jack, "It only took eight months before we decided it was cheaper to share an apartment." Sounds like a good reason to get married, wouldn't you agree?

In 1950, Jack began his chemical engineering employment with the British Chemical Company. He and Lillian had two sons, Philip and John, who were enrolled in English boarding schools for boys. In 1965, when Jack's employer built a facility in Geismar, Louisiana, Jack was sent for the startup. He took the opportunity to continue working with his company in various parts of the US. Their sons moved from England to join their parentsafter they completed their education.

Lillian Finds a New Calling

When Jack and Lillian moved to the US, Lillian gave up teaching and had time to pursue her interest in art. Her work was so well received that sales led to an art career. Jack proudly said her very first painting, titled *Tree,* is in his St. James Place apartment.

Retirement and an Active Lifestyle; St. James Place

Jack and Lillian continued an active lifestyle after his retirement at age 62. They enjoyed swimming and long walks in national parks across the US, as well as other activities.

When the Bartles made the decision to move to St. James Place, they signed papers for an apartment in the Evangeline building, which was under construction. Within six or seven months, Lillian became helpless from a rare fatal disease, and she died before the apartment was finished.

Whether to Move to St. James Place Alone

Jack considered not moving to St. James Place after Lillian's death. Looking back, he believes that would have been the wrong decision. He enjoys the weekly bridge competitions with a roomful of residents. Most importantly, he found the on-campus swimming pool and other physical activities such as shuffleboard, which have helped him gear up to become the Baton Rouge Hall of Fame Senior Olympian that he is today.

Read more about Senior Olympian Bartle in a later chapter of this book, "A Morning with Senior Olympians Julia Hawkins, 101, and Jack Bartle, 93."

Takeaways

The power of an air force is terrific when there is nothing to oppose it.
—Winston Churchill

A terrorist is someone who has a bomb, but doesn't have an air

force.
　　—William Blum

War is not only a matter of equipment, artillery, ground troops, or air force; it is largely a matter of spirit, or morale.
　　—Chiang Kai-shek

LT. COL. JOSEPH WILLIAM CARMENA

It is obvious that Bill desired to serve his country, first joining the Merchant Marine, 1946–47, then serving as a reservist in the US Air Force in 1950–51, followed by twenty years of active duty, including service in the Korean War and four years at NATO headquarters in Italy. He received numerous decorations and was an avid traveler to thirty-four countries and islands.

Marriage and Family

Wow! I had to catch my breath trying to recount his service. Fortunately, Bill found time to marry Eva Kathleen Schafer of Bismarck at the Air Force base in North Dakota. They have two sons, four daughters, and eight grandchildren.

In 1971, when Bill retired from the Air Force, they moved to Louisiana. He worked independently, plus took positions with Exxon and Ciba-Geigy, prior to retiring again in 1995.

This Guy Never Slept!

Bill's life has not been all airplanes, although he earned both private and commercial licenses. He has sung in four operas, performed on stage, been an extra in four movies, and did three TV stints!

Bill reminded me he wasn't a Greatest Generation World War II veteran. I told him his story did not work in my section "War and Marriage" either. All who read the next chapter, "Ageless Warriors," will see why his story was placed here. Who else used his skills—the quickest, the most quoted, and the most photographed—none other than Bill Carmena!

Takeaways

The biggest adventure you can ever take is to live the life of your dreams.
—Oprah Winfrey

What I love most about this crazy life is the adventure if it.
—Juliette Binoche

Adventure is not outside man; it is within.
—George Eliot

AGELESS WARRIORS

Ancient warbirds take St. James Place veterans on a flight back in time. Here are excerpts from George Morris's article in the Baton Rouge Advocate *from May 1, 2017:*

Eight retirees, all military veterans, got to take off and ride over Baton Rouge last Thursday in a Boeing Stearman PT-17, an open-cockpit biplane used to train prospective pilots in World War II. Some had flown in a Stearman before, including Bill Carmena, 88, who nearly blew the opportunity to ride in it again.
    "I thought it was too good to be true," Carmena said. "I was a little tardy signing up when they said they had free rides in a Stearman. I said that's impossible because I'd seen in aviation magazines where they said, 'Fly in a T-6 for $500.'. . . I said I'd better check on this."

*****

Over Tiger Stadium, the LSU lakes, the Mississippi River, and the State Capitol, St. James Place veterans flew with Ageless Aviation Dreams Foundation before landing. Let's pick up the article:

    [Bill] Carmena is a Korean War veteran and LSU ROTC graduate. In 1944, he and other Catholic High students got a job loading camouflage netting onto rail cars at the old Sharp Station Army depot. "We called ourselves the Saturday Commandoes," Carmena said. "'I think they paid us something like 25 cents an hour to work."
    The bonus, however, came when the job ended. The student workers were given a ride in a Stearman at Harding Field. . . .
    Stearmans were not fast, but were extremely maneuverable. Many were used after the war as cropdusters. There are two seats, one behind the other.
    "We took off and got over the boondocks, and they had air communication—just a rubber tube back to my ears," recalled Carmena of that first flight. "He said, 'You ready? Strap yourself in.' He did loops and barrel rolls, all these maneuvers. He said,

'Are you all right?' I gave him the thumb's up and we did a few more, and then we came back."

Seventy-three years later?

"Déjà vu all over again—without the acrobatics," Carmena said.

Bill Morgan, 86, brought the ID card that belonged to his father, Marion H. Morgan Jr., who served in World War I and was trained in open-cockpit aircraft of that era by Jimmy Doolittle, who later achieved fame by leading a surprise raid on Japan in World War II. Hal Filgo, 89, a Marine World War II veteran, said he used to attend Stearman fly-ins in Crowley and was able to bum a few rides.

"It's fun," Filgo said. "It's my favorite airplane. I like the two wings and I like the open cockpit."

Jack Bartle, 93, was born in England and joined the RAF in 1943. Since virtually every available airfield in his country was launching combat missions, he was sent to Grosse Ile, Michigan, to train with the US Navy, and his first training came in Stearmans. . .

Bartle was the first of the St. James Place residents to fly in the Ageless Aviators Stearman, which was piloted by Tim Newton, a retired Air Force pilot who now flies internationally for Federal Express. The trip took them to Tiger Stadium and back. The Stearman is equipped so that it can be flown from either seat.

"I really enjoyed it," Bartle said. "He did let me fly it for a little while, and I realized how much concentration you need on a small plane like this just to fly straight and level. It reacts so readily to minor atmospheric changes. It wasn't a bumpy day by any means, but you find you've got the stick wiggling around. . . . It brought me back."

Will Roussel, Jerry Black, Sidney Flynn, and Bert Knight also flew that day, among the 1,000 veterans Ageless Aviation expects to ride in the organization's three Stearmans this year, Newton said. Everyone in the organization is a volunteer.

"We do this because we love it," Newton said, "and it's the right thing to do."

LT. SHAUN McGARRY:
HONORING OUR VETERANS

Shaun McGarry served in the Vietnam War and in Desert Storm. He has a deep respect for fellow veterans who gave their all to protect our country and to preserve its heritage. He actively supports veteran affairs through membership in the Military Officers Association of America and the Military Order of the World Wars. He also helps with a large Baton Rouge–area celebration on Veterans Day each year at Parkview Baptist Church.

From the Rice Paddies of Vietnam to the Sands of Saudi Arabia

After receiving his commission as a second lieutenant in the Army Reserve, from the Infantry Officers School in Fort Benning, Georgia, Shaun received orders to deploy to Vietnam. There he served as a US advisor to Vietnam infantry units in the Mekong Delta.

Obviously, Shaun was too young to serve in the Korean War, yet he had an opportunity to travel to South Korea in 1984 for two weeks' training as a reserve officer. In 1990, he was called to active duty in the Gulf War, often referred to as Operation Desert Storm. As he said, "I went from the rice paddies of Vietnam to the sands of Saudi Arabia." He served in active duty from February 1968 to October 1970, which in the Army count system is three years' duty, and in the Army Reserve for seventeen years, from 1974 to 1991.

Shaun's Family Roots

Shaun's Irish forefathers migrated from Canada to Vermont, along with thousands of others seeking large swaths of farmland. Shaun was born in Rutland, Vermont, and was the only child of Katherine and Bernard McGarry. He was born September 5, 1942, nine months after the Japanese bombed Pearl Harbor. Following the declaration of World War II, his father served as a Navy lieutenant, leaving Katherine and infant Shaun behind.

Shaun was a graduate of Holy Cross High School in New

Orleans. He was employed by Texaco in Columbus, Georgia. In 1971, he transferred with Texaco to Montgomery, Alabama, followed by Baton Rouge in 1989.

Buying Home Insurance Leads to Marriage; Paris Honeymoon Interrupted

While insuring his Baton Rouge home, agent Katie Brown caught Shaun's eye. In May 1990, they were married, blending their family of five sons and two daughters.

Katie Brown McGarry's account:

"I never dreamed that I would be a war bride, but it happened! I had been single for twelve years. After the end of my first marriage of seventeen years, having two young daughters, I worked really hard to provide for their needs for three years. After opening my Allstate agency, I met Shaun when he was referred to my agency for insurance. After ten months of dating, we married in the Aldrich Chapel of First United Methodist Church in Baton Rouge. We went to Paris on a delayed honeymoon. Our second day in Paris, we saw on CNN that Saddam Hussein had invaded Kuwait. It really didn't get much of my attention. Although Shaun later said that he knew what would likely happen, he did not say a word at the time. He had just transferred his Army Reserve unit in Alabama to the 321st Material Management Center in Baton Rouge. His new unit had been trained for desert warfare, so he knew he would possibly be called for active duty very soon. Upon returning home, there was a message on the answering machine that his unit was on standby for active duty. I was really shocked, as I had no idea he could be sent to war. A few days later, the call came for him to report to the Reserve Center, and their unit was sent to Fort Polk for refresher training and then on to Saudi Arabia."

"During the time Shaun was gone, I had three college students living with me, my two daughters and Shaun's oldest son. I was so glad to have them with me. They helped bridge the loneliness of not having my husband with me. Shaun's assignment was as a purchasing agent, which kept him out of the front lines and close to his base of operations. The facility that they were housed in had telephone connections, and we were able to talk quite often. The connection was not always good and the phone bill was expensive, before today's internet and cell phones. When CNN announced that the war had begun, I wanted to know that Shaun was okay. I later learned why he didn't answer, as they were under attack."

"His unit was the last to come home after the short war was over. His unit returned to Baton Rouge after almost eleven months of overseas duty, just in time for our first wedding anniversary."

During his tour, Shaun was promoted to lieutenant colonel. He retired from the Army Reserve having completed twenty years of military service. Shaun is still serving his country in retirement. He is active in two veterans' organizations that support high school and college ROTC units, and youth leadership programs.

Takeaways

Since the Revolution, eight generations of America's veterans have established an unbroken commitment to freedom.
    —Steve Buyer

When the peace treaty is signed, the war is not over for our veterans and their families. It is just starting.
    —Karl Marlantes

I want people to get involved with veterans.
    —Max Martin

Section 3

Military Women at St. James Place

WOMEN IN THE WORLD WARS

World War I

When the war began, large numbers of women were mobilized to fill civilian jobs of men who had gone to war. According to Wikipedia, almost 23,000 women served as Army and Navy nurses in military hospitals stateside, as well as overseas, over the course of the war. The first American women enlisted into the regular armed forces were 13,000 who were admitted into active duty in the Navy. They served stateside in the same roles as men and received the same pay, $28.75 per month. They were recognized as veterans after the war ended.

In her book *Women Heroes of World War I*, Kathryn J. Atwood wrote, "During the conflict that was placed before them, [these women] not only gained the gratitude of many in their generation, but they proved, for the first time on a global scale, the enormous value of a woman's contribution, paving the way for future generations of women to do the same."

World War II

The women who participated in World War I had been virtually forgotten some twenty-three years later, when the US joined World War II in 1941, after the Japanese bombed Pearl Harbor.

As reported on the History website (www.history.com): "During World War II, some 350,000 women served in the U.S. Armed Forces, both at home and abroad. They included Women's Airforce Service Pilots. . . . Between 1940 and 1945, the female percentage of the U.S. workforce increased from 27 percent to nearly 37 percent, and by 1945 nearly one out of every four married women worked outside the home."

ST. JAMES PLACE RESIDENT WOMEN WHO SERVED IN THE MILITARY

Mary Ann Larson

A weekend warrior, Mary served in several units, with jobs differing from warehousing to advanced supply bases. Her units changed as she was promoted and transferred for her federal civilian positions.

Mary was born and raised in Detroit, Michigan. After receiving a promotional letter declaring the reader was not too old to join the Navy, Mary challenged the premise and was immediately enlisted. Boot camp was in Algiers, Louisiana. From there, she served in Memphis, Tennessee; Washington, DC; and Mississippi; she was discharged in 1996. Although Mary had earned a BS in business education, she was over thirty-five, too old to be considered an officer. Mary is the only member of her family to serve in the military.

Josephine "Jo" Salter, LTJG Nurse, WAVES

Jo served for two and one-half years during the Korean War, stationed in Jacksonville, Florida; Buford, South Carolina; and Corpus Christi, Texas.

She was born in Lincoln County, Kentucky. Because there was very little money to be earned in those times, and her friends wanted to be in the military, Jo was motivated to join. She and her friends took the physical, but Jo was the only one to pass.

Jo had five brothers and a sister in the military. Two brothers in the Navy, one brother in the Army, and a sister who was a Navy nurse all served in World War II. During the Korean conflict, Jo had a brother in the Army, while she served in the Navy.

Irma Moore, Pharmacist's Mate Second Class Petty Officer, WAVES

Irma Keith was born and grew up in Hopkinson, Iowa. She enlisted in the Navy in 1943 in Cedar Rapids, Iowa, and tested in Des

Moines. In September, she attended three weeks of boot camp at Hunter College in New York City. She took a six-day trip by train to the Naval Hospital, known as Oak Knoll, in Oakland, California. Her next duty station was Hawaii. She sailed on the *Matsonia,* a converted cruise ship, which she referred to as having great food! In November 1945, Irma started home in a Navy hospital ship. She remembers the song "Kiss Me Once, Kiss Me Twice, and Kiss Me Once Again," which was played continuously. After the ship docked in San Francisco, she was sent to Great Lakes, Michigan, where she was discharged in December 1945.

Irma's father served in World War I as a drummer for a band from Great Lakes. He traveled all over the world. Irma believes it was her father's service that motivated her to enlist.

Her husband, Lou, served in World War II as a gunner's mate with the US Navy.

June Lank

June Lank enlisted in the Navy in 1943, and served at the women's Marine barracks and Navy barracks. She was honorably discharged as a pharmacist's mate (PhM) in 1946. She wanted to do her part in the war while waiting to marry her college sweetheart, Bob Lank.

June and Bob were married in November 1946 and lived in Bastrop, Louisiana, until June 1948, when Bob joined the LSU School of Veterinary Medicine.

June was born in 1920 in Liberal, Kansas. Her parents, G. L. Light and Mae Lathrop, had two other girls and two boys. June graduated from Kansas State University in 1943.

The Lanks moved to St. James Place in 2001. Bob died in 2017.

Violet Lux (deceased)

Violet was a Navy singer and helped entertain troops during World War II.

Jackie Tandy (deceased)

Jackie was a former servicewoman and a World War II veteran.

To learn more about these ladies, view Baton Rouge channel 33's "Hometown Heroes":
http:www.brproud.com/news/local-news/hometown-heroes-june-irma-jo-violet-and-mary

Takeaways

No nation can rise to the height of glory unless your women are side by side with you.
 —Muhammad Ali Jinnah

Men always want to be a woman's first love—women like to be a man's last romance.
 —Oscar Wilde

There are only three things women need in life: food, water and compliments.
 —Chris Rock

Part II

Socialization of Seniors

Section 1

Personal Reflections on Senior Care through the Years

Born perhaps with a compassionate heart for others, I began to realize in my late thirties that my in-laws would soon require assistance with medical needs. In retrospect, I wonder if there should have been a meeting of siblings and spouses to develop a flexible plan, aimed to share the responsibilities while carefully preserving the dignity of their elders. Would such a meeting work? Would there be deniers of the need, or indifference to sharing of the responsibilities? Although my in-laws had three sons and daughters-in-law in town, others seemed oblivious. We all had dependent children. The sons were all working, and I was the only wife working outside the home, managing my home-design and contracting business, Regrets, no; resentments, thankfully, no! If others felt guilt, that was theirs to deal with.

    After ten years, my mother-in-law, who had survived her husband, passed away. Less than two years later, my parents moved to Baton Rouge at the advice of their doctor, and lived in the Catholic Presbyterian Apartments until my mother's death nineteen years later at age 94. With both brothers living out of town, I gladly took the responsibility.

    When I had to leave the high altitude of Mexico for health reasons, I chose to move to St. James Place to live, rather than my country home an hour away. I was 80 years old and still driving. I wanted socialization, a place to continue my volunteerism, and the opportunity to *age in place,* in a continuing care retirement community, as my needs changed. When macular degeneration ended my driving, my needs were met by St. James Place. They provide transportation to doctor's visits, thus freeing my only child of this responsibility, and I enjoy walking to the nearby grocery store for other needs.

THE GUEST HOUSE (NURSING HOME), 1966–1971

In 1965, my father-in-law's doctors directed that he be moved from the hospital where he was being treated, as they could no longer help him. Facing reality as my mother-in-law's health was also failing, I assumed the familiar family responsibility expected of me and moved my in-laws to the Guest House, a facility in Baton Rouge. Some of the family made accusations about putting parents in a nursing home.

My father-in-law, Mr. Smith, had been referred to by his fellow Standard Oil employees as "Smoky." His years of smoking caused failures of both heart and lungs. For five years, I drove him numerous times from his rural Greenwell Springs home to the Stanocola Medical Center.

After Mr. Smith died, a female roommate shared the room with my mother-in-law. All was well until the roommate began holding hands with a man in the Guest House living room. Mrs. Smith, along with some of the other residents, felt disgraced by such behavior. The hand-holding continued, and the formerly grouchy male resident became pleasant with the other residents, and especially to the staff he previously verbally abused.

There were no doorknobs or privacy locks on the resident doors at that time. As I recall, the doors had push plates like those on hospital or dining-room doors. Thus the ultimate disgrace occurred when staff found the lovers in his bed. Yes, you guessed right as to what happened next! He was isolated to his room and became even more verbally abusive with the staff.

Twenty months after Mrs. Smith died, my parents moved to the Catholic Presbyterian Apartments in downtown Baton Rouge.

THE CATHOLIC PRESBYTERIAN APARTMENTS, 1973–1992

As an aside, can you imagine a collaboration between Catholics, Presbyterians, and the federal government? Dr. Voss (who has become a friend to all since moving to St. James Place) suggested I take my parents to see the Catholic Presbyterian Apartments shortly after construction was finished in 1972. (Shortly after my mother died in 1992, the facility became eligible for Section 8 residents.)

As Parkinson's disease began to confuse my father's mind, and heart disease became more pronounced, Mother and Dad moved from their quiet north Louisiana farm to an exciting new adventure. Their eleventh-floor corner apartment overlooked the State Capitol grounds and the Mississippi River by day, and by night Dad marveled at the panoramic view of the brightly lit Standard Oil Refinery, now Exxon Refinery. They loved to go with me to my West Feliciana country home and gardens, where I came to know my dad, for a few years, after a childhood when he worked six days a week, farming to feed and support our family.

For a number of months, Dad often spent his days walking down to the Capitol gardens and visiting with the many tourists. Each apartment had its own kitchen, and my mother found time from her usual housekeeping chores to volunteer in a telephone ministry with homebound seniors. Dad died two and a half years after their move.

Mother, the middle child of nine, was the only one to go to college. She graduated from Louisiana State Normal School, now known as Northwestern State University, and became the principal and teacher of a one-room school for children through the sixth grade. She taught there until her marriage to my father.

After Dad's death, she was asked to head the Resident Council of the 13-story, 195-unit apartment facility, a key position she would hold for seventeen years, until her death at age 94. I referred to her as the *mama of the mamas,* as the residents were predominantly women.

The day she died in her apartment, she was rolled out feet first, as she had requested. My daughter had come earlier that morning with a bouquet of flowers picked by her five-year-old quadruplets and their three-year-old sister. I went back to gather her few pieces of jewelry, poems she had begun writing at age 90, and her spiral-bound recipe and diary notebooks. I still treasure these and use some of the recipes.

Mother had been married since 1924 and had lived in her and my father's own home until they moved to the apartments fifty-five years later. Mother was a widow for seventeen years, and viewed socialization between widowed men and women as fodder for her diary.

Section 2

Eat, Drink, and Remarry

I never saw the pillow with the embroidered words, *Eat, Drink, and Remarry,* reportedly in one of the lounge chairs in the lobby of the Duplantier Auditorium at St. James Place. You will read how some seniors in long marriages, after the death of a spouse, begin to socialize and remarry. Many of today's seniors are remaining physically, sexually, and mentally more active, as the longevity rate continues to climb.

      Apparently living with a spouse through sickness and death does not discourage some from seeking that close companionship in another marriage. *Till death we doth part* is an idiom from the 1662 Book of Common Prayer and is closely associated with the wedding vows.

NONAGENARIAN BERT KNIGHT MARRIES OCTOGENARIAN DORIS AKERS

In June of 2016, wedding bells rang at Baton Rouge's First United Methodist Church when Bert Knight married Doris Akers, a petite former cheerleader. Family members gathered in the beautiful Aldrich Chapel for the exchange of vows, Rev. Brady Whitton presiding.

The lunch and myriads of photo ops that followed the ceremony did not end until after 3 p.m. Branson, Missouri, their honeymoon destination, was over five hundred miles away. Bert knew that was too long a drive to share their first night together. Bert, a former research scientist who had helped develop the hydrogen bomb during the Korean War, had done his research and had well-laid plans for their romantic honeymoon. They would stop over in Natchez, Mississippi, on their way to Branson.

First Erotic Rendezvous, Enhanced by Ants

Well, sorry to say, Bert's well-laid honeymoon plans went a little astray. In his excitement, he forgot that there are few freestanding restaurants in Natchez, apart from those in hotels and plantation homes. So they ended up ordering dinner at Big Fat Mama's Tamales. The popular eatery was jam-packed, with most patrons smoking. To be able to breathe, the newlyweds retreated to the patio. In an otherwise pleasant venue, Doris managed to plant a foot on a small anthill! I failed to ask whether their first erotic adventure of the night happened before or after their server brought their tamales.

Well, it was like this. Doris began feeling *things*. Alas, it was ants. Bert doesn't recall what the lotion was that he found in his car. Whether it was the lotion, or his fingers applying it, we will never know, but the burning and itching faded quickly. I hope the tamales didn't get cold in the *heat of the moment*. . . .

But the most important details of their honeymoon night they did not reveal. I had laughed so much at the intimate details of their first *erotic adventure* (after all, I do have a bad heart condition) that I dared not to ask.

On the Road Again to Branson, Missouri

With over four hundred miles to go, Bert drove to his prearranged hotel destination in Branson. He noted that for an unknown reason, possibly noise, they were shown to a room farthest from the other occupants. He equally bemoaned that it was a ten-minute walk through mazes to reach his car. Otherwise, they enjoyed the musical venues, and all too soon, it was time to hit the road back to Baton Rouge. In an attempt to shorten the way home, Bert took a straight shot to Baton Rouge along country roads with many miles between fuel and cold-drink stops. Doris, not having visited such Mississippi backwoods areas, was perhaps as shocked as were the beer-drinking locals as they watched this pair of seniors, as though they were carrying a banner declaring, "Newlyweds!"

How the Romance Began

Bert, ever ready with his camera, took pictures of all new arrivals at St. James Place. He remembered Doris Akers as a "cute one" when he took her picture in 2011. He managed to be seated next to her in Snazzy Singers, a St. James Place choir of over thirty residents.

Bert said he had good genes, as one family member lived to age 103 and another to almost 100. Now we understand why he remembered the younger "cute one," as he had outlived his two wives.

The Courting Began, *Sort of*

Bert the researcher/planner hit a few bumps in the road leading toward romance. First, he issued several invitations to dinner, followed by politely asking Doris if he could kiss her good night.

After a successful kiss, he invited himself over to watch the evening news. Doubtless Bert had more in mind, as he arrived with a bottle of wine tucked under his arm. Considering that both Bert and Doris have small frames, after Bert popped the cork, I doubt they could remember the top TV news story. A few more invitations to dinner . . .

Ready to Pop the Question

Yes, confident Bert said he hemmed and hawed before he asked Doris to marry him, and immediately presented a diamond ring. He said, "Doris was less than excited, but she kept the ring!"

He waited as the weeks passed, while taking her to dinner, with no mention of *the ring*. After about six weeks, Bert had worried long enough, and perhaps in a "put up or shut up" mood (Doris's son Jim had told him she was very slow to make up her mind), he asked Doris, "Do you still have the ring?" I was so excited that I forgot to ask how the dialogue continued, yet I do know Bert had to have gone back to his garden home with a grin on his face!

Family Backgrounds

Doris was born on a small, Depression-era farm in southwest Missouri. She was a petite baton twirler and a leader of the band in high school. She went to Drury College, earned a BA in education, and sang in the college choir. Later she received a BS in counseling at Louisiana Tech University. She has two sons and a daughter. In 2011, two years after her husband died, she moved to St. James Place. She has made five long trips to Australia to visit her daughter, including before and after her daughter's delivery of a baby boy.

Bert was born in Turner, Maine, on a dairy farm. He earned a BS in chemistry from Bates College and a physical chemistry PhD from Harvard University. He has no children.

Newlywed Glow

As Doris and Bert sat talking with me, by the look on their faces and the hand holding, it was obvious how happy they were after six months of marriage. Sure, the garage is still filled with furniture after Doris moved from her apartment. She wears a sling following rotator cuff surgery, but *what the heck*. This is a couple, both from rural backgrounds, finding many things in common, yet most of all, they have each other as best friends and lovers.

For more about Bert Knight, visit "Weekends with Whitney" at https://www.youtube.com/watch?v=ZDbOLpsmyhM.

The February 1, 2017, issue of *225 Magazine* also featured the Knights.

Takeaways

Behind every great man is a woman rolling her eyes.
  —Jim Carrey

Age is something that doesn't matter, unless you are a cheese.
  —Luis Buñuel

I'm for anything that gets you through the night.
  —Frank Sinatra

WALKING THEIR DOGS:
ARTHUR AND JOYCE DICKERSON

It was a beautiful day on the campus of St. James Place when Joyce Jackson's dog Boppy, and Arthur Dickerson's dog Maxi, first met with their masters in tow, on the other end of their leashes. The foursome must have gotten along, as they continued to meet regularly, until Arthur posed a serious offer. . . .

A Romantic Proposal

Arthur is a man of few words, but when he does speak, he gets right to the point: "Since we walk our dogs together every day, we may as well get married." To some, Arthur's suggestion may not seem very romantic, but I surmise it was *very* romantic to both dog and people lovers, each in their own right.

    (I confess I was the sissy taunted by two brothers with all that creeped and crawled. Besides, our house was too small for our family of five, with no room inside for pets.)

Wedding under St. James Place Historic Live Oak Tree

The longevity of the over 2,000-year-old live oak was symbolic of the combined 125 years Arthur and Joyce had shared with their former spouses, both of whom died in the St. James Place health care areas. They had experienced *till death do us part.*

    I lead music with Joyce each week in those areas. I asked her why she considered marrying again, and was surprised by her answer. I decided I better run it by Arthur before publishing it. I told him Joyce's answer was, "To be taken care of," and he immediately said, "I don't care, and I am still taking care of her."

    They were indeed skilled in their 125 years of marriage. Now, Joyce is 92 and Arthur is 91. They have enjoyed eight years in their second marriage, proving that we are never too old to seek the pleasures of love and companionship.

Takeaways

Proof that our dog can be our best friend, finding us a soulmate!
   —Robert Browning

Never be afraid of doing the thing you know in your heart is right, even if others don't agree.
   —Elizabeth Berg

For me and my wife, it was love at first sight.
   —Jeff Bridges

FAMILIES THAT PLAY TOGETHER STAY TOGETHER: WILL AND MARGARET ROUSSEL

Will is the youngest of eight children,
Father of three girls and three boys,
Grandchildren, 19,
Great-grandchildren, 20.

Margaret is the youngest of nine children,
Mother of three girls and one boy,
Grandchildren, 10,
Great-grandchildren, 4.

Now you understand the title. It only takes one family member to call and suggest a fun event and everyone within driving distance, on a moment's notice, joins in the fun.

It is easier for Margaret's children living in Prairieville and New Orleans than those in Texas and Washington, DC. Will has a son and a daughter living in Baton Rouge, with others in St. James Parish and Georgia. Putting Will's and Margaret's families together, *wow!* I understand family reunions number about seventy and, thankfully, showcase many family talents, including a baker/bride who baked and decorated her own elaborate wedding cake!

Their Separate Moves to St. James Place

Margaret and her husband Sidney Vail moved to a St. James Place garden home in 2001, and Sidney died in 2004. Will moved to his St. James Place garden home in 2004, a year after his wife, Carolyn, died.

Both Margaret and Will joined other residents for happy hour and dinner most evenings. In 2005, Bert Knight and his wife Olga (now deceased) invited Will to bring a date to the dance club's dances, along with John Firestone and wife Ruby Anne (now deceased), and Tom Oswald and wife Margaret (now deceased). This was Will and Margaret's first date.

Absence Makes the Heart Grow Fonder

Shortly after that first date, Margaret went to visit friends for three weeks in England. As we know, *absence makes the heart grow fonder,* while they conversed by email. Margaret remembers her homecoming as her garden home was filled with family that had evacuated when Katrina ravaged New Orleans in 2005.

Not surprising, while our courting couple was in a coffeehouse, Will told Margaret it was time for them to look at rings.

They received marriage counseling with Catholic priest Father Burns and Episcopal minister Father Holland. These sessions were rather amusing as Will was previously married for fifty years and Margaret for fifty-one years.

Father Holland told them they could give him pointers as he had been married for a much shorter time. They were married at St. James Episcopal Church.

Traveling with the "Eat, Drink, and Remarry" Couples

Largely an "eat, drink, and remarry" group, the Roussels, Oswalds, Firestones, Knights, and Al and Shirley Schroeck (both now deceased) enjoyed playing cards and taking day trips, both before and continuing after their marriages. Their trips with other St. James Place residents included Boston, the St. Lawrence River, Nova Scotia, and Quebec. In the Christmas season they enjoyed San Antonio and the many festive canal barges. A favorite trip was to Las Vegas with hopes of competing in *The Price is Right Show.* They dressed in Mardi Gras attire, but their combined total of 105 years of marriage was not sufficient to be chosen to compete. In 2006, Independent Living residents elected Margaret and Will as king and queen of the St. James Place Mardi Gras parade and celebration. It was another occasion for their extensive family to come and join in the festivities.

Margaret's Family Roots

Margaret was born in Alvin, Texas, the youngest in a family of nine. Her father, Thomas Smith, was a dairy farmer. She went to business school. After her children were grown, she furthered her education at LSU-NO, followed by employment as a secretary for All Saints Episcopal Church for nineteen years. She helped direct the church's top fundraiser—selling their cookbook.

Will's Family Roots

Will was born in St. James Parish. His father, Morgan Roussel, worked for the Louisiana State Department of Highways until his early death, leaving eight children. Will, the youngest, was ten. He was seventeen when his mother died.

After high school, Will enrolled at LSU and in ROTC, majoring in political science. Upon graduation, he enrolled in Officer Training School to become a second lieutenant, subsequently serving in the Marines in the Korean conflict in 1951–1952.

After his release from the Marines, Will worked as the director of personnel and customer relations with Kaiser Aluminum in their three locations—Baton Rouge, Chalmette, and Gramercy. He retired at age 72.

Takeaways

There can be hope only for a society which acts as one big family, not as many separate ones.
　　—Anwar Sadat

I come from a big family of storytellers and, growing up, I liked hearing about the years before I was born.
　　—Molly Antopol

When you're the mom in a big family comedy, you have to get your personality when you can.
    —Bonnie Hunt

ESTHER LYNCH, AN INSPIRATION TO ALL SHE MEETS

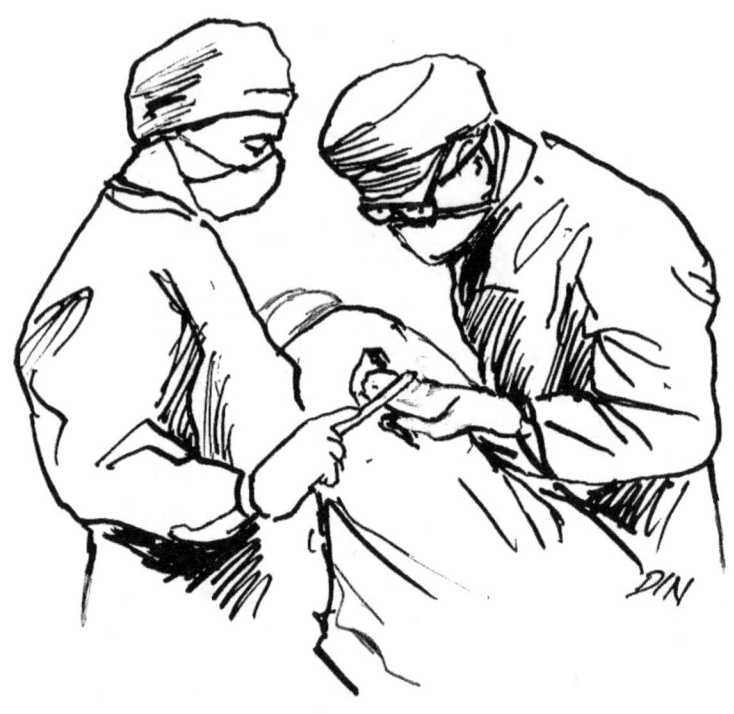

Some people have a pleasant magnetism, a friendliness that is contagious. Such a person is Esther Lynch. I first met her in the cafeteria at St. James Place in 2008, shortly after she moved from a condo community. A people person, she soon realized her condo neighbors were younger and went to work, leaving no one to socialize with all day long. This precipitated her move to St. James Place.

We have enjoyed short visits as our paths have crossed in the nine years since she became a resident. Unfortunately, I never framed an opportunity to really get to know Esther until I interviewed her for this book. The interview was to be about her marriage at age 76 after moving to St. James Place, for the "Eat, Drink, and Remarry" section of this book. Never did I imagine that Esther had survived life blows that would have sunk many into depression, time after time—any of which could have sabotaged normal lives. Her Christian faith and joy have been an underlying part of our short chats since I have known her.

Esther Becomes a War Bride, Raises a Family

After graduating from Iota High School, Esther worked in a merchandise store. While glancing wistfully out the store window, she saw a handsome uniformed soldier approaching, hopefully coming to see her! She had not met Philip Miller when they were both students in school. He was arriving home after his 1947 discharge from the Army.

They were married a year later and moved to Lake Charles, where Philip worked as a dispatcher at Exxon's wholesale terminal. There fuel was barged in and distributed by tanker trucks to Exxon gas stations.

Esther received a nursing degree from the Lake Charles Technical School and worked as a nurse while raising their children—a son, Michael, and three daughters, Harriet, Leslie, and Mona.

Esther and Philip had just returned from a wonderful vacation when Philip died of a massive heart attack, ending twenty-five years of marriage. He was 42.

Esther's Early Life

Esther Roy was born in the interesting small town of Iota, Louisiana (population 1,500 according to the 2010 census). One name the early settlers gave Iota was Pointe aux Loups, French for "Wolves' Path." Cleve Roy farmed in Iota and married Lucy Gott. Esther was one of their four daughters, and always yearned for a brother. (I had two brothers and yearned for a sister.)

Picking Up the Pieces of Her Life

After Philip died, Esther, encouraged by two surgeons who had seen her talents as a surgical nurse, trained to become a surgical assistant, a first in Louisiana at the time. She furthered her education in Denver, San Diego, and Detroit. She alternated working, side by side, with the two surgeons who had inspired her to be a surgeon assistant.

Esther Finds Marital Happiness; Picks Up the Pieces of Her Life Again

Esther later married Newton Lynch, who had two grown children, a daughter and a son. He was an engineer for General Electric worldwide. They had many enjoyable trips together to his GE assignments in various countries. After retiring, they enjoyed stateside travels and cruises on the Caribbean. Suddenly Newton became ill, was hospitalized, and died a week later. They had been happily married for twenty years.

Esther sold their home in Lake o' the Pines Community in Longview, Texas, and moved to Baton Rouge, where her daughters Harriet and Mona live.

The Curse of Rheumatoid Arthritis

Perhaps I had not heard of rheumatoid arthritis in my late thirties, when Dr. Weiss, at Oschner's Clinic in New Orleans, diagnosed me with it. I soon gained deep compassion for those who have developed the disease. The only way I can describe it is that you burn and hurt at the same time. Ester said there are other kinds that have different symptoms.

Esther was only six when she was diagnosed. Her only treatment was half of an aspirin at bedtime. She remembers many nights of crying with pain, her mother, sometimes alternating with Esther's two sisters, rubbing her legs.

In 2005, Esther received further diagnosis of neuropathy and psoriatic arthritis. She experiences good days interspersed with days of debilitating pain.

Ten years ago, she began infusion therapy. Every five weeks she, along with thirteen other sufferers, sat in recliners in a large circle to receive medications intravenously. Esther would later learn that the nurses had discussed "Miss Esther and Mr. Pete" (Poirrier), who had both lost spouses through death. Their plan was to gradually seat the two nearer to each other each session, until they had them sitting side by side.

Romance Blossomed Quickly

Esther noted the fishing magazines that Pete brought to each session and asked if he was a fisherman. Pete quickly responded, "Oh yes! How did you know?" She replied that her deceased husband was a fisherman and read those same magazines. Pete said he had been going fishing more often rather than sitting home alone since his wife died. Their conversation turned to lunch, with Pete suggesting they go to the Piccadilly Cafeteria after therapy. It was easy for Esther to say yes as she noted his broad smile framing his beautiful teeth.

Fate Was in Their Corner

Fate was in their corner at Piccadilly, as there was a pianist playing some wonderful romantic songs. Pete admitted he had taken note of Esther's good looks from the beginning when he sat on the opposite side of the circle.

Pete began visiting Esther almost daily at her St. James Place apartment. Noting her shortage of clothes-hanging space, doubtless looking ahead and handy with his hands, Pete added more hanging rods. Not only was Pete innovative, but he began, and continues, to zealously take care of Esther, despite his own health problems. Fortunately, his health has not prevented his ability to drive. They are able to go to movies, doctor's appointments, and other activities, both on and off campus.

I knew this relationship was getting serious when I began seeing Pete, over six feet tall and a large build, holding the leash of Esther's small Pomeranian dog, Fancy, for a morning walk.

Esther seemed a bit puzzled when I asked several times who popped the question. I should have understood that from day one, both in painful debilitating illnesses, this was a couple who wanted to be together daily for as long as they both shall live. Their illness had brought them together, for which they are eternally grateful!

Plans for a Quiet Wedding Turn into a Big Celebration

It was to be a small, quiet wedding performed at the Amana Christian Fellowship church in Maurice, Louisiana, by Esther's grandson, Rev. Terrell Reed. They arrived at the church with their extended families. Two of Esther's three daughters, Harriet Jones and Mona Delatin, and their five children were in attendance. Esther's three sisters also came: Anna Reed, Alverda LeJunne, and Yvonne Simar. Pete's three sons, Gregory, Kevin, and Eric Poirrier from Pierre Part, attended with their three children. There was a lovely wedding reception, including flowers and a big wedding cake.

It is heartwarming to see a couple, Esther 85 and Pete 73, still very much in love after almost nine years of marriage. Their love grows stronger as they minister to each other when one has a pain-filled day.

Takeaways

Every day is a gift from God. Learn to focus on the Giver and enjoy the gift!
　　　—Joyce Meyer

The heart is a thousand-stringed instrument that can only be tuned with love.
　　　—Hafiz

She had been ready to love this man from the first time she met him, and was more ready when she knew he felt the same way.
　　　—Author unknown

Part III

The Choice Is Yours: Live Life to Its Fullest or Just Exist

Section 1

Shedding of Responsibilities: Time to Enhance Your Life

After I made the decision to move to St. James Place in 2008, I no longer had to worry about getting the lawn mowed, calling a plumber to fix a leaky faucet, a painter—the list could fill a page.

Medicines are delivered to our door by a nearby drugstore. Although I still drove, I could take free transportation to medical appointments, without concern for a parking spot or the weather. The newspaper is dropped at my door now, there are few dishes to wash, and a housekeeper comes to clean once a week and change bed linens.

Yes, after all the years, shedding responsibilities has left quality time for family and friends and the humanitarian work to which I dedicated my life at age 75.

I am truly independent, and my time with family is not centered on medical and grocery shopping. We have an in-house marketplace, and I enjoy a short walk to our adjoining neighborhood stores.

LIVE LIFE WELL
by Janet Dewey, Sales Counselor, St. James Place

These three words represent the goal of most senior citizens who, after a lifetime of working and raising a family, transition into their retirement years. They are also the motto of St. James Place, a continuing care retirement community (CCRC) in Baton Rouge.

Yet, the way that seniors face the opportunities and challenges brought about through aging can determine just how well they will fare in their mid and late retirement years.

We've all met people who are absolutely determined to live in their home . . . forever. They fear that moving will compromise their independence, despite the fact that the home of times-gone-by where family gathered for dinners, parties, and game nights isn't quite the busy, fun place it once was. Add in decreased socialization and isolation as friends become less mobile, and the fact is that "home alone" can become quite lonely at times.

Other seniors facing similar challenges become determined to make proactive choices for their retirement years. Specifically, they want a plan in place for future healthcare changes and to make choices before a crisis occurs when their children will be forced to make often difficult decisions.

Then much to their surprise, these forward-thinking seniors come to understand that they actually enjoy the socialization, involvement, and new family they make after moving to a retirement community.

Planning for the Future

Many of us view ourselves as healthy and think that we will never need long-term health care. However, according to the National Clearinghouse for Long-Term Care Information, at least 70% of people over age 65 will require long-term care services at some point in their lives and more than 40% will need care in a nursing home.

Seniors do have options . . . some better than others!

1) Do nothing and stay in their home until a crisis occurs—not advisable!
2) Move in with their children—not the practice it was generations ago.
3) Purchase long-term care insurance—this will help pay for assistance during mid to later retirement years.
4) Investigate a senior living community—a proactive choice that can enrich early as well as later senior years.

Continuing Care Retirement Communities (CCRCs)

Most people are familiar with assisted living or nursing care centers. They can provide valuable help when needed, but they come at an ever-increasing price that many seniors have a difficult time affording. The national median cost of one year in a private nursing home room is 49% more than the median household income in the United States (Genworth 2011 Cost of Care Survey, conducted by CareScout).

CCRCs offer seniors the option to live independently in the near term, yet establish a plan should health changes occur as they age. Additionally, research shows that seniors living in CCRCs actually live longer, two and a half years longer, and attributes this increased longevity to several factors revolving around the concept of wellness: the level of socialization, attention to nutrition, and emphasis on fitness.

CCRCs must, by definition, offer a full continuum of care, from Independent Living to Assisted Living and nursing care. Care for seniors with dementia is typically included in this continuum. There are approximately two thousand CCRCs in the United States, some on a pay-for-services basis and others requiring an entry fee, which helps ensure a predictable fee structure through all years of residence and health care.

Researchers often look to CCRC residents to develop model social and wellness programs for senior citizens. When asked why seniors decided to move into a CCRC, their answers include the following:

• *The senior(s) or adult children are planners; they prefer to be proactive instead of reactive.* As one resident of a senior community stated, although she was healthy, it would be foolish not to consider future changes in her health. Developing a plan for future health care needs may be difficult for parents facing their mortality or for adult children assuming a different role in their family dynamics. However, once a plan is in place, families often report less stress and concern about future emergencies.

• *Seniors don't want to be a burden on adult children.* A CCRC resident recently commented that her move to a retirement community was her "gift to her son." The reality is that planning early allows seniors to make informed decisions about where they choose to spend their "freedom years." Retirement communities can range from a hometown favorite location where long-time friends enjoy late-retirement living, to a destination community for golfers or snowbirds.

• *They want to avoid the cost and headache of ongoing home maintenance.* After cutting tree limbs and cleaning up debris from a hurricane, one 70-something CCRC resident pledged he wanted to be free of home maintenance and to travel without care about someone guarding his home. Maintenance headaches such as the air conditioner going out, the seasonal gutter clean-out, bursting pipes—"I want no more of it!"

• *They want access to future health care as needed and at a predictable, locked-in cost.* Very few people believe that the cost of long-term health care will actually decrease in the future, yet taking action to pay for future costs now is simply impossible for many. Unable to rationally accept the fact that after a lifetime of working and caring for children and others they will not be able to afford assisted living or nursing care, many people simply choose to ignore the potential financial exposure of years of long-term care. The CCRCs that offer a plan for prepayment of a portion of long-term health care address the concern about paying for future care. This type of plan usually entails a substantial entry fee and level monthly payment (with allowable adjustments for inflation). Often compared to an unlimited, long-term-care insurance policy, these CCRCs can provide assurances for future care.

• *Intangibles: health benefits, social stimulation, sense of community, staying active, involvement in various projects.* "I found a new family!" That's how a CCRC resident described new friends in his retirement community. It's a refrain heard over and over—friendships are really not so hard to make if one is open to the notion, as evidenced by the number of late-life marriages. There's no age limit on the value of companionship, and those who think a person is ever too old to get married are "misinformed," as a 93-year-old newlywed recently commented! Another intangible of retirement community living is the enjoyment of a full activity calendar. From daily bridge dates to billiards, book clubs, musical performances, continuing education classes, holiday celebrations, fitness classes, yoga, exercise programs, art, and woodworking, there is always something to do at a retirement community.

Planning Ahead

In a February 16, 2011, article written for *Forbes*, elder-law specialist Bernard A. Krooks identified five phases of retirement planning. The first two phases focus on saving diligently, taking advantage of tax-deferred opportunities, and converting savings into an income stream when nearing retirement. In Phase III (early retirement), seniors are challenged to create clear communication channels with family members and to make decisions in a calm, supportive way. Phase IV work (mid-retirement) includes looking at what steps you would like your family to take should your healthy condition decline significantly. According to Mr. Krooks, "It takes courage to dive into a conversation about giving up and transferring control." Phase V (late retirement) is the time when all the planning done in prior years makes this transition as "manageable and life affirming as possible."

Pay Now or Pay Later

In so many ways, getting old is not for sissies! And many people experience sticker shock when they begin to consider the cost of long-term health and residential services. National averages for long-term care costs as calculated for 2016 by Genworth Financial (www.genworth.com) are as follows:

Home Health Aide: $3,861/month
Assisted Living Facility: $3,628/month
Nursing Care: $7,698/month

Add in the costs of medications, personal care products, and insurance premiums, and it's easy to see how a senior's retirement savings can quickly become depleted and lead to support by adult children. CCRCs that contractually provide lifetime access to a full continuum of care are based on a century-old concept developed by faith-based and charitable organizations. Evolving over many years, the current funding approach of most CCRCs involves an entry fee based on actuarial projections of the minimum amount required to provide long-term care as contracted. And paying for this care in today's dollars, not future dollars, is an attractive opportunity.

It is important to distinguish between services provided in some CCRCs and other hybrid-type senior communities through a rental-only plan. While attractive to many people as they typically do not require a substantial entry fee, they also do not guarantee future care or the cost of such care. For more resources, visit www.mylifesite.net.

Again, pay now or pay later!

The Crystal Ball Effect

While Dorothy in *The Wizard of Oz* was able to see Auntie Em in the crystal ball, reliable crystal balls seem to be in short supply these days. Planning for the future must be based on the best available information as to family longevity, aging trends, disease processes, and other factors.

As one resident of a senior community said, "I'm a healthy 75-year-old woman. But I would be foolish not to plan for the possibility that my health could change." CCRCs, while not inexpensive, can be a prudent, cost-effective, and satisfying solution.

Section 2

How Two Generations Chose Senior Living: The Judge Jess Johnson Family

I never met Judge Jess Johnson, who was born in 1887 in Washington Parish. In 1910, while he was in his third year at LSU, he heard a Louisiana legislator speak and took him at his word when the congressman said to look him up when he visited Washington. So Jess went and astonished the empathetic legislator, who did follow through and obtained Jess a job with the Library of Congress, followed by other positions in the nation's capital, while he continued his studies to obtain his law degree at Georgetown University.

After World War I broke out, Jess served as a sergeant major in the Judge Advocate General's Corps. After the war ended, he worked as an attorney in Baton Rouge and was elected district judge in 1950.

ADA DOWDELL JOHNSON

Ada Dowdell, born in 1902 in Pointe Coupée Parish, would later become Jess's wife. When she was a small child, her father moved his family to his hometown, Auburn, Alabama. She earned a teaching degree at the Woman's College in Montgomery, Alabama. A friend wrote to her about a teaching opportunity in Brusly, Louisiana, but when she arrived, it had already been filled. She applied for a position at Baton Rouge High School and was hired. Years later, after marriage and her two sons were in high school, Ada taught English at LSU for a number of years.

Never Underestimate the Wiles of a Woman

After several years of courting and tired of waiting for a proposal from Jess, Ada took a teaching position for a year with United Fruit Company in British Honduras. After six months, Jess wrote Ada and asked her to come home and marry him. Their younger son, David, said he still has a special place in his heart for bananas as they remind him of his audacious mother.

Marriage and Family

Ada's marriage plan worked! She and Jess were married in December of 1926 in Auburn, Alabama. Jess bought four lots on Esplanade Avenue in Baton Rouge's new Goodwood Plantation development. The home they built on one lot was where Jess Jr. was born in 1927, followed three years later by David. Two lots were used for a vegetable garden and to raise chickens, ducks, rabbits, and a cow.

The other lot became the neighborhood playground, where Jess Jr., David, and their friends played rough-and-tumble football, baseball, and even did some pole vaulting. A well-stocked first-aid kit was kept nearby. David said these were wonderful years as they put in practice the leadership goals of the Boy Scouts.

My Observations

Wouldn't it be beneficial if more vacant city lots could be used as vegetable gardens and playgrounds, providing a sense of community where neighbors knew each other and kept an eye on the safety and camaraderie of their youth? Judge Johnson did. Why can't we begin selling this idea, rather than have our children become hangouts on city streets?

Judge Johnson Retires, Serves as Duty Judge

After Judge Johnson's retirement, he was appointed as an appellate judge in New Orleans and later appointed duty judge, which continued until his death in 1975 at age 87. Jess Jr., obviously consoling himself while nursing an injured right knee, spent a week in his father's bed.

Ada's Senior Years

Ada continued to live in the family home until 1983, when she was 81. St. James Place opened in 1983 as Louisiana's first retirement community. Ada chose a third-floor apartment with a balcony overlooking a beautiful courtyard, the same courtyard I enjoy from my ground-floor apartment. At that time, there were only two buildings on the 52-acre campus. Ada was an Independent Living resident and continued her hobbies of sewing, reading, growing violets, and traveling. She opened her apartment home to visitors and family for twelve years.

St. James Place had a nursing unit to care for Ada's needs the last six months, until her death when near age 93.

Takeaways

Happiness held is the seed. Happiness shared is the flower.
    —John Harrigan

The qualities I most admire in women are confidence and kindness.
—Oscar de la Renta

The age of a woman doesn't mean a thing. The best tones are played on the oldest fiddles.
—Ralph Waldo Emerson

JESS AND ADA JOHNSON'S FIRST-BORN SON, JESS JOHNSON JR.

Born in 1927, Jess Jr. aspired to follow in his father's footsteps. He met Peggy Settoon in high school, and on their first date they rode the ferryboat back and forth across the Mississippi River, enjoying the skyline of Baton Rouge.

(This was a romantic, inexpensive venue for many courtships to blossom, until the ferry closed after the downtown Baton Rouge bridge was built. Many of us remember those fond times, which we were quick to share with out-of-town guests. This simple pleasure was enhanced by the city lights after nightfall. Remember the gate closing after the cars were in place, the engines revving up and the whistles blowing, announcing our departure! Now the jam-packed Interstate 10 overhead is prone to further delay by traffic accidents—the price of modernity.)

Courtship Leads to Marriage

After Jess entered LSU, his romance with Peggy blossomed. They married in 1950, and Jess is quick to praise Peggy, and her salary, for helping make it possible for him to finish his law degree from LSU. He volunteered and served as a first lieutenant in the Korean War, and had no overseas assignments. He proudly pointed out that his service in the Judge Advocate General's Corps mirrored his father's service in World War I. (In my interviews with Jess, his pride and admiration of his father were poignant, obviously fueling his desire to follow in his father's footsteps.)

After discharge from the Army and a brief time practicing law in Baton Rouge, Jess Jr. accepted a position with Shell Oil Company in New Orleans. In the interim, two sons were born, Richard in 1952 and Eddie in 1954. Both, like grandfather and father, became attorneys. Richard's wife Marsha is also an attorney. They have two children and live in Prairieville. Jess and Peggy's younger son, Eddie, and his wife Mary have two children and live in New Orleans. Mary has taught health and wellness at William Carey University in Hattiesburg, Mississippi, and formed her own health company. Jess was transferred to Washington, DC, by Shell Oil in 1971, and became Shell's vice president of government relations in 1981.

Peggy, perky and quick-witted, is an aspiring artist, I am told. While in Washington, she served as vice president of the Hospitality and Information Service under the auspices of the secretary of state, to help families of diplomats assimilate into the American culture.

Retirement

After Jess retired at age 60, he and Peggy moved from Washington to the Siesta Key barrier island of Sarasota, Florida, where Jess loved to golf and fish and Peggy enjoyed the lush landscape and abundant fauna.

In 2005, yearning to see their sons and grandchildren more often, they moved back to Baton Rouge to the Country Club of Louisiana. Jess fished the lakes when he was not playing golf on the extensive fairways. Peggy enjoyed their home, especially the long sunporch where she was content to sit for hours reading and watching the birds, squirrels, and raccoons lured to her feeding station and fountain. She also became an avid artist.

Fighting Reality of Getting Older, Jess Becomes the Family Chef

Jess had once considered leasing one of the new garden homes being built on the St. James Place campus while his mother Ada lived there—"only to have available when we decided to move," he quickly added. This idea was brushed aside until Peggy began to have tremors that impeded her walking ability. They visited St. James Place again, but Peggy adamantly refused to move from their home in the Country Club. After several years, Peggy's macular degeneration eventually made reading the controls on kitchen appliances unsafe and Jess assumed the responsibility of family chef, preparing daily meals. He recounted how he would wake up during the night and worry about what to cook, making a grocery list, and shopping. He recalled, "I got so darn tired of cooking!" Despite his efforts, he and Peggy continued losing weight. Jess said he gained a healthy respect for women and their multiplicity of chores.

Jess's Continuing Battle with Himself

Once again, they returned to St. James Place. This time they selected a two-bedroom apartment in Assisted Living, where Peggy could receive needed care. They discussed the possibility of having the small covered patio enclosed for a sunporch. They were referred to me, a resident, and I designed a garden especially for Peggy's enjoyment. Jess, the vigilant attorney, asked that my landscape plan be approved and signed by our CEO.

After much deliberation, Jess and Peggy signed a contract giving them thirty days to make up their minds. Before he left, Jess told me adamantly, "I don't want to make myself do anything I do not want to do!"

The decision to leave their spacious home and move to a two-bedroom apartment in a retirement community was overwhelming. Yes, you guessed right. On the thirtieth day, Jess asked for the return of their deposit and went back to lost sleep, planning menus, and cooking. . . .

Second Thoughts

Jess and Peggy both finally realized that they had made a mistake. Peggy's condition was not improving, and Jess's overworked and worn-out right knee was not getting better. I wasn't surprised when Jess called and told me the apartment they had originally chosen was still available. He returned to sign a contract and made plans to move after St. James Place finished some repair work. Jess's physician advised he must have his knee replaced.

It was a tough time, psychologically and physically, to move from their home to a retirement community. Their son Richard and his family continued living in his parents' home until their own home was repaired, following the August 2016 south

Louisiana flood.

Jess and Peggy immediately bought two power chairs, so they could go to their choice of restaurants at St. James Place.

Jess's Knee Replacement

Jess was hospitalized for knee surgery, then released to the St. James Place Health and Wellness building for rehabilitation therapy. Soon after returning to their apartment, Jess developed a swollen and painful right foot. A staph infection had affected both knee and foot, necessitating a number of antibiotic infusions. Fortunately, Jess is now pain-free and able to resume playing golf.

Stroking the Muzzle of a Colt

Sensing Jess and Peggy's depression (during the time he was having infusions), I took a day off from book writing for a much more important diversion for Peggy and Jess. Diane Stewart, who provides care services for Peggy, drove us to my family's pastoral West Feliciana gardens, studded with historic live oaks and lakes. I drove a motorized golf cart to share over three hundred acres of beauty with my friends.

A colt, larger than its beautiful quarterhorse mother, approached Peggy's side of the golf cart. Stroking the white streak on the colt's muzzle, Peggy felt a joy that she has expressed many times to others, while living in her memory through the days when she is confined to her bed.

Takeaways

There is only one happiness in this life, to love and be loved.
    —George Sand

You are the master of your attitude.

—Roy T. Bennett

Living in the moment means letting go of the past and not waiting for the future. It means living your life consciously, aware that each moment you breathe is a gift.
—Oprah Winfrey

JESS AND ADA'S YOUNGER SON, DAVID JOHNSON

David, the second son of Jess and Ada, did not follow the attorney path of his father and brother. After graduating from Baton Rouge High School, David chose Duke University in Durham, North Carolina, for college because he was awarded a full Navy scholarship.

More than Studies Going On

In Durham, David attended Watts Street Baptist Church, where he met a beautiful student, Anne Kennard. They met again on the way to a BSU retreat. David still remembers his thoughts as he sat in the back seat of the car looking over Anne's shoulder: "Boy, I bet I could get interested in that young lady." As Anne was a freshman and he was a junior, they had years ahead to finish their education.

On the Duke campus, David and Anne lived two miles apart. In the absence of a car, for two years David took a bus to see Anne, except when he could catch a ride. One memorable trip they took by car with other students was to the University of North Carolina at Chapel Hill and the German rathskeller.

David says he borrowed a care for their first "real" date. By "real," David meant the two of them alone, where they could, as he said, have "smooching opportunities." They discussed their future together, while facing the reality that they had to finish their education before they married. By the way, I forgot to ask where they went that night in the borrowed car. . . .

Proposal from the South Pacific; Wedding in Washington, DC

After David received his degree from Duke, he was commissioned a 2nd LTJG and sent to Navy Supply Corps training. He and Anne were engaged in November before he joined his first ship, the aircraft carrier USS *Boxer*. The next summer he wrote Anne and asked her to marry him when the ship came home to San Francisco. It took thirty long days before he received Anne's yes, as she was in Paris with her family where her dad had his Air Force assignment.

Arrangements for their wedding were made long distance. Both of their families flew to Washington, DC, for the wedding at Calvary Baptist Church on December 11, 1953. As Jess Jr. was in the Army's Judge Advocate School in Charlottesville, Virginia, he requested two days off to be the best man in his brother David's wedding.

A Cross-Country Honeymoon

They honeymooned by car, visiting David's parents, Judge Jess Johnson and wife Ada, whom Anne had met on several occasions. From there they visited other relatives as they continued cross-country to San Francisco.

When David's ship returned to the Pacific and the Korean War in June, Anne spent three months with his family in Baton Rouge until her parents, Gen. Bill and Marian Kennard, returned from Paris. Anne's father was a doctor who served twenty-five years in the Air Force.

David's 38-Year Career

After his three years of active naval duty, David and Anne returned to Baton Rouge. He worked in the computer department of Ethyl Corporation, 1955–1986, in Baton Rouge, and transferred to the Richmond, Virginia, office until his retirement in 1993 at age 63.

Anne and David have a close-knit family with three children. David Jr., a nuclear power plant modification scheduler, and wife Patti have two daughters. Patti works as a ministry assistant at their church in Granbury, Texas. Their daughter Jessica, a graphic artist, and husband Steve have two children, including the only grandson. Their last-born child, son William, an associate pastor and program manager, has two daughters. Carter, his wife, enjoys her vocation as a nonprofit manager. Anne and David have one great-grandson.

Retirement Years

Dr. Kennard died at age 67, when Anne's mother was 65. She continued to live alone in her home until age 87, when she could no longer take care of herself and her home. She adamantly refused to move to a retirement community, saying they served dinner too early; plus she did not want to leave her garden. Thus began an eleven-year ritual, with Anne and David moving in for three weeks, alternating with Anne's sister and husband for three weeks, which continued until her death at age 98.

During their free three-week periods, Anne and David went on both private and Elderhostel trips, now Road Scholar. The mission work of their church, Richmond activities, and family kept them busy.

"Like living on a cruise ship"

After Anne's mother died, she and David signed a contract to move to Ashby Ponds, a retirement community in Ashburn, Virginia. After just eight years, it has 1,200 independent residents. It is located in the beautiful hills of northern Virginia. They did not want to disrupt the lives of their children to take care of them and were happy to quit the commute from Richmond. They enjoy their many friends and activities at Ashby Ponds. David is quick to say, "It is like living on a cruise ship!"

The motto of Ashby Ponds, *Add Living to Your Life*, is synonymous with the St. James Place motto, *Live Life Well*.

Takeaways

You can't blame gravity for falling in love.
    —Albert Einstein

The Navy has both a tradition and a future—and we look with pride and confidence in both directions.

—Adm. George Anderson

A good Navy is not a provocation to war. It is the surest guaranty of peace.
—Theodore Roosevelt

Section 3

Choosing to Live Life Well: Surround Yourself with Beauty and Music

These are two absolutes when I choose where to live life in its fullness, regardless of what age I am (my 89th birthday recently). And, oh yes, I must have people in my life, no isolation here! Beauty, music, and people, like strings of a fine violin.

In my inspirational memoir, *He Lays the Stones for Our Steps*, I chose to share stories I had written for my grandchildren with the world, after God woke me with the book title and plans for revenue from book sales to promote Rotary humanitarian work. My editor, with these family stories in hand, chose to add an appendix, for the enjoyment of fellow gardeners, of how I approached and developed my fifteen private gardens, beginning at age fifteen. Gardens have been an essential way for me to surround myself with beauty. Nine years ago, when I returned to Louisiana from the high altitude of Mexico, the family compound gardens I had developed on seventy acres, in the rolling hills of West Feliciana Parish, were being cared for by my family. I was free to enjoy more people, while pursuing humanitarian work.

I made an easy transition to St. James Place, a 52-acre development with a garden lake, framed by woodlands, with twelve acres devoted to three-story housing. Within a half-hour, I chose a ground-floor apartment opening into a large courtyard, where I could develop a patio garden, I haven't turned my back on the past, as I share with residents, on a motorized golf cart, tours of the West Feliciana gardens and homes, an hour away.

Music is everywhere, both on and off campus in a university town. Researchers have found that music is the medium for quality of life, including those with Alzheimer's.

FROM CARNEGIE HALL TO ST. JAMES PLACE: GWEN BRUTON

Gwen Bruton is a perky, attractive lady with shiny red hair, and a twinkle in her eyes as she smiles. To honor the title of her story, let's start on the giant stage of Carnegie Hall, flanked by three balconies, all seats filled with Sweet Adelines from across the United States.

Gwen was the lead singer in the Cajunettes quartet of Baton Rouge's chapter of Sweet Adelines. Out of the 58 competing quartets, the Cajunettes placed 28th.

Birth of the St. James Snazzy Singers

One Sunday afternoon in 2008, after Gwen had moved to St. James Place, Mary Jane Kahao invited a few friends over, including Gwen, and Dorothy and Al Bankston, a former Baptist minister. When Mary Jane called me, I told her I was still in my housecoat, recuperating from recent surgery, and she insisted I come as I was.

Mary Jane had a beautiful baby-grand piano in her spacious apartment, across the hall from my own. When she started playing, we sang hymns and oldies, and talked about missing such informal sing-alongs. We made a pact to get together to sing regularly.

As Gwen began to realize some other residents would also enjoy singing, she inquired about the possible use of the Convocation Room, which has a grand piano. Mary Jane's daughter suggested the name, Snazzy Singers.

Now, nine years later, the choir of over thirty continues to flourish, entertaining at resident birthday parties, singing in the Health and Memory Care areas, plus other engagements off campus.

Gwen's Early Years in Central Texas

Not surprisingly, Gwen was a demanding and hypersensitive three-year-old. As her mother played the piano for the local church, she convinced precocious Gwen that the choir absolutely could not perform without her sitting on the front row, often with her hymnbook upside down.

She had a younger sister, now deceased, who bossed her around. Gwen, I am sure, bossed her as well. Her brother, seven years older, knew better than to hang around, as his two sisters had taken after their mother.

At first, Gwen said she hated herself, and then, in deep introspection, said, "To me, I felt my life was hopeless. However, I was determined to take advantage of every opportunity."

Education and Achieving an MRS

After high school, Gwen's formal education continued at the University of North Texas. She also studied dance, while earning her BS degree in education, to become a teacher.

After graduation, she was awarded a graduate-assistant scholarship to earn an MS. Instead, she earned an MRS. Her daughter Belinda was born from the union.

Her husband was recalled into the Navy for a second tour of duty during the Korean campaign. After his tour, they moved to Baton Rouge, where he was employed in industry.

On the Way to a Music Career

In 1959, Gwen had applied for a Sweet Adelines chapter in Baton Rouge. She formed the Cajunette quartet, which was very active, performing several years in concerts in various towns.

Gwen applied at the local school board for short-term employment as a secretary. When asked how long she wanted to work, she replied, "Long enough to make $300 to go to Denver to serve as mistress of ceremonies for the Baton Rouge chapter of Sweet Adelines."

In Denver, Gwen discovered she had a talent as mistress of ceremonies, and continued with engagements nationally. She was truly in her element.

Gwen's singing in the Cajunette quartet ended when the group was performing at a private party. She said the smoke literally took her voice away.

She has an amazing record of service with the Sweet Adelines, first directing the Baton Rouge chapter for twelve years, followed by twelve years directing the Lafayette chapter.

Professional Careers

During these years, Gwen became director of human resources for the state of Louisiana. As the position required a master's degree in special education, she enrolled at LSU, alongside her daughter, Belinda, who was an honor student.

Gwen developed a special education curriculum and traveled the state to implement classes in the schools. She was also instrumental in helping develop the Special Olympics for handicapped youth. She directed the Special Olympics in six parishes for fourteen years.

Moving to St. James Place

Gwen moved to St. James Place in 2006. She loved to greet newcomers with, "Hello. You must be a new resident. I am Gwen Bruton," offering her hand.

One such greeting at Sunday brunch changed two lives forever! They were both at the salad bar, when Gwen made her usual newcomer greeting, to Richard ("Dick") Charles Robert. The following morning, when Dick arrived at exercise class, there was only one chair left, by that beautiful redhead, Gwen Bruton, with those flirty blue eyes. . . .

They became close friends for two years, prior to their Thanksgiving trip to Waco, Texas, to Gwen's family reunion.

While they were in Texas, Dick shocked Gwen when he said, "We need to talk about marriage." Gwen had been divorced for thirty-six years, and getting married was not on her mind! Dick, a devout Catholic, further fueled the fire, saying he wanted their wedding to take place in a Catholic church. Gwen had to have time to think. . . . She agreed to his proposal, while saying she wanted only family members to receive invitations.

Her family was small. Belinda, married to Dr. Dale Redmann, had one child, two grandchildren, and one great-grandchild. Dick had a large family of thirty.

Dick moved into Gwen's apartment and used his own as an office. They enjoyed the comradery of the St. James Place residents, plus their volunteerism. Dick died in 2014 after a brief illness.

Snazzy Singers Entertain at N.O. 8th Air Force Reunion

Dick had served in the 8th Air Force during World War II. In 2011, when he was in charge of the 8th's reunion, he booked the Royal Sonesta in New Orleans. They had never had musical entertainment at previous reunions, but you can bet your bottom dollar, Gwen seized the opportunity to act as mistress of ceremonies and showcase her choir, the Snazzy Seniors. We were a hit, and Gwen encouraged both American and visiting airmen, and their wives from England, to join us in singing some of the wartime songs. We were overnighted at the Royal Sonesta, further enjoying our night in the Big Easy.

Takeaways

Music expresses that which cannot be said and on which is impossible to be silent.
—Victor Hugo

Music washes away from the soul the dust of everyday life.
—Berthold Auerbach

Music is a moral law. It gives soul to the universe, wings to the mind, flight to the imagination, and charm and gaiety to life and to everything.
—Plato

THE CAMELLIA LADY: MARY JANE KAHAO

Writing again about Mary Jane Kahao, I want to pay tribute to her gifts of giving. True, her impromptu gathering that special Sunday afternoon continues to bring joy to the Snazzy Singers, as well as those privileged to hear them sing.

Mary Jane was known for her involvement with the St. James Camellia Memorial Garden. She visited the garden regularly year-round, wearing a big sun hat, with work gloves and pruners in hand. Each camellia shrub was carefully examined (most likely talked to as I do to plants in my apartment garden). She selected and removed buds to encourage the development of larger blossoms, and called the Baton Rouge Camellia Society when the plants needed spraying.

Baskets of Camellia Blossoms

When flowers began to open, she took her pruners and a wide basket made for blossoms, gently arranging her camellia display. She brought the basket to our coffee shop so residents could choose their favorite blossom, a ritual that she continued each season.

A Celebration of Just *a Little More Time to Live* . . .

When Mary Jane's cardiologist said her heart was failing, hospice care was begun in the hospital, prior to her being moved to a local hospice facility. She rallied and, after several days, was moved to our St. James Place Health and Wellness building (a nursing facility). I joined the family one afternoon at her bedside, in an obvious yet unacknowledged celebration of *a little more time to live*. . . .

"You have to do this for her"

I had heard that Mary Jane asked to have a hospital bed put in her apartment, where she wanted to die. When I walked past her apartment, assuming noon was perhaps the best time to find her awake, her granddaughter answered my tap on the door. She insisted I step into the bedroom to see Mary Jane, although she was asleep, with family members sitting by her bed.

As I left, walking down the hall in tears, her granddaughter called out, "Ms. McDaniel, come back, she's awake!" I told her I was too distraught. Her answer was emphatic: "You have to do this for her." I slowly turned and walked back, and went to the opposite side of her bed. Her eyes were open, her breathing eased with oxygen. Only God can give us words at such a time. I put my hand on her shoulder and told her, "I'm glad you have come home. I went by your camellia garden this morning [on the way to our neighborhood shopping area]." I continued, "The Camellia Society has been out and sprayed for fungus."

She passed away two days later, *with assurance her camellia garden was being taken care of.*

Takeaways

When you see flowers, your day is brightened. It is like sunshine!
—Marcus Koole

It is good to be blessed. It is better to be a blessing.
—Author unknown

We make a living by what we get, but we make a life by what we give.
—Winston Churchill

LEGENDARY JAZZ ARTIST JIMMY JULES

I probably would not have met Jimmy except for another love, gospel music. I boarded a St. James Place bus to attend a gospel music festival held annually at Zion Baptist Church, on Baton Rouge's East Boulevard, next door to First United Methodist Church. (The annual festival is held in various venues each year.)

    There were a few single seats left in the church, and I slipped into one behind a lady wearing a hat. I first tried to start a conversation with those sitting by me, to no avail, so I tapped the shoulder of the lady, complimenting her hat. Our conversation led to St. James Place. Once her husband, Romales Stewart, understood that was the name of a retirement community where I live, he said the jazz band he plays with plays concerts for seniors and children, sponsored by the Jazz Association of America. Romales is the drummer and business agent for the Jimmy Jules Jazz Band, now known as the St. John Icons.

Louisiana's First International Peace One Day Observances

Our Capital City Rotary held the state's first observance of International Peace One Day at my home church, First United Methodist. I asked the Mount Zion Church Choir to fill our choir loft, and they, as well as Jimmy, sang several numbers accompanied by his band. Ms. Unyoung Kim, a South Korean, played the violin and provided classical arrangements. Jimmy and his band returned to headline the concert the following two years, benefiting local and international humanitarian outreaches through Rotary.

    Jimmy's voice, deep and grave, is akin to Louis Armstrong's. Nicholas Gott referred to his voice as "deep, rustic, and magnificently strong. A whisper from him could easily fill a room."

The Jazz Foundation of America Rescues Jazz after Katrina and the Beat Goes on . . .

When New Orleans was inundated by Hurricane Katrina,

donations began to flood into the Jazz Foundation to help support musicians from the city known as the "birthplace of jazz" as well as surrounding areas. There is such a love of jazz that these donations have continued. Once a month, the Foundation pays each musician $100 to play for an hour for seniors and/or children.

The Jimmy Jules Jazz Band from Reserve, Louisiana, is well known in Baton Rouge. I have booked and gone with them, acting as MC, several times most years, since I met Romales Stewart eight years ago.

Visiting Jimmy at His Sugar Mill Home

As a very devoted fan, I wanted you readers to meet him. Jimmy had told me he lived in the same house on Sugar Mill Plantation where he was born eighty years ago. His frame house was easily identified as it is painted a pleasant blue color, perhaps reminiscent of the blues they play.

Jimmy met my friend and me, formally dressed and wearing white shoes, as he had been to two funerals that morning. He led us into his dimly lit recording studio. I was eager to hear his music once again, and to amaze my friend who loves the old original jazz. I asked Jimmy to play and sat back to enjoy that wondrous voice singing, "He's Got the Whole World in His Hands," "It's a Rainy Night in Georgia," and "Walking to New Orleans."

I was excited to have a one-on-one with him. Jimmy was not born to play music and had no thoughts of a music career. He expected to follow in his father's footsteps in the sugarcane fields, rightfully proud of his father's call to fame for developing the first sugarcane planter, which allowed an expansion of the world's top sugar-refining area in the 1920s.

As a teenager with no pocket change, he sometimes was successful in convincing a club doorman to let him slip in if he sang a song. His voice was magnetic to many, yet only the cane fields were familiar to Jimmy.

He was eager to tell his story, which, unbeknownst to him,

would eventually lead him away from following in his father's and grandfather's footsteps.

In his last years of high school, his agricultural class teacher kidded him, and after an exchange of words sent him off to music class. I couldn't quite understand such seeming arrogance, until I realized music perhaps was not considered macho and I imagined a humiliated Jimmy walking away as his classmates jeered. The laugh was perhaps on the teacher as Jimmy was awarded a four-year scholarship after he graduated, to study music at Southern University in upriver Baton Rouge. Jimmy was a good student with a bright mind. College also kept him out of the hard days in the cane fields, a little longer.

That Burning Gut Feeling . . . Jimmy's Fate Was Cast

After he studied music at Southern University for two years, Jimmy volunteered to serve in the Army during the Vietnam conflict. He was chosen as the bugler. While talking to Jimmy, I caught a glimpse of the honor and respect he felt, which he wanted to last for the rest of his life. He was hooked, finally realizing that music was his key to life. He was honorably discharged in less than a year as the conflict ended.

Jimmy's burning desire motivated him to meet the top soul artist at the time, Sam Cooke, in Los Angeles. With no thought of the distance to drive in a rather old car, Jimmy cobbled together a few buddies for a band and set out for L.A.

A Six-Month Road Trip

The car broke down in Texas. With little money to repair the car and to eat, the band resorted to playing jazz in local bars and clubs. As word spread, they spent six months playing, with Jimmy singing in larger venues.

Sam Cooke and Jimmy were to finally work together. Jimmy had acquired a following himself, both as a singer and a prolific writer of his own songs. At age 22, he signed his first recording contract and was granted a scholarship to study in California. Cooke had hired him as a writer. But it wasn't meant to be. Just before they were to meet in 1964, Cooke died unexpectedly.

Jimmy played and sang from New Orleans to Los Angeles, from the Cotton Club in Denver, to Newport, Rhode Island, Switzerland and Italy, to name a few places. . . . He cut records with eight labels, including Columbia and Atlantic Records.

He married Rita Mae and they had six children.

My friend and I concluded our visit with Jimmy in his recording studio, driving back to Baton Rouge, reflecting on this legend who lives for his faith and music.

Romales housed their instruments in his Baton Rouge home, which flooded in the devastating 2016 south Louisiana flood. Assuring that jazz will never die, the Jazz Association of America funded the replacement of the instruments and a new van to transport them in.

I have booked Jimmy and his band to play at two other retirement homes since our visit in his hometown of Reserve, making sure that I can continue getting a *fix* from their music—until next time. . . .

Takeaways

If you have to ask what jazz is, you'll never know.
—Louis Armstrong

Life is a lot like jazz. It's best when you improvise.
—George Gershwin

Jazz is about being in the moment.
—Herbie Hancock

SINGING PRAISES TO GOD: CLAUDETTE THIGPEN

Joyce Dickerson, a pianist, and I have led sing-alongs of the old songs and hymns, biweekly and/or weekly, at St. James Place in Assisted Living and Memory Care for nine years.

After one of pianist Don Irvin's concerts at St. James Place, he shared that he had been appointed to the National Alzheimer's Board, the first musician to join the board, as research has proven that music is the best way to bring quality of life. Soon after, in a middle-of-the-night awakening, I was inspired to start our Music and Memories sing-alongs in Assisted Living and Memory Care.

Claudette Thigpen Now Sings Praises, after 65 Years of Being Quiet

Recently, Claudette Thigpen from nearby Baker, a former executive with the regional Social Security Administration, moved to Memory Care with her dachshund Amber. Claudette is a bright 73 years old and an avid reader. The first time she came to our music program, she sat with her finger across her mouth indicating, "Be quiet." Her first-grade teacher had told her she was never to sing.

I returned early the next morning. I found Claudette with a resident who seldom talks, whom she lovingly takes under her wing. They were the only residents remaining in the dining room; an attendant was clearing tables.

I sat down with them and shared the good news that God gave us a voice to sing praises to Him. Claudette recalled how embarrassed she has been all her life when all stood while singing "The Star-Spangled Banner" and she remained silent. After asking what their favorite hymn was, I reached across the table and, holding hands, we sang "Amazing Grace," followed by "Jesus Loves Me." Then I suggested we sing "The Star-Spangled Banner." Claudette, obviously recalling her years of humiliation and embarrassment, shared the sad event that had happened in her childhood, prompting her to raise a finger saying *be quiet*. I walked back to the living room with them and left feeling as though I had been to a prayer meeting!

Whenever I can keep Claudette in the present, she will sing, but she often lapses back in memory to "be quiet." On her better days she laments how not being allowed to sing robbed her of an important part of her life. She also realizes what is happening to her, how she is losing other parts of her life. I brought her an article on Alzheimer's disease in an attempt to help her understand what is happening to her.

Claudette loves to take care of her fellow residents. The previous day, her friend had followed Claudette's lead in not singing. I learned later from a family member she had sung for many years in the church choir and served as pianist when needed. She undoubtedly spent a lot of time with her grandfather she loved deeply as she says her birthplace is Ruston, where he is from, when it is actually in South Carolina.

I do not read music or play an instrument. I sang in the folk choir of the Methodist Church in St. Francisville and more recently in the St. James Place Snazzy Singers choir until my weakened vocal cords prevented my singing an entire phrase. My hope is to continue singing with "my family" in the health care areas as long as I shall live!

New Year's Eve 2016

Tonight I have a date, actually two dates, as I decided to celebrate New Year's Eve with Claudette and her friend! First, a lavish buffet dinner in our formal dining room, followed by song and dance music by Rocky Saxon. Our friend, while seated as we sing each week, dances with her feet unless "Mother" Mary, our St. James Place minister/counselor from St. James Episcopal Church, comes. With a bit of encouragement, we enjoy watching the two dance and twirl. Tonight will be a *ball* of fun! And it was, as I watched Pete Sebastian cross the room to dance with them, ever mindful of bringing joy to others. . . .

Takeaways

Where words fail, music speaks.
    —Hans Christian Andersen

If music be the food of love, play on.
    —William Shakespeare

Music can change the world because it can change people.
    —Bono

Section 4

Personal Enrichment

ART—St. James Place has a weekly art class, using acrylics, and the art workshop is filled most days with artists and budding artists, honing their skills. Every three months a reception is held, and each St. James Place art piece is presented in the Convocation Room, where they remain on display until the next presentation of new work.

LIFE WRITING—St. James Place has a weekly writing group. Original works by residents are read and discussed.
    A previous group I attended helped lead to the publishing of my inspirational memoir, *He Lays the Stones for Our Steps.*

EDUCATION—We learn as long as we live, and St. James Place certainly encourages learning, with over 4,500 volumes filling bookcases, in every area, plus a weekly stop of the parish library bookmobile. There are periodic guest lectures and book signings,
    St. James Place tries to provide a variety of activities for its residents and welcomes Osher Lifelong Learning Institute at Louisiana State University (OLLI at LSU) to the campus. OLLI was originally known as Lagniappe Studies, a group of people 50 years and older who enjoy learning through LSU Continuing Education. The faculty and retired faculty offer classes on multiple subjects. From the beginning, St. James Place provided some classroom space. Membership in the organization grew, and LSU applied for a grant from the Bernard Osher Foundation. Lagniappe Studies then became part of OLLI at LSU, one of a network of 120 university-affiliated lifelong learning programs supported by the

Osher Foundation. A large group of member volunteers provides the program's leadership. There are over a thousand members on the 2017 roll, and twelve classes, from art to presidential elections, are offered at St. James Place.

SPIRITUAL ENRICHMENT—Several church services and Bible studies are held weekly on site. Transportation to downtown church services is provided. Some churches provide their own transportation. A support group meets weekly, led by Nick Abraham, PhD.

THEATER—The St. James Place Theater Room shows movies five times a week, including foreign and vintage films.

STAYING PHYSICALLY FIT—St. James Place has a 5,000-square-foot gym, shuffleboard courts, and much more . . .

GAMES AND GABBING, THEME PARTIES, DINING OPTIONS—The opportunities for socializing seem endless!

RENOWNED ARTIST BYRON LEVY AND WIFE CAROL

Byron and his wife Carol moved to St. James Place after Hurricane Katrina, calling Baton Rouge home since 2005. Over the subsequent decade, Byron enrolled in art courses at LSU, taught art classes, offered workshops, and mounted several art exhibitions. In Baton Rouge and at St. James Place, as throughout his life, his characteristic charm, generosity, and infectious enthusiasm enlarged his circle of friends.

After retiring as president of a paper company in 1983, Byron devoted over three decades to his intense lifetime pursuit of art. An accomplished watercolorist, he has had sketches and paintings exhibited in galleries, museums, and elsewhere in New Orleans since the 1940s, when the *Times-Picayune* published illustrations of the war effort that he mailed to the paper from overseas. He also frequently contributed to *Stars and Stripes.* A cartoonist during World War II, Byron refined his art through the decades, studying with premier watercolorists, including Dong Kingman, Edgar Whitney, and Milford Zornes.

In recent decades he has taught art classes and workshops, working with students of all ages. He was a member of the New Orleans Art Association, the Louisiana Art and Artists' Guild, and the Louisiana Watercolor Society, which awarded him its Lifetime Achievement Award in 2005. Beyond his hundreds of paintings, sketches, and drawings in the hands of family, friends, and private collectors, he produced over 150 sketchbooks, the earliest dating from his first months in military service.

His Art Benefits Alzheimer's Research

In 2017, Byron's wife Carol and son, Ron Levy, a professor at the Peabody Institute of Johns Hopkins University, partnered with St. James Place and the Pennington Foundation to present a symposium on the benefits of the arts for Alzheimer's patients, with a large exhibit of Byron's art for sale, benefiting Alzheimer's research.

Among his other serious avocations, Byron maintained his childhood interest in model aviation. Prior to Hurricane Katrina, he was the senior member of the New Orleans Model Aviation Society.

Following a brief illness in 2015, Byron died, months before his 95th birthday and weeks after his 69th wedding anniversary. He was preceded in death by his parents, Laz Levy and Rita Goldstein Levy, his daughters Carol Jane Levy and Dianne Lynn Levy, and his sister, Tess Levy Schornstein. He is survived by Carol and their three children, three grandchildren, and six great-grandchildren. He was a lifelong member of Temple Sinai in New Orleans and a more recent member of B'nai Israel, in Baton Rouge.

Tracing Their Family Roots

Byron was born in New Orleans in early 1921. He attended Fortier High School and Tulane University, graduating with a BS in engineering in 1941. He worked as an engineer in the design and construction of Liberty ships for the Delta Shipbuilding Company on the west bank of New Orleans, an emergency shipyard mobilized for the war.

In 1943, he enlisted with the Army Air Corps, serving as a second lieutenant with assignments in British Guiana and Guam. After the war, he returned to civilian life in New Orleans. He married his sweetheart, Carol Jane Bauman, in 1946, and with her as his lifelong companion, began his family of five children while embarking on a merchandising career in his father's business, Alco Paper Company.

Carol Jane Bauman was born in in St. Louis, Missouri, of Corinne and Sanford Bauman. She had one sister, now deceased. Her mother was a college graduate, and both parents worked in merchandise store sales, in St. Louis, Dallas, and New Orleans. Carol earned a sociology degree with honors from the University of Texas.

She said her best friend introduced her to four-year-older Byron at the Temple Sinai in New Orleans. She still marvels that she told her mother, "He's nice, but I am not going to marry him."

Their Married Years in New Orleans

Byron maintained an active professional life in New Orleans for almost four decades, managing Alco Paper as it expanded operations throughout southern Louisiana. During these years, he was active in the New Orleans Chamber of Commerce, served as president of the Southern Paper Trade Association, and contributed to a range of other business and civic organizations.

Takeaways

Life is the art of drawing without an eraser.
—John W. Gardner

It is the supreme art of the teacher to awaken joy in creative expression and knowledge.
—Albert Einstein

Nature is the art of God.
—Dante Alighieri

LOUISE COUVILLION, A ROLE MODEL FOR SUCCESSFUL AGING

There is a fountain of youth: it is your mind, your talents, the creativity you bring to your life and the lives of the people you love. When you learn to tap this source, you will have truly defeated age.
   —Sophia Loren

Although Louise's calendar says she is 96, she has defied years with resilience and a zest for life. We can all learn much from her! She is a friend to all she meets, always with a contagious smile, standing erect, even when using her walker.

She said she never expected to have a stroke, but she did, followed by two months in the St. James Place Health and Wellness Rehabilitation Center learning to walk again.

When I called her today to ask a few questions, she was off again on a bus trip to Colorado!

From Paralysis to Walking Again

From paralysis on one side of her body and impaired speech, through tenacity and determination, coupled with three hours of therapy twice a day, five days a week, she regained the ability to walk, aided by a walker. Two months after her stroke, she returned to her garden home. Her speech therapy was successful, and she now uses a walker when walking distances.

Louise's Early Years; Romance and Marriage

Louise Couvillion was born Leah Louise Allen in September 1921 in Leesville, Louisiana. She was still a toddler when her young parents moved to Shreveport and bought a modest house on a quiet street one block from South Highlands Elementary School and the Line Avenue trolley. Louise spelled out her childhood: "I lived in that house until I married, attended that school through the seventh grade, and rode that trolley to music lessons, swimming lessons, the Strand Theater on Saturday mornings for the children's special movies, and eventually to Byrd High School for four years."

She enrolled at LSU, where in her junior year she met her future husband, James Borden Cobb, better known as Jimmy. They both graduated in the spring of 1941, and Jimmy, who had four years of ROTC, was immediately commissioned and sent to Fort Bragg, North Carolina.

A Christmas Wedding

They were married at Christmas that year, and Louise followed her husband to North Carolina, then Quantico, Virginia, and then to Newport News. Jimmy was transferred to this Marine base for training in combat loading of ships and then to Newport News to put the training into practice.

It was from there that a flotilla of Navy vessels, anything that floated and could carry men and equipment, sailed one night in late October 1942. This was part of the invasion of North Africa. It would be three years, almost to the day, before Louise saw Jimmy again.

Louise went home to Shreveport, got a job at KTBS as a writer and fill-in announcer, and spent her evenings playing bridge with other war widows or working at the Shreveport Little Theater both on and backstage.

She decided it was time for a change of scenery and moved to Dallas, where she went to work for a public relations agency. That's where she was when Jimmy returned in November 1945.

"Neither was quite the same person"

Getting reacquainted and settling down was not easy for them. Neither was quite the same person.

Jimmy came home with a lot of ideas but no specific plans. That problem was solved when he visited his friend and former mentor at Shreveport Engraving Co. Jimmy had edited the LSU yearbook, *The Gumbo*, and had worked with the engraving company staff and knew the process. He was offered a job there that day, and the publishing business became his career.

They settled in Shreveport, and their two children, Jim Jr. and Delia, were born there. Some years later, the engraving company was in the process of changing ownership, and Jimmy decided to accept an offer from a competitor, Taylor Publishing in Dallas, although it meant moving the family to their branch office in Alexandria. Those were good years.

After Jimmy suffered a massive heart attack at age 37, he recovered and went back to work. "His precarious health situation became the unacknowledged center of family life," Louise says.

She began an enjoyable career teaching at a junior high school a few blocks from home. At first she taught ninth-grade speech and began producing one-act plays to present to the entire student body. Then she taught English and social studies in three-hour blocks. When the school was fully integrated, she taught reading and language arts to seventh and eighth graders.

Jimmy died in 1968 at the Texas Medical Center in Houston. He was Dr. Denton Cooley's second heart transplant and the eleventh in the world. Unfortunately, he was allergic to the drug used to prevent rejection of the new heart, and lived only three days after the transplant.

Louise continued to teach school, but soon discovered that she needed to upgrade her credentials, and eventually her income. She commuted the sixty miles to Northwestern in Natchitoches for her MA in English. That accomplished, she was hired as the secondary language arts supervisor in the State Department of Education. She moved to Baton Rouge and has lived here since 1977.

In the meantime, son Jim finished college and began graduate work at the University of Virginia in Charlottesville. He married and became the father of Austin, Louise's only grandchild. Daughter Dee chose the University of Oregon, graduated, and moved to San Francisco. She was a paralegal until she decided she would rather be a lawyer, and she came to Baton Rouge to attend LSU Law School, bringing her "California boy" husband with her.

Back in Shreveport, Louise's mother fell and broke her hip. She realized that she could no longer maintain a house and yard and reluctantly agreed to move to Baton Rouge so that Louise, who was still a full-time working woman, could look after her.

While all these life changes were taking place within the family, Louise quietly married Ed Couvillion, her old high-school boyfriend from Byrd High days. She had been a single woman for sixteen years. "I was lucky, lucky to have Ed willing to join the family," she said. He was her "strong right arm." At one point, her mother was wheelchair bound and daughter Dee was diagnosed with breast cancer during her second year of law school. "We all leaned on Ed." Dee lived only eighteen months after the diagnosis.

In the next year, one loss followed another. Louise's mother died, and Ed developed multiple illnesses, lost a leg, and died in 2005.

Moving to St. James Place

Now living alone and taking care of a house and yard, Louise began to consider moving to Virginia to be near her son Jim. However, Jim developed lung cancer and died in 2008. Louise moved to St. James Place that same year.

With many talents to share, she soon launched a new five-year volunteer career as curriculum chair for OLLI Continuing Education classes at St. James Place. (A virtual full-time job, I observed.)

"Jimmy's War"
(I requested more details.)

From the time he landed on the western coast of North Africa until the 47th Infantry marched into Bizarre some eight months later, his 9th Infantry Division had been in combat mode.

The ship that Jimmy loaded was an old destroyer. They landed at Safi, a port city on the Atlantic coast of Morocco, south of Casablanca. Their mission was to occupy the city and make the harbor safe for landing tanks. From there they began the 1,000-mile trek across Morocco and Algeria to join the British fighting the Axis forces in Tunisia. Lack of transportation was a problem, and they rode some days and walked the others. They endured weeks into months of dirt, bad food, foxhole sleeping, and sporadic engagement with German forces. In Tunisia, Jimmy's 9th Division, 47th Infantry was in the battle for Kasserine Pass and later El Guettar.

At one point, he received a battlefield promotion to company commander. He was 23 years old. When French North Africa was finally in Allied hands, Oran, Algeria, became the major port for supplies coming into North Africa headed for Italy. Jimmy's textbook French and shipping loading experience put him in charge of a pier there. When the French Riviera became the R&R location for war-weary men and women, he again found knowing the language useful. He managed several villas, including General Eisenhower's and a hotel for nurses, from late 1944 until his homecoming in November 1945. "Tough duty," Louise adds.

My Observations

It is perhaps redundant for me to say that there is no way we can personally fathom what our servicemen and women endure in times of war, fighting to preserve our freedom, nor the impact on the lives of loved ones waiting for their return.

This week in a medical waiting room, a woman kept saying she did not believe in war. I reminded her that none of us do, while saying that we would all be under Communist dictatorship if brave, freedom-loving soldiers had not sacrificed for us. She never acknowledged what freedom means. . . . It is so easy for some to live in the lap of luxury, in a me-and-mine world. . . .

Takeaways

Education is the most powerful weapon you can use to change the world.
   —Nelson Mandela

The brain is like a muscle. When it is in use, we feel very good. Understanding is joyous.
    —Carl Sagan

Regardless of age, don't just sit and watch the world go by, get in the parade!
    —Author unknown

MARJORIE COLOMB:
MISTRESS OF CEREMONIES AND TOUR DIRECTOR

Marjorie Colomb was a prominent tour director and patron of the arts in New Orleans, during her career days. She, as did many, relocated after Katrina.

We at St. James Place enjoy her ever-positive spirit, full of joy, never lacking something to say! She is in her element when she introduces her friend and noted pianist, Ronnie Kole, in concert, in the St. James Place auditorium.

Slow Learners May Never Learn, When a *Tour Director* Is on Board

No need to learn when Marjorie is on board! She continues her career as tour director, meriting laughter that we all benefit from.

She made the bus trip with fellow residents to the New Orleans World War II Museum, which made it even more memorable as she assumed the role of tour director. Marjorie expertly directed our driver when to change lanes for better traffic flow on Interstate 10, and when and how to turn to reach the museum.

Returning from the museum, Marjorie continued instructing our bus driver. After we arrived back at St. James Place, I told our driver that she was a very slow learner, requiring Marjorie to resume her role as tour director!

I have laughed much more since moving to St. James Place, and this trip was no exception. Marjorie does brighten our days. We need more residents like her, but possibly not in the same room at the same time. . . .

This morning I asked Jackie, who cleans my apartment weekly, if she knew Marjorie. "Oh yes," she said. "I cleaned her apartment for years, and as I came down the hall each Tuesday before 8, Marjorie would be peering down the hall, lamenting that no one was out there," ignoring Jackie's reminder that it was early morning. She always found Marjorie fully dressed. Jackie sees me in my housecoat, midmorning.

Marjorie Now Holds Court Early Mornings in Assisted Living

Marjorie's current apartment in Assisted Living is right across from the living room, where numerous concerts and other events take place. Her apartment is also steps away from a choice of two dining rooms. I am sure Marjorie is now truly in her element, out early, holding court, as other residents come, some perhaps not so wide awake, for 8 a.m. breakfast.

Takeaways

One laugh, hopefully more each day, helps keep the doctor away.
—Charles Hunter

Smile, and the world smiles with you; cry, and you cry alone.
—Stanley Gordon West

A day without laughter is a day wasted.
—Charlie Chaplin

DIFFERENT STROKES FOR DIFFERENT FOLKS: JOHN WHITSON, A TRADITIONALIST

John Whitson and wife Frances moved to St. James Place in 2001, and Frances died prior to my moving here in 2008. I have met Mr. Whitson in the halls (I never refer to him as John), dressed impeccably in coat and tie, on his way to happy hour, followed by dinner in the St. James Place formal dining room.

Residents at St. James Place are free to eat in a choice of restaurants, all with cloth tablecloths and napkins. A traditionalist like Mr. Whitson chooses the formal dining room, with attentive wait staff to serve each course, continuing the lifestyle he is accustomed to. On Mondays, when the formal dining room is closed, rather than eating at our cafeteria, Mr. Whitson has an attendant drive him around town, most likely to stop at one of his longtime favorite formal restaurants.

The Pragmatist

I asked Mr. Whitson's permission to compare lifestyles available in senior communities. I lean toward the practicality of a pragmatist, giving extra time to my many endeavors.

Sure, I occasionally enjoy dressing up and eating at a formal restaurant. You will find my apartment furnished with fine French antiques from our thirty-five-year Fireside Antiques business, now run by third-generation Laura Roland. My luscious apartment garden is enhanced by containers, statues, and other garden appointments from France, England, and Greece.

However, for meals, I revert back to my childhood on a farm where our main meal was at noon, with fresh fruits and vegetables. Our cafeteria at St. James Place is near my apartment, boasts an extensive salad bar, and has friends to visit with. This informality takes less time from my dedication to humanitarian outreaches, on and off campus.

I am a morning person and not an afternoon napper. As I face more health issues, I recall resident Carmel Mask saying years ago, "When it gets around five or six in the evening, I begin to fold up my tent."

I refer to whether you come to a retirement community to

live life abundantly or to wait to die. . . . Choose carefully where you wish to spend what could be *"one of the best periods of your life!"*

Concerts, Theme Parties, Stateside Foreign Travel

Mr. Whitson and I share the love of travel. He said when he was fourteen, his parents took him by train to Miami. Recalling his first cruise at age ten, cruising from below Niagara Falls to Montreal, he said in those days a hotel room cost ten dollars.

After he went to work with Ethyl in Baton Rouge, his work assignments brought him to New York City. He and coworkers saw Broadway shows in the '50s, seated on a last-row balcony seat, for five dollars.

St. James Place sponsored an Atlantic crossing from Barcelona to New Orleans. (We flew to Barcelona.) Theater and music, equal to any Broadway production, were my favorite activities. Jerry Black and I were the only two St. James residents to watch the entire LSU-Alabama game, on the three-story screen, with the Tigers beating the Crimson Tide, ending at 2 a.m. our crossing time!

Of course this Royal Caribbean cruise ship was the world's largest, until they built one larger. We enjoyed the ship's "main street" where you could shop, eat, and sit to watch a parade go by. . . . On another St. James Place cruise, we explored the Caribbean.

Mr. Whitson said he has enjoyed perhaps fifty cruises, virtually touring the entire world. Defying his late 90s, he made more ports of call with his daughter, to Russia, North Africa, and Iceland.

More about Our Traditionalist, Mr. John Whitson

On Sundays I see Mr. Whitson at First United Methodist Church, sitting in his usual aisle seat with one or more family members. Until a few years ago he insisted on driving his own car; now his stepdaughter picks him up. Pragmatist Cheri, I take St. James bus transportation to Sunday school and church, since macular degeneration put an end to my driving four years ago.

John's Early Years

John was the only child of Franklin Forrest Whitson and Helen Long, both of whom were only children. His father had a privately owned lending agency. That meant the family was well-to-do, compared to many living on our farms of mortgaged land. When I told Mr. Whitson my father said that during the Great Depression, he negotiated with the Federal Land Bank to save his 80-acre farm, Mr. Whitson said my father was very fortunate.

He had a distant relative, a doctor whose wife was also a doctor, who bought 12,000 acres of these mortgages. The couple became very wealthy when crop prices rose during World War II, and farmers were able to buy more farmland. During the war, to prevent her husband from being drafted, his wife closed her medical practice, thereby creating a shortage of medical personnel in town if her husband were called to serve.

Roles of Women in the 1920s and '30s

Mr. Whitson spoke of his mother, who never said what she wanted and then became angry if things did not go as she wished. His mother was ever mindful of the social discourse, such as hearing that engineers could always get a job after college, so John took his first chemistry classes at Purdue University and said, "It was ok." He graduated with a BS in chemical engineering, and had no luck finding a job. He went back to Purdue for another year, prior to taking a job as a chemical engineer with Ethyl in Baton Rouge. He married Rae Mickey, and they had one daughter, Helen Rae.

My Mother's Roles in the '20s

My mother, Ruth Nygaard, worked her way through Louisiana State Normal School, a college for teachers in Natchitoches, the oldest town in the Louisiana Purchase. In the 1920s, one-room schools for elementary students, through age six, were a focal point of rural communities. Mother was both school principal and teacher.

When World War I soldiers marched in Farmerville, Louisiana, celebrating the war's end in 1918, Arthur McDaniel spotted Ruth in the crowd. He rode horseback to court her for six years before they married in 1924. Married women were not allowed to teach, so she gave up her teaching career. (Once married women were allowed to teach, they had to quit if they became pregnant.)

Our parents encouraged us to get a college education and find our passion, away from the poor farm life they were thrust into when their sawmill burned. After college, we three children formed our own successful businesses.

Friends Travel Together, Remarry

Mr. Whitson said his wife, Rae, was good friends with Frances, the wife of Henry Wall, a former coworker. They planned a cruise to Buenos Aires and Rio de Janeiro, Brazil. In Rio, Henry died unexpectedly, apparently from Lou Gehrig's disease, although the coroner reported the cause of death was a heart attack.

Years later, Rae died, and the two surviving spouses, with similar interests, married prior to their move to St. James Place. Frances died from a stroke, leaving her two daughters and three sons, a combined family of seven grandchildren and seven great-grandchildren.

When I asked Mr. Whitson what he thought of being almost 99, he said it was fine, except he hated being responsible for housekeeping. He is blessed in life and fortunate, don't you agree?

Takeaways

Shared dining fortifies us.
    —Deng Ming-Dao

Dining should be something that isn't always taken extremely seriously.
    —Graham Elliot

Fine dining is an occasional treat for most people.
    —René Redzepi

A MORNING WITH SENIOR OLYMPIANS JULIA HAWKINS, 101, AND JACK BARTLE, 93

When Jack and I went to pick up Julia at her home in University Acres, I asked her to show Jack her bicycle "museum." The collection starts with one of her earliest bicycles and ends with the three-wheeler a grandson gave her when she cracked an elbow several years ago. Apparently, Julia was a little indignant about the gift as she told him she would never ride it. The last one is a shiny new bicycle given to her by a granddaughter, which, because of Julia's tiny erect frame, her legs are too short to mount. She keeps extra bicycles so her three grandchildren and her great-grandchild can ride along with her.

Julia Begins Senior Olympics Competition

Julia began competing in the Senior Olympics by qualifying in the Louisiana State Olympics held in Baton Rouge, where she won a gold medal in cycling, the 1 Mile, 5K, and 10K. Then she competed and won a bronze medal in cycling in the San Antonio Nationals. She won gold medals thereafter in cycling, 5K, and 10K in nationals in Tucson and Orlando. When she competed in nationals held in Baton Rouge, she was the only woman in her age category.

For many years she continued her daily cycling for three miles, weather permitting. She decided to broaden her skills by adding a 50- and 100-yard dash to her daily routine. She said she got the idea that she might as well compete when she was gardening and ran inside to answer the telephone. She marked off 50 and 100 yards on the quiet street in front of her home and stayed in shape for the Olympic competition. She began competing in these categories in the 2016 state competition in Lake Charles, at age 100. Perhaps Julia was sending a strong message that she was of age, not over the hill, and a competitor to be reckoned with! She won a gold medal in the 50-yard dash and in cycling.

I fear my 88-year-old body could not measure up to Julia in her 80s, much less at her youthful 101. Perhaps some of you readers can identify with my lack of athletic prowess!

St. James Place Sponsors Senior Olympics

When St. James Place got involved with the Senior Olympics in 2002, Jack Bartle volunteered to help in the competitions. The following year, he brought home six gold medals in accuracy throws and race-walking in the Louisiana competitions and became a Baton Rouge Hall of Fame athlete.

Accidents Hit Our Heroes, Can't Keep Senior Olympians Down

Cycling was one of Jack's events until 2006 when he fractured his wrist. He switched to field events and shuffleboard competitions.

Julia dislocated her elbow while riding her bicycle near her home, and her daughters asked her to stop competing. That is when her grandson gave her the three-wheeler, which she refused to sit on, much less ride on!

Takes Grit, Tenacity, and Dedication

Jack said, "It's not all fun and games. It requires a daily mindset of staying in the best possible physical condition, as well as practicing your competitive skills, while trying not to break anything!"

Our Seniors' Upcoming 2017 Nationals in Birmingham

Jack and Julia are looking forward to the Birmingham nationals this year. Julia qualified in cycling and both the 50- and 100-yard dash. She has decided not to compete in cycling as there is a 100-foot incline in the tract and she is a flatlander. In the 100-yard dash, I predict, Julia will show Birmingham competitors that age is only a mindset. She will also likely set a historic Senior Olympian record as a 101-year-old gold medal winner!

Jack, age 93, will be traveling to Birmingham with a 65-year-old competitor, his son John, competing in cycling.

Jack's Years of Competition

Jack entered his first competition in the Virginia nationals in 2003 in the race walk, followed by cycling in the Louisville nationals in 2007, and discus and shot-put in the California nationals in 2009. In the Houston nationals in 2011, he competed in shot-put, discus, and shuffleboard. He received his first gold medal in shuffleboard in the 2013 Cleveland nationals.

Family Cheerleaders

Senior Olympian family members make great cheerleaders, and are very helpful in transporting equipment across the US to nationals. Murray was an ardent fan of his beloved Julia and accompanied her to all of her competitions until his death in 2012. Jack recalled the nationals in Houston, where several generations of one family, dressed in identical t-shirts bearing the name of their winner, composed a big cheering section.

My Observations

It is not all pomp and ceremony, as I listen to Julia and Jack talk of the consistent daily dedication it takes to stay on top of your game. Jack noted that the 55-year category moves much faster than, and is perhaps not as vigilant as, the oldsters. After this great morning with these two positive, fun-loving Senior Olympians, *age seemed to disappear*. As we went to the cafeteria for lunch, they were much like two high school students, walking buoyantly, on the way home from a ball game. . . . Julia has maintained an amazing erectness, and no stranger would believe her true age of 101!

    Do they have health issues? Have they had disappointments or lost parents and younger loved ones through death? Their answers, and ours, are a resounding, "Yes!" They are not giving up on life and focusing on such challenges. Are we?

Takeaway

Harness the power of today.
Seize the blessings of today!
Make something happen, enhance your life,
Make someone laugh, help a friend, love, love, love!
          —Steve Maraboli

JULIA HAWKINS BREAKS TWO SENIOR OLYMPICS WORLD RECORDS

Julia is an encouraging role model for all of us seniors, proving once again the value of finding purpose and passion in our lives. That gives us meaning for being alive! That spirit spills over in all of Julia's activities, and radiates outward to those fortunate to know her. Her uplifting joy and love of people is contagious.

Now for an excerpt from the USA Track and Field press release, July 15, 2017:

101-Year-Old Julia Hawkins Sets Second Pending World Record in One Month at 100m at USATF Masters Outdoor Championships

BATON ROUGE, Louisiana—The full age range of Masters athletes was on display Saturday as 2008 two-time Olympian Walter Dix, 31, and newcomer Julia Hawkins, 101, reigned supreme in the 100m at USATF Masters Outdoor Championships.

Julia "Hurricane" Hawkins (Baton Rouge, Louisiana) ran an inspiring 100m race in 40.12, alongside fellow Baton Rouge native, 92-year-old Mary Norckauer, and 82-year-old Christel Donley (Colorado Springs, Colorado). . . . While Hawkins is the oldest female competitor in the history of USATF Masters Outdoor Championships, she just recently picked up running as a hobby when she turned 100.

Hawkins was a sight both on and off the track, as spectators and local media requested photos and interviews with the latest sprints star. When asked how she maintains her lively spirit, Hawkins said that "an exercise program keeps you alive, active and mentally sharp."

Takeaways

Sports do not build character. They reveal it.
   —Heywood Hale Broun

Winners never quit and quitters never win.

—Vince Lombardi

Success is where preparation and opportunity meet.
　　—Bobby Unser

Part IV

Living a Life of Significance, with Purpose

Section 1

Purposeful Living

From "The Essence of Aging"
in my book, *He Lays the Stones for Our Steps:*

Odds are we will live a whole lifetime longer than many of our ancestors. It's a new frontier, and we are breaking new ground. Most people are unprepared and are searching for meaning in midlife. The young seek to be loved; as we get older, we are looking for love that arrives in self. The greatest mistake of mistaken identity relates to success, money, status, and fame. If these are the most important things in our lives, how long will we last after retirement? The average person dies within two to seven years after retirement. Many lose their purpose in life and retire *from* something rather than *to* something.

For everything there is a season, and a time for every matter under heaven; a time to be born, and a time to die, a time to plant, and a time to pluck up what is planted.
—Ecclesiastes 3:1–2

Bob Buford's book *Finishing Well* is about moving from a life of success to one of significance. The result is a long, extended life that can be our richest season. He quotes Dan Sullivan: "Simply checking out and coasting is not an option." In order to restore some vitality and excitement in your life, you must have a *higher purpose*. You've got to pour yourself into a larger overriding goal that will occupy your time and talents. Retirement is not in the Bible. The dictionary definition is to "take out of service." Bob calls that *reactive retirement*. He recommends *creative retirement* by retiring from the things you dislike doing and focusing your attention on what you love doing. You'll plunge into some of the most important work you will ever do.

SOUL PURPOSE:
SENIORS WITH STRONG REASONS TO LIVE OFTEN LIVE STRONGER
by Judith Graham, "Navigating Aging," Kaiser Health News

After making it through the maelstrom of middle age, many adults find themselves approaching older age wondering "what will give purpose to my life?" now that the kids have flown the nest and retirement is in the cards.

How they answer the question can have significant implications for their health.

Over the past two decades, dozens of studies have shown that seniors with a sense of purpose in life are less likely to develop Alzheimer's disease, mild cognitive impairment, disabilities, heart attacks or strokes, and more likely to live longer than people without this kind of underlying motivation.

Now, a new report in *JAMA Psychiatry* adds to this body of evidence by showing that older adults with a solid sense of purpose tend to retain strong hand grips and walking speeds— key indicators of how rapidly people are aging.

Why would a psychological construct ("I feel that I have goals and something to live for") have this kind of impact? Seniors with a sense of purpose may be more physically active and take better care of their health, some research suggests. Also, they may be less susceptible to stress, which can fuel dangerous inflammation.

"Purposeful individuals tend to be less reactive to stressors and more engaged, generally, in their daily lives, which can promote cognitive and physical health," said Patrick Hill, an assistant professor of psychological and brain sciences at Washington University in St. Louis who wasn't associated with the study.

But what is purpose, really? And how can it be cultivated? Anne Newman, a 69-year-old who splits her time between

Hartsdale, north of New York City, and Delray Beach, Fla., said she's been asking herself this "on a minute-by-minute basis" since closing her psychotherapy practice late last year.

Building and maintaining a career became a primary driver in her life after Newman raised two daughters and went back to work at age 48. As a therapist, "I really loved helping people make changes in their lives that put them in a different, better position," she said.

Things became difficult when Newman's husband, Joseph, moved to Florida and she started commuting back and forth from New York. Over time, the travel took a toll, and Newman decided she didn't want a long-distance marriage. So, she began winding down her practice and thinking about her next chapter.

Experts advise that people seeking a sense of purpose consider spending more time on activities they enjoy or using work skills in a new way. Newman loves drawing and photography. . . .

"Not knowing what's going to take the place of work in my life—it feels horrible, like I'm floundering," she admitted, in a phone interview.

I didn't ask myself did I have a larger purpose in life — I asked myself what gives meaning to my life.
—Barry Dym

Many people go through a period of trial and error after retirement and don't find what they're looking for right away, said Dr. Dilip Jeste, senior associate dean for healthy aging and senior care at the University of California–San Diego. "This doesn't happen overnight."

"People don't like to talk about their discomfort because they think it's unusual. And yet, everybody thinks about this existential question at this time of life: 'What are we here for?'" he noted.

Newman's focus has been on getting "involved in something other than personal satisfaction—something larger than myself." But that may be overreaching.

"I think people can get a sense of purpose from very simple things: from taking care of a pet, working in the garden or being kind to a neighbor," said Patricia Boyle, a leading researcher in this field and professor of behavioral sciences at the Rush Alzheimer's Disease Center at Rush University Medical Center in Chicago.

"Even small goals can help motivate someone to keep going," she continued. "Purpose can involve a larger goal, but it's not a requirement."

Older adults often discover a sense of purpose from taking care of grandchildren, volunteering, becoming involved in community service work or religion, she said. "A purpose in life can arise from learning a new thing, accomplishing a new goal, working together with other people or making new social connections when others are lost," she said.

Tara Gruenewald's research highlights how important it is for older adults to feel they play a valuable role in the life of others.

"I think what we often lose as we age into older adulthood is not a desire to contribute meaningfully to others but the opportunity to do so," said Gruenewald, chair of the department of psychology at California's Crean College of Health and Behavioral Sciences at Chapman University. Her research has found that people who perceive themselves as being useful had a stronger feeling of well-being and were less likely to become disabled and die than those who didn't see themselves this way.

"In midlife, we contribute to others partly because it's demanded of us in work and in our social relationships," Gruenewald said. "As we grow older, we have to seek out opportunities to contribute and give to others."

Some researchers try to tease out distinctions between having a sense of purpose and finding meaning in life; others don't. "Practically, I think there's a lot of overlap," Boyle said.

After Barry Dym, 75, retired a year ago from a long career as an organizational consultant and a marriage and family therapist, he said, "I didn't ask myself did I have a larger purpose in life—I asked myself what gives meaning to my life."

Answering that question wasn't difficult; certain themes had defined choices he'd made throughout his life. "What gives meaning to me is helping people. Trying to have an impact. Working with people very closely and helping them become much better at what they do," Dym said in a phone conversation from his home in Lexington, Mass.

In retirement, he's carrying that forward by mentoring several people with whom he has a professional and personal relationship, bringing together groups of people to talk about aging, and starting a blog. Recently, he said, he wrote about discovering that he feels freer now to "explore who I am, where I came from and what meaning things have to me than at any other point of my life."

And therein lies a dilemma. "I feel of two minds about purpose in older age," Dym said. "In some ways, I'd like to just shuck off that sense of having to do something to be a good person, and just relax. And in other ways, I feel deeply fulfilled by the things I do."

Reproduced from *Kaiser Health News*, August 31, 2017. Kaiser Health News is a nonprofit news service covering health issues. It is an editorially independent program of the Kaiser Family Foundation that is not affiliated with Kaiser Permanente.

INDIA, MOSCOW, USSR, AND HONG KONG: AP BUREAU CHIEF HENRY BRADSHER

His wife Monica does the writing this time:

When I think back about a marriage with more blessings and narrow escapes than I ever could have expected, I can't help thinking that God has been guiding us the whole time. "Marry in haste; regret at leisure," goes the old warning, but we ignored it and have been together 54 years! Our story falls into distinct periods based on where we lived: India, Russia, Hong Kong, Virginia, and Louisiana.

India, 1963–1964

A short trip into Canada from the Chicago area where I grew up was the only experience I had in a foreign country. So it's no wonder my father was concerned about his daughter preparing to spend a year in India on a Fulbright Fellowship. He dropped me off at JFK Airport in New York in June 1963 without mentioning his fears or that he had contacted people who might keep an eye on me. I didn't think I needed looking after. I was 21 years old and the proud recipient of a BA with high honors and a Phi Beta Kappa key, from Swarthmore College. Although I was not a know-it-all, I thought I was capable of learning anything if I put my mind to it, and I was fascinated by the history of India. My ambition was to become a professor, to research and write books about India.

I traveled to India in a group of newly minted graduates of American universities who were to teach conversational English, helping high school students develop accents that could be understood outside of India. We stayed in the International Center, a pleasant hostel in New Delhi, for a month studying Indian culture and methods of teaching English as a second language, before being sent to other Indian cities. The hostel's cafeteria served only vegetarian dishes, which tend to be even spicier than other Indian food. Eager to learn everything I could about India, I sampled all the dishes—and developed blisters on the inside of my mouth! I also lost ten pounds in successive bouts of "Delhi Belly" (diarrhea).

One day I was called to the hostel's only phone. The correspondent for the *Chicago Daily News,* where my father wrote editorials, invited me to dinner. "Humph," I thought, "Daddy must have asked this guy to check on me." But I accepted the invitation and spent a boring evening with the man (who was short, fat, balding, and old, maybe 45) and his wife and two children. It was like visiting a home in the United States. I was interested in India, blisters and all, not in a typical American family. It never occurred to me that it might be useful to learn how my own family someday might manage to live abroad. After all, having a family was not remotely on my horizon. I dutifully wrote a thank-you letter to the *Chicago Daily News* correspondent and thought to myself that my father could now relax about me and stop interfering.

Henry has written about meeting me in his book *The Dalai Lama's Secret and Other Reporting Adventures: Stories from a Cold War Correspondent.* Returning from a reporting assignment to his home in New Delhi, he found a couple of pieces of mail. One was an invitation to a farewell dinner dance for Ambassador John Kenneth Galbraith at the American Embassy. The other was from the headquarters of the Associated Press news agency, his employer. As Henry describes it in his book, "Stan Swinton, the head of AP's worldwide business operations, had written on June 21 a short note to enclose a letter that he had received. Stan said the letter was from the man with whom he had shared an apartment when they were young AP newsmen in Detroit in 1940 and 1941. Stan asked me to help his friend if help were needed. The letter had been written June 19 by Fred J. Pannwitt, who was now the chief editorial writer for the *Chicago Daily News*. It was the letter of a proud father, but a father with a certain unease about his daughter's venture into the unknown. Fred said he would appreciate it if the AP bureau chief in India could help her, perhaps by introducing her to interesting people."

The next time I was summoned to the hostel phone, the caller was the AP bureau chief, Henry Bradsher. "Oh no," I thought. "Daddy has done it again!" But this time, the invitation was to a glamorous event for Ambassador Galbraith, one of my heroes! I'd read some of his books. "Yes, I would love to go," I said, but as I told him, I had nothing to wear to a formal dinner dance. I had only one good dress with me, sleeveless and slightly above the knee, far from formal. It was impossible to buy a new dress. Stores in India had no ready-to-wear dresses; Indian women wore saris. I guessed rightly that an American woman at an American Embassy party should not show up in a sari. In desperation, I bought a shawl from a street vendor to cover my bare arms and went to a fancy hotel to have my hair done. The shawl was cheap, but my hair, naturally light blonde, looked great piled high on my head.

    On the night of the dance, my date showed up in a summer tux, white jacket and black trousers. He was tall, slim, and handsome and had a full head of hair. This was no boring evening. We danced a lot, especially enjoying the polka. At the end of the party, Henry asked me to go out with him again. And we wound up going out nearly every evening until just one week later, over dinner at the fancy hotel where I'd splurged on a hairdo, he told me that the next evening he planned to ask me to marry him. He wanted me to have some time to think it over. Think it over? *I was so in love I couldn't think at all.* I asked all my girlfriends at the hostel what I should do, and they all thought it was wonderfully romantic. Of course I should marry him! After a sleepless night, I accepted his proposal.

    We waited two weeks for responses to letters to our families before getting married. My parents could not come to India but gave their blessing, writing that they had raised me to make good decisions for myself. I didn't know until later that my dad went into high gear researching who Henry was and everything anyone knew about him, and could find nothing but good deeds and success.

    The wedding could not have been simpler. By Indian law, we had to be married by a Christian magistrate, and the only one available was the assistant commissioner of housing (loans) in old Delhi. The consular officer from the US Embassy attended and gave us an official American marriage certificate. We had to swear we had no other spouses, and Henry had to pay a fee of about $8.00.

Young people today are even more shocked by this story than my parents and friends were at the time. To get married to someone you have known only three weeks seems like the height of folly and rash behavior. But I knew Henry and he knew me, from all those long talks we had. I have had no regrets for fifty-four years. Now doesn't that story sound like prevenient grace?

USSR, 1964–1968

As AP bureau chief in New Delhi, Henry was responsible for news coverage not only in India but also in Pakistan (including what is now Bangladesh), Nepal, Bhutan, Ceylon (now called Sri Lanka), and Afghanistan. He took me to see all of them except Afghanistan before the AP decided to transfer him to the capital of the USSR, an even bigger and more important place. He hoped to become Moscow bureau chief. I had lived in India only eight months. Henry managed to pay back all that had been spent on my travel and stay at the hostel. He liked to say that buying me from the US government appealed to his swashbuckling instincts. His many Indian friends found it all quite understandable that he had paid a bride price and married someone from the same sub-caste—journalists.

We had a few weeks to get ready for the move to Moscow. I decided to have some clothes made by the tailor who had made my close-fitting white shantung silk wedding suit and several dresses. His little shop was near our home, and he did good work very fast at amazingly low cost. The tailor was a big burly man, a Sikh with a beard and turban. He was also deaf and dumb, so we communicated through pantomime. I would bring fabric and draw a sketch of what I wanted. He took my measurements and smiled and nodded. A week later, I would return for a fitting and any adjustments. But this time, the dresses I planned to take to Moscow didn't fit! He was terribly distressed. He measured me again and showed me that his original waist measurement had been smaller.

How could he have made such a mistake? I acted out rocking a baby in my arms, and his worried face relaxed into a huge grin. He understood that I was pregnant, and he made adjustments. Then I had him make some very loose-fitting wool dresses for Moscow's winter 1964, later in the pregnancy. That turned out to be a good thing because there was no nice clothing to buy in Moscow. Russian women made their own dresses, and most of the fabrics available then tended to shrink and were not colorfast.

What to Expect in the USSR in 1964–68

We spent a few weeks in London learning some very basic Russian. We were briefed there about what to expect in the USSR. There might be attempts to get us into trouble so the Soviet government could expel us as spies. If someone offered to sell something cheap on the street, we were not to buy it. The seller could be a government agent trying to get us arrested for black marketeering. We couldn't find our own housing. Soviet officials assigned apartments. All apartments assigned to foreigners were bugged, and the building entrances were guarded by KGB policemen who kept track of comings and goings and prevented ordinary Russians from talking to foreigners.

Our first home in Moscow was an apartment assigned to *Newsweek* magazine. The AP bureau chief whom Henry hoped to replace was still in an apartment assigned to the AP. The *Newsweek* correspondent had been summoned to New York, where he was fired for embarrassing the magazine by partying with so many Russian women that Soviet officials had complained about his behavior. Those women kept calling the apartment looking for him. I learned to say in Russian, "Patrick went to America," but they didn't believe me, thinking I must be a rival.

Not knowing he was about to be fired, the correspondent had left most of his belongings behind. I had to pack them up and send them to New York at *Newsweek*'s expense. I shipped closets full of clothing, a whole case of men's cologne, various prophylactics from his medicine cabinet, as well as lots of broken-down stereo equipment. The apartment bore evidence of wild partying—broken lamps and stains on furniture. When I turned on the lights at night in the kitchen, every surface was crawling with roaches. I would say to them very loudly, "I see you spying on me with your beady little eyes, you nasty Communists!" I hoped whoever was listening to our apartment would hear me and wonder. There were no repercussions. I cleaned and cleaned, and put down boric acid powder, the only anti-roach solution I could find, which didn't do much good.

Communist Ideology, Party Politics Prevent Change

We arrived in March when it was still snowy and very cold. I went to a grocery store and came home with a very small, scrawny chicken and some potatoes. The potatoes looked fine, but when I cut them open, I discovered they were all black inside. Frozen. I learned from wives of other correspondents that food in the government stores was far inferior to what I could buy in the peasants' market, where farmers sold what they had grown on their small private plots. The great power of private enterprise was on vivid display, but Communist ideology and Party politics prevented any change for many years to come.

I was somewhat bored and lonely. Henry worked long hours, and I had no real friends. In another country I would have gotten a job or gone back to studying for a graduate degree, but the Soviet government did not allow spouses of foreigners from NATO countries to work in Russian enterprises or attend Russian universities. One night at a dinner party given by Indian diplomats, I met a Russian professor of Indian history. Oh, joy! We had a stimulating conversation, and I offered to come help him in his research as a volunteer. He agreed enthusiastically, but the next morning someone at his university called to tell me he had gone to the US to a conference and would not need my help. I never saw or heard from him again. I hope he didn't get into any serious trouble. No doubt the KGB thought I was a spy.

Henry Promoted to AP Bureau Chief of USSR; Birth of a Son

In June, Henry finally moved into an AP apartment—without me. I had gone back to my parents' house in Evanston, Illinois, in May to await childbirth. I had arrived in Chicago very pregnant with no husband in sight, a bit embarrassing since my parents had yet to meet him.

Henry sent me a telegram that the baby's home would be on Narodnaya (People) Street, so I knew he had been promoted to chief of the most important overseas AP bureau in the world. I was happy for him but missed him dreadfully.

Henry knew I was safe, and he felt his new responsibilities at work acutely. He feared some critically important story might break at any time, preventing him from leaving his post, so he said he would "try" to come see the baby and me soon after the birth. He wouldn't promise for fear of having to break the promise. My parents were not impressed by his priorities, especially when I became depressed after our son arrived, weeping uncontrollably, still unsure when or whether he would come see our child.

Henry did come, within a week, and he was a very proud and happy father of Keith Vinson Bradsher. In one way, I think it was good that I went through that spell of unhappiness. I finally grew up. I was no longer the weaker partner, a sort of child bride taking all direction from my brilliant husband. I now had a great responsibility of my own, rearing this adorable baby boy.

Life of an American Wife, with a Newborn—Moscow in the 1960s

Life in the AP bureau chief's apartment was much better than in the *Newsweek* apartment. Our household goods arrived from India after six weeks at sea and more weeks traveling from the Baltic Sea port at Leningrad. We had disposed of all our furniture in India, bringing only books, phonograph records, carpets, and Henry's treasured Tibetan art. Our apartment now felt like home.

I studied Russian with a tutor once a week and memorized

vocabulary while giving little Keith his bottles of formula. He was a serene and happy baby, but I was anxious to know that he was making normal progress. Lacking a pediatrician or any quick communication with my mother, I practically memorized the popular American book on childcare by Dr. Benjamin Spock.

I had two other guides to raising a baby—Tonya Savina, the building custodian, and our weekday helper, Svetlana Razuvaeva. They were both mothers about fifteen years older than I was, and they had compassion for this young American who lacked basic skills in motherhood, shopping, and cooking. We paid Tonya to babysit when we went out at night. We hired Svetlana through the Soviet government's Agency for Provisioning the Diplomatic Corps. No choice but to take whomever they sent, but we were blessed with sweet Svetlana.

Many years later, I was able to visit these women in Moscow. They told me then how they had had to attend monthly meetings with the KGB in which they were expected to report on our activities, especially anything that might be spying or anti-Soviet. They felt much more loyalty to us than to their supervisor and played stupid, reporting perfectly normal activities at boring length.

Svetlana cleaned our apartment and did some cooking, but her main job was doing laundry—boiling diapers on the stove, washing clothes in the bathtub and drying them on an elaborate rack hung from the ceiling in the tiny room that also housed the ironing board. She ironed everything, including underwear and cloth diapers. On weekends and holidays, I had to do these things and appreciated her help all the more.

Having a Second Son, Russian Style

Svetlana's diaper duty doubled when I had a second son, Neal Clifton Bradsher, just before Keith's first birthday in July. Our family doctor was a US Marine doing his medical residency at the American Embassy. An energetic young bachelor who wanted to learn about Russian medicine, he urged me to have our baby in

Moscow. In May, Henry and I toured the well-known women's hospital where top ob-gyn specialists took unusual cases from around the country. Diplomats and other foreigners were directed to that hospital. There were three beds to a room with a bathroom and a refrigerator in case family members wanted to supplement hospital food. We decided that I would stay in Moscow for the birth rather than fly to Evanston with baby Keith. Although I was very obviously pregnant, our tour guide failed to mention that the elite hospital closed every summer "for renovations"! By the time we found out, it was too late in the pregnancy for me to fly.

I had written some articles for the AP about life in Moscow. I thought I might write a long one or even a book about having a baby Russian style. I never wrote the article, because the experience was so awful that the authorities might be very displeased by my description, and it might even hurt Henry's career.

Rodil'ny Dom (Birth House) Number 13 on Leninsky Prospect featured rooms with ten beds, packed together so the patients had to crawl off the foot of the bed to get out. As a foreigner, I was privileged to share a room with only three other patients, all foreigners. I could speak Russian with the Bulgarian, but had no common language with the woman from Yemen or the one from Turkey. However, we all made happy noises over each other's cute babies. The Yemeni infant looked just like Gamal Abdel Nasser, then president of Egypt.

Hoping to mix with Russian patients, I asked our nurse if I could join a class on how to take care of a baby since I didn't know Russian methods. She showed up at my bedside with a doll and gave me a brief private lesson on how to swaddle an infant. No mixing allowed with Russians who lacked security clearance!

We foreigners were allowed to use the staff toilet, which was filthy, rather than the one used by Russian patients, probably even dirtier. Both Neal and I came home with serious infections.

Diplomatic Social Events

As AP bureau chief and wife, we were invited to diplomatic receptions at the Kremlin. I went to a few of them, but begged off after realizing that few women attended. Henry had to work the room, gleaning bits of Kremlin gossip from diplomats. I stood around and observed with nobody to talk to. One time I was able to get close to the velvet rope separating dignitaries from more ordinary attendees. I was only a few feet from USSR Premier and Communist Party Secretary Leonid I. Brezhnev and his chief guest, Britain's Prime Minister Harold Wilson. I had seen newspaper coverage, only in black-and-white in those days. In person, Brezhnev's scarlet face beneath his bristling black eyebrows startled me. Wilson, on the other hand, was pale, just like his newspaper image.

Ambassadors frequently gave dinner parties and often included Henry, representing the press, since the AP was the largest press agency in the world. Soviet officials didn't hold press conferences or grant interviews, so socializing at such parties was important to Henry's work. Entering the dining room of one of these ambassadorial mansions, we would see the seating chart for the long, long table. Henry and I always ranked last behind all the diplomats. We were seated across from each other in the middle of the table if the ambassador and his wife were at either end, or, if they were in the middle, we would be miles from each other at opposite ends.

Henry was young for a bureau chief, and I was younger still. All the other guests usually appeared to be my grandparents' age. Sometimes that was an advantage. The Swedish ambassador kept flirting with me and telling everyone that I looked "just like our Swedish girls back home"! At another grand party, the ambassador's wife instructed the waiter to serve dessert to me first, an unusual departure from protocol. I soon understood that all the other guests were in on a secret. The dessert was a frozen delight in a huge, beautiful amber crystal bowl. The waiter lifted his big silver spoon to serve me and, to my horror, shattered a corner of the bowl onto my plate! Everyone laughed uproariously at my shocked face. The bowl was made of sugar.

At another dinner, a Burmese ambassador felt it his Buddhist duty to warn me all evening long about the dangers of vanity. Little did he know how far from vain I felt. I had bought only one long dress in London, not guessing I would need more. One night as we were dressing to go out, Henry remarked that he'd seen my dress so often he was beginning to think it was his!

The down side for me of these elegant dinners was that we were expected to reciprocate, a terrifying thought. I had never learned much about cooking at home, nor had I learned in our first months of married life. In India, Henry had a "cook bearer" named Emmanuel, who prepared delicious meals with a primitive stove and an oven without a temperature gauge. He didn't want me in his kitchen. Putting on a dinner party in Moscow took the better part of a week. I made some parts of the dinner early in the week and froze them. Rolls had to be made from scratch with a little cake of yeast, no Fleischmann's packets or ready-to-bake crescents. Finding food and figuring out what to make was a challenge. I had bought two cookbooks in London—my mother's favorite, *The Joy of Cooking;* and Mrs. Beaton's nineteenth-century classic that began its recipes with advice like "first, catch a chicken." I needed really basic directions, but I would go through the index of both books and find only a few recipes that didn't include ingredients that were not available in Moscow.

On the final day, I would buy flowers for the table in the farmers' market, knowing the flowers would barely last the night. Through the long winter, flowers were flown to Moscow from southern parts of the Soviet Union. I heard that enterprising Armenians would charter a whole plane, fill it with flowers instead of passengers, and make a profit in the Moscow market. Without Svetlana, I would never have managed to raise two babies and put on those dinner parties for ambassadors.

Operas and Ballets at the Bolshoi Theater

Learning the Russian language and developing an appreciation of Russian culture helped make up for the difficulties we encountered in Moscow. Henry was able to get good seats at operas and ballets at the Bolshoi Theater. I joined a little group of correspondents' wives who visited at least one museum a month. By the beginning of our fifth winter there, I was content with our life, but several events made me eager to leave.

Henry was denounced in the government newspaper *Izvestia* when he covered a demonstration by Russian dissidents. His articles about the fiftieth anniversary of the Bolshevik Revolution pointed out failings as well as successes, further irritating authorities. One day, not long after Israel's success in fighting Arab aggression in the Six-Day War, Henry learned from a very high Soviet official that the USSR was not eager to re-arm Syria, which had lost the Golan Heights and left an embarrassment of defeated Soviet tanks scattered across the plain below. Henry's AP articles were big news across the Middle East, as well as in the West. We were getting angry calls from the Syrian Embassy in the middle of the night.

An Unwelcome Gift

On Christmas day, 1967, we received an unwelcome "gift." After a pleasant evening out with the United Press International correspondent and his wife and little boy, we found our parking lot full, because other foreigners in our building had parties. We parked in the alley just out of sight of the KGB guard. A half hour later, after I had put the boys to bed, we were summoned back to the parking lot. Someone had placed a bomb under the front right fender of our VW Beetle! Because the gas tank was completely full, it didn't explode, but the blast blew a hole into the passenger side of the car and broke sixteen windows of our Russian neighbors' apartments.

Nobody was ever charged with the crime, which received no news coverage inside the Soviet Union. Since all kinds of explosives and weapons were tightly controlled by the KGB, we assumed the gift was intended to scare us into leaving. And I was ready!

Henry's Nieman Fellowship to Study at Harvard

We stayed a few more months in the Soviet Union, until Henry won a prestigious Nieman Fellowship to study at Harvard for the following school year, 1968–69.

I had long since given up my dream of becoming a university professor. Instead, I had become fascinated by our sons' development. As an elementary school teacher, I would be able to work wherever in the world we might be sent. I applied to the Harvard Graduate School of Education and was thrilled to be accepted into the master of education program.

Compared with Moscow, living in Belmont, Massachusetts, was easy. Most Americans do not truly realize how blessed we are with opportunity and plenty. The grocery store seemed like a miracle—so many choices! It was the most pleasant kind of culture shock. I missed Svetlana and Tonya, but we didn't need help. We had a washer and dryer! The boys went to a Lutheran preschool. Henry's Nieman gave him his choice of courses to audit, with no papers to write or exams to pass. He mainly studied Chinese history, politics, and economics.

I enjoyed my courses at Harvard, especially those focused on remedial reading. For my favorite course, on children's cognitive development, I wrote a long research paper on bilingualism, using some examples from our sons' learning Russian as well as English. For a course on assessment, I had to give an IQ test to an inmate in the maximum-security prison in Walpole, Massachusetts. At the end of the test, the inmate helped me on with my coat, slid his hands around my neck, and asked if I knew that the Boston Strangler was in that prison! (He was.)

Since I had so much homework, Henry cleaned up the kitchen every evening. For years afterward, he liked to tell people, "I put my wife through Harvard by washing dishes!"

Protesters' Reminders of the Communist Youth League

Many Harvard students were so upset about the escalating Vietnam War that they put their time into protests instead of studying. In some of my classes, students would march in, treat the professors extremely rudely, and tell us we should be ashamed for not demonstrating. They reminded me of the Komsomol (Communist Youth League) in the USSR, and I did not appreciate their interfering with my chance to earn a master's degree. Although I had a lot of doubts about our entry into the war, I had heard enough anti-American propaganda in Moscow and didn't need to hear more in my own country.

Henry Employed by the *Washington Star*

After our academic year at Harvard, Henry accepted a job offer from the *Washington Star* newspaper. We moved to Arlington, Virginia, and enrolled Keith in kindergarten. Henry didn't know whether he would be sent to cover news in Africa or in East Asia.

For me, there were several months of frustration not knowing how to prepare for our next post and not being able to begin teaching after learning so much at Harvard. I took an evening class in oil painting that helped my mood. So did house hunting. I was longing to put down roots, to have a home to return to. We bought a house and rented it to a family just before we moved . . . to Hong Kong.

Hong Kong (December 1969 to February 1975)

Our five years in Hong Kong were productive and happy. We moved several times, but most of those years we spent in an apartment with a great view of the harbor. I reconnected with a Swarthmore College classmate living there, and we and our husbands bought a Chinese junk. It didn't have the traditional batwing sail. Instead, it had a diesel engine. We were able to escape from crowded beaches to explore outlying islands—until the junk sank at its mooring during a typhoon.

Household help was inexpensive, and I was lucky to hire

dear Ah Pui, a teenager who was an amah (helper) in training, a job known in local slang as a "make-ee-learn." She lived with us, going home to the island of Cheung Chau on weekends. She cooked amazingly good fried rice and other Chinese dishes, kept our apartment tidy, did the laundry in our washer and dryer, and looked after the boys when Henry and I were both out. She had not gone beyond elementary school but amazed me with her ability to remember long telephone numbers and detailed messages, sometimes several of them at once, without writing anything down.

Teaching at the American Hong Kong International School

Keith attended a British school near our apartment for a year, but when I landed a job teaching at the American HKIS (Hong Kong International School), I moved our children to that school. I taught sixth grade and had opportunities to make a lasting difference working with other teachers who became lifelong friends. We created an outdoor education week for the sixth grade that is still held today.

I particularly enjoyed developing dramas with our sixth graders, having them improvise dialogue and then writing their words down for them as the script. One year the three sixth-grade classes put on a musical that drew on my years in Russia. The story line was based on the folktale "The Little Humpbacked Horse," but it included classic Russian songs like "The Volga Boatmen." A group of girls who were taking ballet after school did their own choreography for a dance to music from Stravinsky's *The Firebird*. I found teaching science the most creative work of all, helping children develop their own projects while learning basics of research and designing experiments.

Henry's News Coverage in Dangerous Places

The only difficult part of living in Hong Kong was that Henry's work took him far away. Unlike Moscow, where his office was across the hall and he came home several times a day, and

Belmont, where he washed the dishes, Henry was away nearly half the time, often in dangerous places. He covered many aspects of the continuing Vietnam War, including traveling in Cambodia, Thailand, and Laos as well as Vietnam. He visited Okinawa when the United States returned control of the island to Japan. When rebels in the Philippines turned violent on the island of Mindanao, Henry was there. He was the runner-up for a Pulitzer Prize for his coverage of the 1971 Pakistani civil war that resulted in East Pakistan breaking away to become Bangladesh. In February 1972, he accompanied President Nixon on his famous trip to open relations with Communist China. A year later, Henry won the George Polk Award for reporting and analysis of Chinese affairs.

    Communications in those days were nothing like today's satellite and digital connections. When Henry was away, the boys and I rarely had any messages or calls from him. When he did try to call, the connections were so bad that he couldn't understand our children's high-pitched voices. In case of emergency, I had instructions to call the *Washington Star* editors in DC, who could get a message to him. Only when he returned from hair-raising adventures did I find out what he had been doing.

    One time, when I knew Henry was in Vietnam, the TV news showed an explosion in Saigon at an office building where foreign correspondents worked. I didn't find out for days that he had not been there at the time. One of the reporters, who had worked for Henry in the AP bureau in Moscow, had gone to work for CBS. He and his TV team were killed by rocket fire in Cambodia. I learned later that the percentage of newsmen killed in the Vietnam War was higher than that for officers or enlisted men in the armed forces because the journalists and photographers were always in the hottest spots. Like the wife of a soldier, I spent a lot of time worrying about Henry, wondering how I would cope if something happened to him. Ah Pui became like a sister to me, and we remain friends to this day.

The Bradsher Family Moves Home to Virginia

In February 1975, the Vietnam War was winding down but not quite over when the *Washington Star* decided for financial reasons to shut down their last foreign bureau—Henry's. We had to leave Hong Kong in the middle of the school year, moving back to the house we had bought in Arlington, Virginia. It was not an easy transition for Keith and Neal, who now walked to a nearby public school where they were complete outsiders. When they told other children that they had come from Hong Kong, the response was laughter. Hong Kong Phooey was a dog character on Saturday morning cartoons. When the other children talked about the Redskins, Keith and Neal looked blank. They knew nothing about American football.

I missed teaching but knew the top priority had to be helping our kids settle in. This was our ninth home in eleven years of marriage, counting temporary places like the *Newsweek* apartment in Moscow. We had to buy a car, beds, and all sorts of suburban stuff that we'd never had before—lawn mower, rakes, snow shovels, etc. While we were waiting for our Chinese rosewood furniture and other household effects from Hong Kong, I spent a lot of time refinishing floors and cleaning fingerprints and crayon marks left by our last tenants. Real estate values had soared in our absence. We realized that we could not have afforded to buy the house had we waited until our return.

Teaching at the National Cathedral School

Other things had also changed. Henry had some idea that I might not need to work, but it seemed that all the women my age with children in school were working. It was lonely in our empty house all day, so I began looking for a job. The Arlington public school system wanted novice (cheap) teachers, not ones with a master's degree and five years' teaching experience. Private and parochial schools paid less but didn't have the same regulations. By the time our furniture arrived, I had found a job teaching at the all-girls National Cathedral School across the Potomac River in DC. The boys were accepted by its brother school, St. Albans. Now all four of us were commuting into DC.

I loved the four years I spent teaching at NCS, a wonderful community of teachers, administrators, clergy, and parents devoted to excellence. The girls were bright and fun to teach, and I had freedom to be creative. I taught fifth and sixth grades in a departmentalized setting; each class went from teacher to teacher. My specialty was history—American in fifth grade and Ancient in sixth. We put on original plays and "happenings" that other classes could visit. One year, the fifth graders reenacted the Continental Congress, culminating in signing the Declaration of Independence.

Changes Evolving in Journalism; College for Sons

Henry's work changed with the journalism business. The dollar was worth less and less as other countries' economies grew. American news organizations closed most of their foreign bureaus, preferring to send journalists and photographers abroad to wherever the breaking stories were. Henry often traveled with the secretary of state, sometimes with the president. He didn't enjoy waiting around for briefings with dozens of other reporters, and he didn't think most of them had enough experience to understand the cultures behind the news. It seemed to him that TV news in particular had become more and more superficial. The headlines often seemed to be dictated more by the drama of photos or videos than by more important developments that were less visual.

Our boys were excelling at St. Albans. Summers were taken up with swim team practice, tennis matches, and diving competitions at a neighborhood club. We began to visit college campuses. My entire salary at National Cathedral School was going next door to pay tuition at St. Albans. Looking ahead at the looming cost of two boys in expensive colleges, I began to think about changing careers.

A New Role with the National Geographic Society

A Swarthmore classmate who had been working at the National

Geographic Society ever since our graduation began inviting me to evaluate work in progress in the Educational Media Division, which used NGS resources to produce filmstrips and other materials for schools. This consulting work was fun, and other editors also asked me to come look at their progress. In June 1980, I went to work at NGS as an editor of school materials.

That fall, when Keith had just earned his driver's license, he began driving himself and his brother to school. It was a big responsibility, and at times Keith resented the fact that Neal could still sleep on the way to St. Albans. Two years later, Keith was in college and Neal had to wake up early and drive himself to school.

Newspapers Begin Succumbing to TV News

I loved my new job and earned a small raise and promotion in my first year at NGS. But just after I got the job, Henry was forced to make a career change: the *Washington Star* went out of business. An excellent newspaper with a long history as the best paper in DC, it succumbed to the same pressures that killed other afternoon papers across the country, including the *Chicago Daily News,* where my father managed to retire just before it closed down. The afternoon papers were killed by evening news on TV and the difficulty of delivering newspapers during rush hour. The *Washington Post*, a morning paper, absorbed only a few rookie (low-paid) reporters and the most popular syndicated columnists from the *Star*.

Until this point in our marriage, Henry's career had dictated where we lived and when we moved. Realizing that I had just found a really exciting job and that the boys were at a crucial point in their education, Henry decided not to seek employment outside of Washington. I have been ever grateful that he put us ahead of what he might have preferred to do. In February 1982, he found work with the CIA.

At National Geographic, my boss, George A. Peterson, noticed that filmstrip sales were starting to falter. Videos were gaining popularity, but the TV division retained control of that medium. George asked me to research what we could produce for schools that would run on a computer. I leaped at the opportunity and wound up producing some award-winning software.

Another Swarthmore classmate, Dr. Robert Tinker, and I joined forces to apply for a grant from the National Science Foundation to create National Geographic Kids Network, which became a series of hands-on science units that allowed children to collect data and share it with distant classes online. Our software enabled the kids and their teachers to display the data as graphs and maps and to send email letters to their "research team" of a dozen widely separated classes. I was able to get grant support from telecommunications companies to pay for subscriptions for poorer schools and foreign countries to be sure the research teams had contact with very different places. The American classes were especially excited to get emails from Russia, which I was able to arrange just as the USSR was opening up under President Mikhail Gorbachev.

Trips Back to Russia

Our president, Ronald Reagan, signed an agreement with Gorbachev to improve relations between the two countries by exchanging large exhibits. In 1988, I was recruited to serve as a computer specialist for the American exhibit the month it spent in Tashkent, Uzbekistan. Stopping in Moscow on my way home, I formed a partnership with some Russian scientists trying to reform education in their country. Over the course of the next decade, I made at least one trip to Russia each year, developed lasting friendships with several Russian scientists and teachers, organized workshops for teachers in fifteen cities across Russia, and observed the changes and struggles of Russians as their country fell apart. The fact that I had had a baby in Moscow in the 1960s was an instant icebreaker. That meant I knew what they had been going through in the Communist era.

Meanwhile, at the CIA, Henry was studying Russia's continuing efforts to spy on other countries, even while its government changed dramatically. When some of my new Russian friends came to visit, he had to report contact with them. No doubt, some of his CIA colleagues harbored suspicions of my new friends, but they never stopped us from hosting them, and none of my friends proved to be spies. Henry was allowed to make two trips to Russia in 1991 and 1998, using a diplomatic passport. I wasn't allowed to tell my friends where he worked.

Retirement in Baton Rouge

As Henry's 70th birthday approached, I began urging him to retire while he was still able to travel and enjoy life. When I suggested various places we might live, he always said, "We don't know anyone there." It became clear that the only place he wanted to live was his hometown, Baton Rouge. I had already retired and had my own little consulting business, which I could continue wherever we lived.

We made the big move in the spring of 2000. Within a year, we became involved in volunteer work. I joined the board of LSU's International Hospitality Foundation, which helps foreign students get settled and learn about our community and country. Henry replaced me on the board when my term ended. We have enjoyed hosting students, having them come to dinner on a regular basis, and taking them on swamp tours and visits to New Orleans. Henry gets a kick out of asking them about recent events in their countries; they are always surprised that he knows so much about their hometowns. I have served on the board of Volunteers in Public Schools, and both of us have tutored young children at Bernard Terrace Elementary School, where Henry attended first and second grade eighty years ago. I have led church missions to Ekaterinburg, Russia, and have hosted teams of Russians journeying to Louisiana to help repair homes after hurricanes. We have both taught courses through LSU's OLLI program for seniors, and we have both given lessons about the world in the Rings and Ivy Sunday school class at First United Methodist Church.

We love Louisiana and have made many friends here. Although the state has many problems, it also has the friendliest people I have ever met. It has been a privilege to live here and share what we have learned about the world with Louisianans.

My Personal Note

I first met the Bradshers at the Rings and Ivy Sunday school class Monica mentions above. Monica was modest in her listing of her and Henry's volunteerism. I am awed by their intellect, zest for life, and involvement in service to others, despite both facing their own mortality in the past two years, as chronicled by Monica in a later chapter. They will still be in the saddle, receiving God's riches through service to others, when death calls. . . .

Takeaways

Journalism is what we need to make democracy work.
—Walter Cronkite

Ratings don't last. Good journalism does.
—Dan Rather

I am grateful to journalism for waking me up to the realities of the world.
—Eduardo Galeano

JACK ("PETE") SEBASTIAN SERVING OTHERS AT ST. JAMES PLACE

Pete Sebastian is a quite gentle man with a passion for others. We see him routinely pushing his stereo system, filled with some of his collection of an estimated one thousand records. His music runs the gamut from honky-tonk to Toscanini's opera. Pete plays records and brings back memories, not only for St. James Place Assisted Living and Memory Care residents, but also for Old Jefferson Nursing Home residents. He never misses an opportunity to "shake a leg," pulling a seated resident with dancing feet onto the dance floor.

He is adept with his hands, a skilled woodworker, and he keeps the Assisted Living clocks and jukebox in fine working order.

Pete's Early Years

Pete was born in Trees, Louisiana, but the family, with two boys and two girls, moved from oil field to oil field in Louisiana and Texas until his father accepted employment in 1942 with the Standard Oil Company in Baton Rouge.

After graduating from Istrouma High School in 1947, Pete met his future wife, Betty Beard, on a blind date. He dated her steadily henceforth, telling his competition, "All is fair in love and war." They were married in 1949 and later adopted a daughter, Lisa, and a son, Terry.

Pete Sings Honky-Tonk

After enrolling at LSU in 1947, majoring in electrical engineering, Pete met fellow students who needed a singer to accompany their four-piece band. When I asked him why he was not singing with us in the Memory Care sections, Pete chuckled and said he only sang honky-tonk songs, such as "The Wild Side of Life," while guys cried over their beer, lamenting lost loves. On a good night in those college days, when they passed a hat, they collected as much as $35! (Sounds like a lot of money, considering I was paid 50 cents an hour typing for the LSU Speech Department during those same years. There were only two jobs available for girls, babysitting or typing on an upright Remington.)

Thus began Pete's deep love of music. As there was no downtown bridge in Baton Rouge until 1968, riding the car and passenger ferryboats plying the waters of the mighty Mississippi River between Baton Rouge and Port Allen was a popular pastime for residents, students and visitors alike. Port Allen had numerous rowdy dance halls. In those days they were called honky-tonks, a forerunner of today's nightclub terminology. The dance halls featured bands with lively music, far more appealing than jukeboxes.

Serving Our Country in the Korean War

Pete also joined the Army Reserve at LSU. Foolishly, he said, he turned down the opportunity for Officer Candidate School.

When the Korean War broke out in 1950, he was sent to Korea to attend a radio school and became the radio chief for the 3rd Battalion, 31st Regiment, 7th Infantry Division. After the war ended, they were told that a majority of their fellow soldiers had been wounded or killed in action during the horrific and bloody war. Pete served a total of eight years in the Army in the active Reserve, two of which were served in Korea.

Career Path and Marriage

Pete left the Army Reserve in December 1953 and was employed at Gulf States Utilities. Following several other positions, he retired from work with the federal government in 1994, at age 64.

His wife Betty died in 1957. He remarried in 2008, and his wife Barbara died in 2013. They had four grown children from their combined marriage.

Moving to St. James Place

After Barbara died, Pete moved to St. James Place, quickly finding opportunities for service, surrounded by a bevy of friends as he began a new life.

To learn more about Pete Sebastian, view Baton Rouge channel 33's "Hometown Heroes":
http://www.brproud.com/news/local-news/hometown-hero-pete-sebastian

Takeaways

The purpose of life is not to be happy. It is to be useful, to be honorable, to be compassionate, to have it make some difference that you have lived and lived well.
—Ralph Waldo Emerson

Music washes away from the soul the dust of everyday life.
—Berthold Auerbach

He who sings scares away his woes.
—Cervantes

MESSENGERS FOR GOD:
JERRY AND NANCY DUMAS

I believe God chooses each of us for His various purposes, bringing unspeakable joy when we decide to live the life of significance and purpose He lays out for each of us. Jerry and Nancy are truly fulfilling their role, carrying His message with action and with words (which many men hesitate to share as Jerry does).

Jerry's obvious admiration for former LSU football coach Paul Dietzel makes one stop and listen. The lessons Coach Dietzel taught, by word and actions, continue to have an effect in lives long after his death. He taught much more than football; he taught his boys how to become Christian men, successful in all aspects of life, mirrored by his stewardship.

Hearing Jerry talk about Coach one morning, as I crossed the gym at First United Methodist Church, led to my interviewing Jerry and writing a chapter, "Coach Paul Dietzel: A Giant among Men," in my book *He Lays the Stones for Our Steps*.

Jerry and Nancy Dumas's Christian Stewardship

Nancy has a master's degree in spiritual transformation from Asbury Theological Seminary, and leads Christian studies. She serves on Asbury's board of trustees. Jerry serves on the board of the Fellowship of Christian Athletes.

Jerry and Nancy's generosity of time and service extends to their monetary giving, which has ranged from a church chapel to church missions, scholarships for aspiring ministers, and more.

Jerry Dumas, LSU Alumnus of the Year

I asked permission to share Jerry's story, which attests to his humility. One day when Jerry called home, Nancy told him he had a letter from the president of the LSU Alumni Association. When Nancy opened the envelope, she told him he was chosen as the 2009 LSU Alumnus of the Year. Jerry immediately said, "They made a mistake." But it was really not surprising, considering Jerry's association with LSU—playing end on Coach Dietzel's

Fighting Tigers football team, giving football scholarships to worthy players, and even making a multimillion endowment to the Ole War Skule. One of the most meaningful scholarships Jerry instituted was a US Air Force scholarship in honor of his younger brother, Col. Charles "Chuck" Dumas.

Jerry's Professional Career

Shy of funds, and with no scholarship, Jerry enrolled at LSU in 1953, majoring in business and natural sciences. His funds ran out and he left LSU at age 22, six hours shy of graduating. He began a 53-year career in the oil and gas industry. (He worked as a mud engineer in the oil fields, as his first job.)

Jerry had learned from his beloved Coach Dietzel how to achieve success in every area of his life. He became a multimillionaire, and is still an active consultant in the oil and gas industry.

His first venture, along with two partners, was an oil-field rental tool company. After attaining full ownership, he sold the company and patent. Subsequently, he purchased the patent and with a partner formed Hydrotech International, a deepwater pipeline repair firm. Hydrotech was acquired by Hughes Tool Company.

Jerry became a group division president of Hughes Tool Company in Houston, one of the world's largest tool companies. He was advised by the chairman of the board that he could not advance further without a college degree, so twenty years after leaving LSU, Jerry studied by correspondence and traveled to LSU weekly by company plane, acquiring his degree in 1984.

I assume that traveling to LSU gave him time to consider if he wanted to continue working for Hughes, or be a business owner once again. You guessed right—he acquired his degree from LSU, and resigned from Hughes.

Jerry and Investors Purchase a Canadian Public Company

Jerry spent five years with Merrill Lynch learning investment banking and tech management. After acquiring Canadian Flotek Industries, he and his investors moved the company to the US as a Delaware Corporation and entered the engineering, manufacturing and sales market, growing the company from $1 million to $250 million. It was registered on the New York Stock Exchange in 2008. Jerry continued as chairman, president, and CEO until he retired in 2009. He continued as chairman of the board until 2010.

Jerry was also recognized as the Ernst & Young Entrepreneur of the Year.

Nancy and Jerry's Methodist Roots

Jerry and Nancy were active members of the First United Methodist Church of Houston, and endowed the building of a chapel for the church.

Jerry had a yearning to move back to Baton Rouge and his many memories as a young football player with Coach Dietzel. Former players meet one Monday each month at Frank's Restaurant for breakfast, reminiscent of the 7 a.m. skull practice for LSU football players, when Coach mapped out the challenges they would face with the opposing team. Former players also attend a weekly Bible class that Coach started at First United Methodist Church.

When Coach and Nancy Dietzel returned to live in Baton Rouge, they joined the First United Methodist Church and the Rings and Ivy Sunday school class I attend. One Sunday, as our class speaker, Coach spoke of the stress and feelings of rejection associated with coaching. His tears brought ours, as he spoke of the acceptance he felt in Rings and Ivy.

Death of Coach Paul Dietzel

Coach Paul Dietzel died in September 2013, nineteen days after his 89th birthday and one day before the 69th anniversary of marrying his wife Anne. Former players served as pallbearers at his funeral.

He leaves behind shining examples of the disciples of Christ he wanted his men to become.

Jerry and Nancy are true disciples and messengers for God. In their retirement years, they continue their service through Baton Rouge's First United Methodist Church.

Takeaways

From everyone to whom much has been given, much will be required; and from the one to whom much has been entrusted, even more will be demanded.
—Luke 12:48

For what does it profit a man to gain the whole world and forfeit his soul?
—Mark 8:36

A good name is more desirable than great riches; to be esteemed is better than silver or gold.
—Proverbs 22:1

Postscript: **Death of Jerry Dumas**

Sadly I write about the untimely death of our friend, Jerry Dumas. After enjoying Christmas at their Vermont home, Jerry slipped on the ice and hurt his head. Not surprising for a former LSU football player, Jerry dismissed the need of seeking medical attention. He died three days later from the injury, on the journey home to Baton Rouge, on December 29, 2017. Funeral services were held at First United Methodist Church on January 4, 2018.

I believe God sent a message through Jerry's death, to remind us our bodies are temples of the Holy Spirit, thus encouraging us to take care of His temple.

T. O. PERRY, A DEDICATED COMMUNITY LEADER

St. James Place gained a leader when T.O. and his wife Linda became residents. They had been in Baton Rouge a long time, first living in Walden before moving to St. James Place in 2013, so Linda could receive memory care in Highland Court Assisted Living. T.O. chose a garden home where they could also spend time together surrounded by their prized memorabilia and furnishings.

T.O. immersed himself in the St. James Place community and served as president of the Resident Association and as the resident representative to the St. James Place board of directors.

Music, the Best Way to Bring Quality of Life to Those with Alzheimer's Disease

I visited with Linda almost biweekly until her death in 2015. In my book *He Lays the Stones for Our Steps*, I wrote about Music and Memories, a God-inspired music program pianist Joyce Dickerson and I began with residents with Alzheimer's disease. I wrote about the miracles music brought as residents recalled past experiences, at times singing when they can no longer speak.

This is my most heartwarming volunteer work. I greet each resident with a hug, talk individually with each, stroke their arms, and kiss their cheek. Staff say they see smiles and laughter—seldom seen—as we clap and accompany our singing with hand movements. Some of these residents I have known during my nine years at St. James, as they have moved through different levels of care. I look forward to our visit each week. May I encourage you to bring back quality of life while singing slowly the old songs and hymns with those needing our attention and love.

Often, I would catch Ed Taylor in the coffee shop, a resident who once entertained on the Mississippi riverboats. Linda was so delighted to have a dance partner as we sang.

T.O.'s Early Years, and Military Service

T. O. was born in Fort Worth, Texas, to Thomas Perry and Ola

Mae Graves Perry. He was an only child but was raised with a cousin, Nell Woodard.

He graduated from LSU in 1948 and spent two years in Korea as an Army field artillery officer, followed by twenty years in the US Army Reserve, obtaining the rank of major.

T.O. and his wife Linda Davis had one daughter, Evs, now deceased, and one son, Thomas O. Perry II, referred to as Tom. He also has one grandson.

T.O.'s Professional Life

T.O. began his professional life as personnel director for ARKLA Gas Company in Shreveport, Louisiana. He and Linda, along with the family, moved to Baton Rouge in 1971.

T.O. retired from Louisiana National Bank as executive vice president of human resources and community relations. The Capital Area Personnel Association recognized his work with the Outstanding HR Professional Award in 1991.

T.O. was an almost full-time civic advocate and dedicated volunteer. He believed in serving others and his community. He worked with dozens of boards in the Baton Rouge area, including Louisiana Public Broadcasting, the Louisiana State Ethics Board, and the LSU International Hospitality Foundation.

In 1995, the Arts Council of Greater Baton Bouge presented Perry with a Distinguished Service Award for his contributions. In addition to many other civic positions, Perry was at one chair of the Baton Rouge chapter of the Red Cross and vice president of the Baton Rouge Area Foundation.

T.O. and Linda were members of the University Methodist Church in Baton Rouge, where T.O. was a lay leader and member of the administrative board. T.O. passed away in 2017 at age 88.

To learn more about T.O., view Baton Rouge channel 33's "Hometown Heroes": http://www.brproud.com/news/local-news/hometown-hero-thomas-o-perry

Takeaways

Without community service we would not have a strong quality of life. It's important to the person who serves as well as the recipient. It's the way in which we ourselves grow and develop.
    —Dorothy Height

Only a life lived for others is a life worthwhile.
    —Albert Einstein

You must become the change you wish to see in our world.
    —Mahatma Gandhi

Section 2

Rotarian Seniors Serving Humanity

We Are Rotarians

We are business, professional, and community leaders
Who are ready to serve and be involved
Without using guns, knives, or bombs,
To get the world's problems solved.

We combat hunger, poverty, disease,
And promote education,
Exchange students and groom leaders
For better global relations.

We address natural disasters
And send our volunteers.
Clubs partner with clubs
Both far and near.

We save hundreds of lives everyday
Celebrating fellowship along the way.
We're a volunteer army working in teams
Giving people hope and activating dreams.

Copyright © 2014 Helen Reisler

MR. AND MRS. ROTARY:
MIKE AND MARTHA COLLINS

When I think of Rotary, my mind immediately goes to Mike and Martha. This has been my experience since I transferred to District 6200 in 2009. Mike, a former district governor, began his third year as foundation chair in 2017–18, while Martha serves as district governor.

Romance and service don't just happen and, rarer still, do not always go hand in hand. Let's set the stage. . . . I asked Martha for a look into the life of the Acadians from Nova Scotia, who settled along the bayous of south Louisiana. . . .

Deep Roots in Cajun Country

Mike was born in a small doctor's office in Golden Meadow, Louisiana, along the banks of Bayou Lafourche, in Lafourche Parish. His father was an oil driller and production foreman, and his mother, a housewife, sold Avon cosmetics for a while. Mike had a brother, Russell, who was older by two years.

His paternal grandparents lived on Bayou Lafourche. They trapped and fished for a living. His maternal grandparents lived on a houseboat, which they moved seasonally to find food and work for their family. They finally settled their little houseboat in Lafitte along Bayou Barataria.

Martha was born in Cut Off, along Bayou Lafourche just north of Golden Meadow. She was the second of seven children. She has five brothers, and the last born was her only sister. After staying home to raise her seven children, Martha's mother went to college and eventually worked as a teacher's aide until she was 79 years old. Her father worked on tugboats, at the sugar mill, and as a school-bus driver.

Martha's paternal grandparents lived in a small plantation cottage called Cloverly Farms in Cut Off. Her dad quit school at age eleven to cut sugarcane with a cane knife for 11 cents a day to help his parents with his three sisters. Martha's grandfather had limited movement because of polio he contracted as an infant. He spent most of his time fixing lawn mowers and other gas engines, even though he had never been trained and couldn't read.

Martha never really knew her mother's parents as they died when she was an infant. Her maternal grandfather was a streetcar operator on the St. Charles Avenue streetcar line in New Orleans during the 1920s. He moved his family to Cut Off around 1942, and sold groceries from a grocery bus that traveled along the bayou to people who had no cars.

That Cute Boy

The bayou community was small, yet Mike and Martha had never met. They went to the same high school; Mike graduated while Martha was in junior high.

Martha first noticed the "cute boy" when he played with the band at her neighbor and friend's wedding, right after graduating from high school. When she was a junior, attending summer school at Nicholls State University in 1972, she noticed him again. He was usually walking at lunchtime with a friend she knew. She made sure to pass them each day and say hello.

One day the two young men were running late for class, and Martha met them just outside the cafeteria. They were carrying apples. *Finally,* she actually laughed and called them "health freaks." That's when Mike, not to miss an opportunity, offered her his apple. With that, Martha's true personality emerged as she snapped it out of his hands, took a bite, and walked away. Now she tells us she didn't know how to talk to someone she was interested in. Really?

Mike, the Aggressor, Armed with an Apple . . .

The next morning Mike was standing at the door of her classroom. She knew he had to go to a lot of trouble to check her class schedule. Excitedly, surprising herself (or so she said), she walked straight over to Mike and said, "What, no apple today?" He asked, "Do you want one?" "Of course I do," she replied. He took her down the hall to another building that was lined with lockers, opened a combination lock, and showed her the interior filled with apples. He explained that he and the young man she knew saved their apples from the cafeteria, let them ripen in the locker, and sold them for 50 cents each.

It was evident as she told their story to me that she was vividly reliving this moment forty-five years ago, when her life changed forever.

We assume they got to their classes on time! From then on, each morning Mike would meet her at her classroom door, with an apple. That was July 1972; their first date was in August.

Mike Pops the Question

In September, Mike asked Martha to marry him. They were married March 3, 1973, and he graduated from Nicholls in May. They have three children and eight grandchildren. Seven are granddaughters, the oldest recently celebrating her thirteenth birthday and the youngest is seven. Their only grandson passed away when he was nine weeks old. His death was the most devastating event in the life of their family. They refer to him as "our little angel who watches over us."

Mike, a Teacher; Martha, a Stay-Home Mom, Finishes College Degree

Mike taught elementary school for seventeen years and was principal for seventeen more years prior to retirement. Martha stayed home with their children, until the last one was in school. She returned to Nicholls and graduated with a degree in elementary education, and taught until 2007.

Mike the Rotarian

Mike became a Rotarian in 1998 and was very active both at the club and district levels. He became an assistant district governor soon after joining Rotary. He received several recognitions from the Rotary Club of Golden Meadow as well as from District 6200 and Rotary International.

Mike the District Governor; Martha Joins Rotary

In 2008–09, Mike served as district governor, the year Martha became a Rotarian in the formerly all-male club. Mike has served in various leadership positions and on several international committees, including the home host committee for the Rotary International Convention, held in New Orleans in 2011. Mike was co-chair of the Fun, Food, and Fellowship Festival at the Aquarium of the Americas. Rotarians visiting from around the world got a taste of boiled shrimp, gumbo, fried fish, and many other south Louisiana foods.

Husband-and-Wife Rotarian Team

In one Rotarian project, Mike and Martha went to Honduras on an eyeglass mission. Together, they made hundreds of pairs of glasses and distributed them to six hundred people.

When Martha was District 6200's First Lady, she headed a literacy project to collect and distribute books to at-risk children, from infants to five years old. Since then, Martha and Mike have distributed an estimated $70 million worth of new, free educational materials for the home libraries of preschool to fifth grade children in Louisiana, Mississippi, Alabama, Kentucky, Texas, Honduras, Guatemala, Haiti, and several countries in Africa. As former educators, the Collinses usually adopt projects dealing with literacy.

Rotary's Prestigious Service Above Self Award

Mike says his proudest moment was receiving Rotary International's highest honor, the Service Above Self Award, in 2011. Only up to 150 Rotarians annually—.0125% of the 1.2 million Rotarians worldwide—receive this award. Martha received the Service Above Self Award in 2012. It is rare for both a husband and wife to be recipients.

Former First Lady Martha, District Governor, 2017–18

Our Capital City Club was honored to have the first official visit of District Governor Martha and First Mate Mike (or as he liked to say, the First Laddy), who is serving his second year as 6200 Foundation Chair.

Martha has made a wager to encourage more giving to the Rotary Foundation, She contends that she will raise more funds for the Rotary Foundation than Mike did during his district governor year. His year broke previous records in District 6200.

Confident she will break Mike's record, Martha plans a pie in the face for Mike at 6200's annual conference! The wager they made was that whoever raised the most money would get to throw a pie in the other's face at the District Conference Down the Bayou Bash. The loser gets to choose their favorite pie. The only worry Martha has right now is that Mike would get Key lime pie, but her favorite is pecan pie. She pleaded with every club to help her avoid pecan pie in her face! They are *two-for-one* Rotarians, and they love it!

Making Their Mark on the World

Martha said she and Mike talk Rotary before they go to bed and when they wake up. When they are in their car, Mike will ask her to turn the radio down so they can talk Rotary. Such is the life of Mr. and Mrs. Rotary, truly making their mark on the world in their retirement years.

Takeaways

An investment in knowledge pays the best interest.
　—Benjamin Franklin

Education is not preparation for life, education is life itself.
 —John Dewey

THE FOUR-WAY TEST

1. *Is it the TRUTH?*
2. *Is it FAIR to all concerned?*
3. *Will it build GOODWILL and BETTER FRIENDSHIPS?*
4. *Will it be BENEFICIAL to all concerned?*
   —Rotarian Herbert J. Taylor

(Translated into over 100 languages and recited at all Rotarian club meetings)

9/11:
HELEN REISLER, PRESIDENT
OF THE ROTARY CLUB OF NEW YORK,
BECOMES A GENERAL

Helen shares her story:

People, all around the nation, put aside their differences on September 11, 2001, to gather together in honor of those who perished, and those who became unintended heroes, when New York City was attacked by terrorists. "Patriots Day," as it has come to be known, will always remind me how we became one family during the tragedy of 9/11.

I could never have imagined that I would be called upon to play an important and visible role in a terrorist attack on my own city.

Most people seem to remember exactly where they were and just what they were doing on that fateful day when *our world changed forever*. I was in my Brooklyn apartment, preparing to preside over a meeting of the Rotary Club of New York, which met at the Princeton Club in New York City.

When I received a phone call on the morning of September 11th from my daughter Karen, insisting I turn on the TV, I realized a historic event had taken place.

When I saw the second plane crash into the South Tower of the World Trade Center, I knew immediately that we were under attack. New York City, under attack? I was frozen to the screen!

The shock of realizing that we might be at war turned to numbness when I realized that the roads, bridges, and telephone lines were closed down. It suddenly dawned on me that I was trapped on an island, separated from family members, and others, who were all in separate locations, including my husband, who was awaiting my return to our Westchester home. It was the only Tuesday meeting I missed that year, and I never felt so alone and isolated. . . .

"Seemed the rest of the world was connecting with me"

Then I remembered my computer and turned it on, hoping to connect with someone I knew, only to be surprised by *what seemed to be the rest of the world connecting with me*. The screen was filled with hundreds of emails from Rotarians all over the globe . . . England, Norway, Australia, South Africa, Italy, Israel, Ireland, Lebanon, Germany, France, and many of our own states. They expressed shock and sympathy, offered condolences and assistance, and asked, "How can we help?" "What can we do?"

Rotarians Donate Almost $1.5 Million

Some wanted to send checks but needed assurance of safe delivery and meaningful distribution. I stayed up late into the night answering questions. When I was finally able to make a connection with our foundation chair, I advised him to open a separate 9/11 Disaster Relief Fund account, which eventually grew to $1,460,912 for the victims.

*****

To chart the timeline of Rotary's historic moments, a 100-foot-wide wall in Hartsdale, New York, was painted by a former Rotary ambassadorial student. Helen's image, by an American flagpole surrounded by children, depicting hope, completes the painting.
Helen continues her story:

My next objective was to keep my members together in all the confusion, inspire them, and coordinate their actions in a meaningful direction. During our first emergency meeting, I created individual committees to address various issues and actively participated in them. At our regular weekly meetings, I distributed the words of patriotic songs to keep up the general spirit and invited various people who were directly affected by the disaster. An injured police officer, the father of a port authority officer who was killed, the wife and young son of a missing firefighter were reminders of why we should be involved. The club meetings became a special haven for many, as well.

One of the committees helped at "the pit." They delivered water and food, masks and gloves, assisted with respiratory problems, and identified victims through DNA. Another did grief counseling, crisis management, and ran a soup kitchen. We attended funerals to stand in for the firefighters who were digging for remains, contacted groups who could identify the neediest, and interviewed each applicant.

Within a few months the monies had been meticulously distributed to carefully selected individuals and groups.

I created and worked with another committee to send forty-five first responders on weekend vacations. These therapeutic getaways were a mental and emotional savior for the first responders who dug day and night, hoping to find survivors, or remains. The best thing we could do for them was give them another temporary environment for a few days. This idea came to me after I heard that a 27-year-old firefighter had committed suicide. Other Rotary clubs, in various locations, were their hosts, providing nurture with Rotary caring.

Eight families of victims were adopted by Rotarians in Michigan for one year. I also coordinated with a Rotarian to have their North Carolina Interact Club invite a group of Stuyvesant High School students who had watched people jumping from the towers, to benefit from a North Carolina vacation.

Ongoing planning and constant coordination enabled us to assist many victims who might have fallen through the cracks. That's why, when people comment on my unintended role as bad luck, I strongly disagree. I feel that it was a blessing to have been in a position where I could use my various skills and feel in control instead of helpless.

Helen's Continuing Involvement

We will pick up the story from here.

Since 2001, Helen continues to honor many requests to speak about her role in the relief efforts of 9/11 and has shared her story in California, Michigan, Missouri, six areas of Texas, Pennsylvania, New York, Holland, Ireland, and elsewhere.

The building of a national Firefighters' Home in Houston

was inspired by a recent presentation Helen made in Dallas. She was invited to be an advisor to the board of directors of the Houston Firefighters' Home and was the keynote speaker at the first fundraising gala.

Helen said, "I am especially proud of the surprise Fire Department of New York trophy and plaque that was presented by Joe Torrillo, a 9/11 hero of the New York City Fire Department containing a replica of the Twin Towers and the words, 'No doubt she was put on this earth, so that a Firefighter could have a Hero.'"

"A retired army general once told me that I had taken similar steps to rally my troops as he had in many emergency situations. I can live with that confirmation."

Reflecting Back . . .

Helen joined the Rotary Club of New York in 1988, one of its first female members. Little did she or the club know that a little over a decade later she would become its first female president. On July 10, 2001, she was installed as the president of the Rotary Club of New York.

Let's join the club in celebrating this historic event in its history. . . . Helen frames the scene and shares the exciting event:

"Since I was to be the first woman president in the club's 92-year existence, it was considered a major historic event. Glasses clicked as champagne toasts were made and congratulatory messages, from a variety of New York City dignitaries, were read. A group of police officers escorted me, followed by my all-male board of directors, to the microphone while Frank Sinatra's 'New York, New York' reverberated throughout the room in honor of the Big Apple."

"After reading aloud my well-planned, extensive agenda, I promised the members that the only major change that year would be a president, at the microphone, wearing lipstick."

No one, especially Helen, could have ever imagined what an important role she would be faced with.

Helen's Roots, Growing Up in Brooklyn

Helen shares some of her background:

I grew up in Brooklyn and went to a public school where I was exposed to children of various backgrounds, religions, and cultures. I observed that no matter where we come from, we seem to have similar basic desires to be accepted, respected, and determine our own destiny as human beings. This insight has proved invaluable to me in my dealings with all types of people in my teaching, media, and business careers. Without emotional intelligence, you can't go very far as a leader.

Growing up during the Second World War, when people's greatest strength was their sense of unity, taught me the effectiveness of teamwork and the importance of spirituality and hope.

My parents, having experienced the effects of the Great Depression, taught me the rewards of delayed gratification, and I was expected to work toward my goals. I learned to conserve money and choose priorities. Never have I felt a sense of entitlement. In fact, I still often hear my father's mantra, "You must prove yourself first." These factors enabled me to rise above a temporary economic setback in my marriage, when we had to change our lifestyle. Although not an easy time, it turned out to be an unexpected and valuable gift. We became closer. From each setback comes growth.

How New York Changed in the 1970s

Teaching was my chosen profession. Although I loved it, sadly, the entire environment changed in New York City in the early 1970s. The fact that I was mugged in my own classroom, by intruders, is a perfect example of those times. I tried my best to be the policeman that certain classroom situations demanded, even attained a master's degree as a reading specialist, which might present me with less classroom drama, but it was time for a change.

Transition from Teaching to the Business World

My unexpected success in the business world gave me new joy and greater individual growth as well. I want to make it clear, here, that *nothing is ever wasted*. The title of my master's thesis was "Critical Thinking and Reading." My teacher training and classroom experience were valuable tools in this new environment.

My success in a small company—rising to vice president as I expanded the business—connected to a position in a large corporation. There is one skill that I believe to be the most important one for survival in life—communication. Good communication prevents misunderstandings, stabilizes relationships, saves marriages, prevents wars, and is invaluable in the process of any negotiation. It is even the deciding factor between life and death in a crisis. This is the one skill that has tied everything together in my own life. Through the videos I produce, the nationwide speeches I deliver, the articles I write, and the modern technology I am involved with, I am able to share so much with others in hopes of creating some harmony and balance in a world of constant change.

Helen's Past and Ongoing Rotary Leadership Roles

Helen's many leadership roles include the following:

• President, Rotary Club of New York, 2001–2002

• District Governor #7230 (Manhattan, Bronx, Westchester, Staten Island, Bermuda), 2005–2006

• Rotary International Alt Representative to the United Nations, 2007–2017

• Panel Moderator, "Rotary/UN Day," 2007–2017

• Moderator, Monthly International Breakfast Meetings at the UN, 2016–Present

• Producer, Multiple Rotary Videos; International Speaker to Rotary Districts, Rotaract Clubs, Interact Clubs, and Model UN Conferences, 2002–Present

• Rotary International President's Representative
• Trustee, Rotary Club New York Foundation and District 7230 Foundation

• Consultant to "Radio Rotary" District 7210

• Public Relations Chair, Rotary Club New York and District 7230 (Zone Public Relations Award)

• Vice President of Membership, Rotary Global History Fellowship

• Member, Rotary Action Group for Peace

• Honorary Consuls Fellowship of Rotarians

• Member, Mediators beyond Borders

Takeaways

A leader is one who knows the way, goes the way, and shows the way.
    —John C. Maxwell

Personality has power to uplift, power to depress, power to curse, and power to bless.
    —Paul P. Harris

Remember the hours after September 11th when we came together as one. . . . It was the worst day we have ever seen, but it brought out the best in all of us.
    —Sen. John Kerry

CLARENCE PRUDHOMME:
ROTARIAN, CHURCHMAN, MOLDER OF YOUTH, AND SERVANT TO MANKIND

Clarence continues to faithfully serve Rotary since joining the Rotary Club of Welsh, Louisiana, in 1990. He first served on the board of directors before becoming president of the club in 1994–95. Under his leadership, the club received the Presidential Citation. Clarence received the Four Avenues of Service citation. He was elected district governor for District 6200 for the 2010–11 Rotary year. Clarence is a multiple Paul Harris Fellow and has served on many committees to advance Rotary service.

An Advocate for Youth

For an amazing twenty-five years, Clarence has been buoyed by the youth he had the privilege of forming and interacting with in Interact Clubs, both on the high school and Rotary district levels. Each year, he chaired a district convention for all Interact Clubs with more than three hundred students attending.

Clarence continues to hone his leadership skills by serving on various committees at district level, attending training at Zone in Boise, Idaho, Tulsa, Oklahoma, and St. Louis, Missouri. On the international level, he received training in San Diego, Montreal, and New Orleans. He serves on the board of directors for his club while using his knowledge of Rotary to serve as district trainer for two different district governors.

Rotary's Highest Honor: Service Above Self Award

In 2017, Clarence received the Rotary Service Above Self Award. Sadly, I missed the ceremony and was told Clarence, with many reasons to be proud, showed his gift of humility through tears as he accepted the well-earned award.

Humility: A Testimony of His Faith

Clarence's dedication to youth stems from his deep faith. He was blessed to grow up as a member of St. Joseph Catholic Church in Welsh. His leadership skills and faith propelled him to serve his

Lord in multiple ways as altar server, lector, extraordinary minister of communion, chairman of the Parish Advisory Committee, and chairman of the Finance Committee. He also chaired and worked many major fundraisers, helped maintain the grounds and facilities, and served as trustee for the parish. In 2010, he was selected as the Distinguished Catholic of the Year from the Diocese of Lake Charles. Clarence's amazing service at St. Joseph's advanced as he became the diocesan section president for the Equestrian Order of the Holy Sepulchre. He has been a member of the Knights of St. Peter Claver for over fifty-six years, serving in Council 48, and a member of Grand Assembly No. 22 of the Meritorious Fourth Degree.

Serving the Disadvantaged and Elderly

Clarence has served in lead worship positions and received the Cartagena Award (highest award from the fourth-degree Knights). He works with the Knights to serve lunch at Abraham's Tent in Lake Charles and has helped prepare Thanksgiving Day meals for approximately one thousand people annually for the past nineteen years. The Knights also provide air conditioners each year to the elderly, sick, and those of limited means. He has delivered and installed units at his own expense in eleven surrounding towns.

Clarence is a member of the Grambling State University Alumni Chapter in Jefferson Davis Parish and has been president for several years. These chapters are responsible for providing scholarships to students and for promoting the growth of Grambling University.

Tracing Clarence's Roots

Clarence's father, Alex Prudhomme, a laborer, and his wife, Sylvania, had seven children, five boys and two girls. They made their home in Welsh, a small Louisiana town plotted in 1880 and incorporated by the first mayor, Henry Welsh.

Clarence graduated from Jeff Davis High School (the only

high school for blacks in the parish) in 1957. He earned his BA in mathematics from Grambling in January 1962. His education continued in numerous professional schools during his military service, and he received his MA in management from Central Michigan University in 1977.

He met his future wife, Geneva ("Kitty") Dugar, from Lacassine in 1953 when they were both in high school. They were married in November 1962. They have two sons and one grandson.

Twenty-Six Years in the Air Force

Clarence's military career began in December 1962. He was commissioned as a second lieutenant through Officer Training School in San Antonio, Texas. Clarence served at all levels of command (including with the inspector general team in Europe) and was responsible for multimillions of dollars of Air Force equipment as he completed twenty-six years of service to his country. Lt. Col. Prudhomme, accompanied by his family, served tours of duty in Montana, Maine, California, Washington, DC, Louisiana, and Thailand, and three tours in Europe, before retiring from Wright-Patterson Air Force Base in Ohio. (I hope Kitty won the Congressional Medal of Honor for packing and unpacking!)

Retirement Years Serving Humanity

Clarence retired from the Air Force in 1989. For the next ten years, he taught mathematics at Welsh High School, where he was selected twice as Teacher of the Year. Quick to recognize potential in his students, he never hesitated to tutor them in classwork, as well as for national examinations.

As if his schedule were not busy enough, he sponsored the largest service club at the school, while working with Rotary Interact Clubs at district level. The Sowela Community College called on him as an expert teacher in transitional math.

I am exhausted just following Clarence's whirlwind leadership in so many avenues of service. He is a gracious, generous, and modest man, and to know him has enriched my world.

Takeaways

Service to others is the rent you pay for your room here on earth.
—Muhammad Ali

The best way to find yourself is to lose yourself in the service of others.
—Mahatma Gandhi

Someday is not a day of the week.
—Janet Dailey

LUCY BOWERS, LSU PROFESSOR OF LAW: CHAMPIONING RIGHTS OF CHILDREN, JUVENILES GIVEN LIFE SENTENCES, AND SEX-TRAFFICKING VICTIMS

I met a new resident, Lucy Bowers (Lucy McGough), one Sunday at the St. James Place brunch. She was standing, ready to leave, and someone at her table said she had been dean of a law school in Virginia. I knew such a woman would not sit on her hands in retirement. Ever on the lookout, I asked, "Are you a Rotarian?" Her "no" brought my immediate, "Do you want to be a Rotarian?" and received a "yes" as she hurried away to her next stop. I would later hear that she had a daughter who had been involved in a Rotary peace initiative in Africa. Rotary's work was not new to her.

Lucy—on Her Third Retirement

At 76, Lucy is *sort of* a retiree. As she put it, "I'm on my third retirement." For thirty years, Lucy was a member of the LSU Law School faculty, ultimately holding the Vinson & Elkins Chair in Law, the first woman on the Law School faculty to hold an endowed chair. She retired in 2012 to become the eighth dean of the Appalachian School of Law in Grundy, Virginia. After three years, she retired from administration to rejoin the ranks of teachers. The LSU Law School welcomed her back with the offer of her favorite Juvenile Law seminar, which didn't start until the spring semester. Lamenting the gap in her academic life, that fall she volunteered to co-teach a newly instituted Parole and Reentry Clinic, in which third-year law students practice law under the supervision of a member of the Louisiana bar. The students represent inmates who are eligible for parole hearings. To meet and interview the inmates, Lucy and her law students made numerous trips to five state prisons, including the infamous Angola State Penitentiary. She and the four women in the course took a special interest in the few women who were parole-eligible.

After the great floods of 2016, the women's facility in St. Gabriel became uninhabitable, and the women were uprooted and bussed across the state to be jammed in the small parish prison in Avoyelles. Lucy and her students ("the Lady Lawyers") followed them there and made several trips to gather information. They calmed and prepared these clients for their impending hearings.

Emory University, 1970–1980

Supervising students who were representing live clients was not a new experience; Lucy had been engaged in student courtroom supervision since the very beginning of her teaching career. During her ten years at Emory Law School in the 1970s, she had developed a Juvenile Court representation clinic. Here at the end of her career, she had come full circle, returning to the heady experience of watching fledgling lawyers learn to fly away. She understood that teaching theory was critical to the professional growth of law students, but introducing students to poor citizens without lawyers, desperate in need of a lawyer's representation, was a life-changing opportunity. As a law student herself, Lucy had been active in the civil rights movement and also in legal services/legal aid services. She believed passionately that powerful professionals like attorneys had the civil obligation to nurture justice for all citizens.

Lucy Enters Emory Law School, Graduates with Distinction

Lucy did not always want to be an attorney. In fact, she was the first member of her family to become a lawyer. In 1962, she graduated from Agnes Scott College with an English major and the Phi Beta Kappa seal on her diploma. But in those dark days, professional doors were closed to women; even finding employment was difficult unless the woman wanted to teach in elementary or secondary education or to become a secretary. Lucy did not want to teach (which is ironic in view of the path her life took), and so she became a secretary for three months until she knew she had to do more. By a fluke, while rather casually reading the bulletin boards at Emory Law School (which like Agnes Scott is in Atlanta), she encountered the much-beloved Dean Ben Johnson. In those days there were entry slots known as dean's admits, which, just as the name implies, are available to the dean of the Law School to use at his discretion and usually to reward a generous donor or powerful politician.

After they had talked for about an hour, Dean Johnson told Lucy that he had one such admit left and offered it to her, on the condition that her grades at Agnes Scott were as represented. The fall term of the Law School began the following Monday. Lucy called her father, a franchise holder of Coca-Cola Bottling Company in western Kentucky, and he agreed to send a check! Suddenly she was a law student, and that day, she bought *Black's Law Dictionary*, then the Bible of law students. That weekend, she read into it, encountering for the first time all those wonderfully arcane legal terms. Most were and are still in Latin. (Mercifully, she had taken four years of Latin in high school and eventually ended up doing most of the translations for her classmates who had stuck to modern languages.) Life seemed to be settling into place as she began her studies.

Lucy loved law school, although it was "cool" to complain about hundreds of pages of reading assignments or the Socratic method, then used by all faculty to train students to think like lawyers. Lucy was one of only three women in a student body of about three hundred. There were two black men. Dean Johnson was determined to diversify the student body, and they were in the vanguard. Lucy graduated with distinction and had several firsts, including first woman on the law review and first grades in three courses. Though she had not dreamed of being a lawyer, as had many of her male classmates, it was a perfect fit for her mind and sensibilities. The women's movement was gaining strength; change was everywhere. These were the glory days of the Warren Court, when the Supreme Court was responding to issues of abuse in the criminal justice system—the right to counsel for indigent accused (*Gideon v. Wainwright*), the right against self-incrimination, requiring cautions about constitutional rights when being interrogated by the police (*Miranda v. Arizona*), the right to counsel and all adult constitutional rights for juveniles facing the possibility of incarceration (*In re Gault*). Those were heady times.

Created Emory Neighborhood Law Clinic

Lucy practiced law briefly and then received a postgraduate fellowship (the Reginald Heber Smith Community Lawyer Fellowship) at the University of Pennsylvania. That period of study set the course of her professional interests that would last throughout her career. She returned to Atlanta to create the Emory Neighborhood Law Clinic, supervising law students who represented indigents in civil cases such as housing disputes, disability benefits claims, and family law problems.

Awarded Harvard Law School Fellowship in Urban Law

After two years of practice, Lucy was awarded a fellowship in urban law at Harvard Law School, where she earned her master's in law. She had decided she wanted to teach after all—*surprise!* Having interviewed with several law schools, she decided to return to Emory and further develop its clinical program. She joined one other female on the 35-member law faculty. She created the Juvenile Defense Clinic and the Interviewing, Counseling, and Negotiation Clinic, while at the same time teaching traditional courses in criminal justice, family law, and trusts and estates. She married and juggled family life with faculty obligations.

First Woman Awarded a Candler Chair at Emory

In her ninth year of teaching, Lucy was named to one of twelve Candler Chairs set aside for the entire university. She was the only woman so honored. One of her colleagues chided her, asking if she knew why she got the chair rather than someone more senior. She acknowledged that being a female in a professional school undoubtedly tipped the scale in her favor. She worried a little about the reverse discrimination and then put the issue aside since the chair came with an extra stipend that came in handy with three small children.

Lucy Marries Law Professor Jim Bowers

In 1980, she remarried, this time to another law professor, Jim Bowers. Because of nepotism rules barring family members from joining the same faculty, Jim left Texas Tech Law School and Lucy left Emory, and they joined the LSU Law School faculty. They remained there for over thirty years.

Professor Lucy McGough Juvenile Justice Award

Following her deep commitment to juvenile law, Lucy chaired a group that wrote the first Children's Code for Louisiana. First enacted in 1991, the Code is a comprehensive compendium of all laws affecting the exercise of juvenile court jurisdiction, including adoption, delinquency, and abuse and neglect. The Code won the Best Legislation Award given by the National Association of Family & Juvenile Court Judges. Lucy also coauthored the Model Juvenile Code of Georgia. She has won many awards during her career. The most cherished is the creation of the Professor Lucy McGough Juvenile Justice Award given each year by the Louisiana Bar Foundation to the foremost juvenile advocate in the state. She has written over forty law review articles and five books.

Death of Her Husband, and a Move to St. James Place

After thirty-five years of a dual career and marriage, her most beloved husband and cheerleader, Jim Bowers, died. A year later Lucy moved into St. James Place, but her zest for life has eased her loss. She never stops. She is an avid civic volunteer who plays just as hard—from cello lessons, which she began in her sixties, to her dachshunds, gardening, and traveling the world.

Lucy Brings High-Profile Speakers to Capital City Rotary

Lucy's LSU students have provided a steady source of guest speakers for the Capitol City Rotary Club. Mark Plaisance spoke to the Rotarians about an appeal he had argued before the US Supreme Court; the day after his speech, the Court announced its decision in his case, *Montgomery v. Louisiana*. The landmark decision ruled that boilerplate statutes mandating a life sentence without parole for individuals convicted of a crime committed before their eighteenth birthday were unconstitutional. As a result of this ruling, over two hundred inmates across the country are entitled to individualized parole consideration.

In view of the scientific findings that the adolescent brain lacks critical neurological development essential to rational and moral decision making, Lucy had always taken a special interest in students like Mark who were slow learners in the fiercely competitive law school environment. For many years, Lucy had offered a special weekly extra session for first-year law students who had achieved disappointing marks in their first semester. Mark was one of those students. He ultimately graduated, passed the bar exam, and developed a successful appellate practice, served as a judge, and ultimately became counsel for Henry Montgomery, who had served nearly fifty years of a sentence when he was ordered released after his parole hearing. Mark highly praised Professor Lucy for taking him under her wing. . . .

Our Rotary club has also been caught up in the lives of Lucy's clients. She invited as a speaker guest Andrew Hundley, who was incarcerated at age 18 as an accessory to manslaughter. He has a riveting life of redemption. He spent most of the next twenty years at Angola and became a model inmate. He obtained his GED and took every available course, both those aimed at teaching a trade and those directed toward psychological healing and rehabilitation. Two years before, Andrew had won parole, thanks to the work of Keith Nordyke, one of the co-teachers of the LSU Parole and Reentry Clinic. Andrew entered Baton Rouge Community College and has made straight A's. He also created a nonprofit foundation that provides educational, employment, and social services to inmates who have been paroled and are reentering society. Andrew has become the clinic's poster child for early parole consideration. He captivated the members of the

Rotary Club with his stories of institutional brutality and the sweet smell of freedom.

Lucy keeps up with many of her former students, knowing her legacy will be the contributions they make.

Sex-trafficking victims are another of Lucy's concerns. Through a recent Capital City Rotary District Grant, members supplied personal items and packed over one hundred backpacks to give to rescued victims across the state.

Praise from Lucy's Former Student, Steve Martin

Steve Martin was a memorable student because he entered law school in his thirties. (Older students often feel estranged from their much younger, more naïve classmates. Lucy was the faculty sponsor for a group of older women who entered law school after becoming parents. The group dubbed itself "The Mawmaws," and a quarter of a century later, they still meet for lunch.) Steve was a steady, eager-to-learn student. He remained a friend after graduation and became the head of the Cyber Crimes Unit in the Louisiana attorney general's office. He brought the Rotarians up to date on web solicitations by pedophiles, sexting, and other cyber crimes.

Steve praised his former teacher: "Professor McGough is a beloved law professor, mentor, and advisor to her many hundreds of students, past and present. To us, she is far more than a nationally renowned legal scholar, law school chancellor, or law school professor. Rather, she is someone who has helped each of us, on our own terms, to use the legal principles and life lessons discussed in her classroom to make our world a safer, better, and more just place. Unlike other respected law professors, Professor McGough took significant time away from her own family to ensure that each of us, and especially those like myself who needed extra encouragement and mentoring during their freshman law school year, could benefit greatly from the extra time she devoted to us, individually and as a group. We are all very thankful for Professor Lucy McGough and the immeasurable impact she has had on our lives. She is a treasure to us all."

A Personal Note

Lucy said she did not like to talk or write about herself. Finally, she relented and wrote her noteworthy story, saying I had the persistence of a terrier!

Takeaways

A teacher affects eternity; he can never tell where his influence stops.
　　—Henry Adams

A teacher takes a hand, opens a mind, and touches a heart.
　　—Author unknown

Carve your name on hearts, not tombstones. A legacy is etched into the minds of others and the stories they share about you.
　　—Shannon Alder

ROTARIAN AND HUMANITARIAN PATRICIA ROBINSON

Patricia ("Pat") Robinson honed her skills as a humanitarian while employed by Blue Cross Blue Shield, now Louisiana's largest employer. She wrote, "While learning to process claims, I followed the example of my parents, working in the community. My mom had gone door-to-door collecting money from neighbors for the March of Dimes. My dad solicited donations for the American Heart Association."

Because Pat was on so many nonprofit boards, she was eventually promoted to director of community relations and executive director of Blue Cross Blue Shield's Caring Foundation for Children. She received several awards and notable positions from community organizations during her time at Blue Cross.

Joins Capital City Rotary Club

It was a natural progression for Pat to become a Rotarian. She joined Capital City Rotary Club of Baton Rouge in 2004. Her leadership roles, Club and District 6200, include:

- Capital City Rotary Club President, 2006–07, 2013–14
- Assistant Governor, District 6200, 2007–09
- Assistant Governor Coordinator, District 6200, 2016–17

Coordinator of Yearly Global Community Day

Pat also led the revival of a community salute to diversity, renaming the event as Global Community Day. Louisiana residents, with items from their native countries, as well as entertainers dressed in colorful, authentic attire, accompanied by music and singing, perform traditional ethnic dances. Members of the Baton Rouge international community offer food from their home culture and display flags. Families, especially children, are given passports to "travel" from one country booth to another, learning several facts, including where each country is located on the map. It is a fun Sunday afternoon when history comes alive, while encouraging appreciation of others who may look, dress, or talk different. A parade of flags of many countries closes the event.

Capital City Rotary hails Global Community Day as a way to appreciate and bring our large, diverse community together. In 2017, twenty-five countries were represented. Pat, with her outstanding knowledge and leadership skills, leads fundraising and logistics for this large event.

In my book *He Lays the Stones for Our Steps*, I acknowledge Pat's assistance in my work as service chair/grants writer, in a section entitled, "Patricia Robinson, My Rotary Sister."

Pat's Community Honors:

- 1995 Graduate of Chamber of Commerce Leadership Class
- 1996 YWCA Woman of the Year, Corporate Category
- 2001 Community Volunteer of the Year—100 Black Men
- 2000 March of Dimes Top Volunteer in the Southern Region
- 2006 Volunteer Activist, Speech and Hearing Foundation

Pat's Childhood in Baton Rouge

Pat grew up in Baton Rouge in a close-knit family, the oldest girl in a family of four girls and two boys. Her favorite class in high school was home economics, and she chose that field as her major at Grambling State University. She was a member of the Home Economics Honor Society and graduated with honors.

Pat married Curtis Robinson Jr. in 1971, and they had three daughters and one son. Curtis is now deceased. Pat continues the family traditions and church activities she grew up with.

Takeaways

We have a responsibility to help those around us and help others in need.
—Virginia Williams

Help others achieve their dreams and you will achieve yours.
    —Les Brown

The purpose of human life is to serve, and to show compassion and the will to help others.
    —Albert Schweitzer

JAY BROWN:
AWARDED THE ROTARY MERITORIOUS SERVICE AWARD

Jay was 37 and at a crossroads, referring to himself as "an exhausted rooster"—too old to continue his eighteen-year membership in the JCs, and according to a Baker Rotarian, Charles Young, too young to join the then "old boys' club" (as it was referred to in the days prior to women becoming eligible for membership). Each time Jay went to Young's cleaning business, Young would give Jay another reason he should or could not join the Baker Rotary—too young (of course), it was too expensive, cannot miss a weekly meeting, and so on. (Readers, almost without exception, you will be welcomed at Rotary meetings with open arms, as we are a service club focused on making a difference in the world.)

Jay did join the Baker Rotary Club, on February 12, 1983, on Rotary's 1,905th birthday. The club is known for its achievements, and Jay's contributions of time and monetary giving are exemplary. The Rotary Meritorious Service Award from the Rotary Foundation honors one person in each Rotary District each year.

Jay Brown and Ginger Vann Join Ranks in Rotary Service

Jay, an attorney in private practice, was running for judge in 2003 when he first met Ginger. She helped manage Jay's campaign.

In 2007, prior to her becoming a member of Rotary, Jay surprised her by making her an honorary Paul Harris Fellow. Ginger joined him at two annual Rotary International conventions.

Ginger joined Baker Rotary in 2007, and the two of them have amazing service records. They have attended nineteen other Rotary International conventions, virtually across the world, since she joined.

In one very uplifting humanitarian cause, Jay and Ginger assisted with National Polio Immunization Day in India in 2015. They helped to reach each child, putting two drops of vaccine in their mouth. India is now polio free.

Jay shared a poignant story of meeting a man around 30 years of age who had been stricken by polio in both legs. He crawled, using his hands to pull himself. The man immediately said, "I am not a beggar, I am an entrepreneur." He had trinkets cut from metal, and Jay bought one for each of the volunteers on the bus.

For those readers who do not know, through the dedication and service of the Paul Gates Foundation and Rotary International, polio has been virtually eradicated around the world. It is gratifying to receive the Rotary monthly emails showing no new cases in the last three countries to be treated, Pakistan, Afghanistan, and Nigeria. Occasionally a wild strain surfaces, so vigilance continues.

Jay Serves as District Governor, 1996–1997

In his acceptance speech for the Meritorious Service Award, Jay noted that he had been a member of Rotary for twenty-two years. He became a Paul Harris Fellow in three years and is a major donor. He has never missed any of the seven hundred weekly meetings in that time, and is glad Young took a chance on nominating him as a member.

The Baker Club, of which Jay is a member, has been in District 6200's top 3% in per-capita giving to the Foundation for the last twenty-five years.

Jay Traces His Roots and Education, Intermixed with the Vietnam Conflict

Jay was born in Baton Rouge to Joseph C. and Mary Kilroy Brown. He writes of their influence: "Many of my present-day attributes can be traced to the fact that I had senior citizen parents. Both of my parents were in their forties when I was born in 1948. My mom and dad married in 1925 and had no children for ten years! My oldest sibling (sister) is 82, my only brother, who was seven years older than me, died in 2009. I often kid that I got to grow up in the cool '60s but had Depression-era financial training, which aids me even today."

After graduating from Baker High School, Jay received his BS in civil engineering at the University of Texas, after which he volunteered for a year as an engineer in the Air Force in Vietnam.

He spoke of his enduring friendship with a young African American airman from Gadsden, Alabama. They were very different, yet like brothers. They volunteered with the embroiled Air Force Red Horse Combat Engineering Unit, rebuilding one-room grass huts with dirt floors that had been destroyed by the Viet Cong. After an attack by the Viet Cong, they withdrew a reasonable distance to the safety of a tree line. When two little children ran across the open field from the safety of the tree line, Jay ran and scooped both into his arms and dropped in a drainage ditch, with only a pistol for defense. His friend, seeing him in distress, ran with two AK-47s, throwing one to Jay, prior to the exchange of gunfire with the Viet Cong, who fled when an Army unit appeared. Jay's excitement in being rescued was short-lived, as he turned and held his wounded friend in his arms as he died. He was one of 50,000 US servicemen who died in Vietnam.

After that tour of duty, Jay received his MA in finance from the University of Southern Mississippi. He reenlisted in 1970, as he would receive $20,000 to serve for four more years. He was sent back to Southeast Asia, where he was recognized as an outstanding airman and engineer. He volunteered for an interesting venture at the main Air Force base in Thailand.

Jay shares his harrowing escape:

Many times I have told people that I do so much volunteer work because I have been living on borrowed time. There are several episodes in my military life in which I had extremely close brushes with death and somehow survived, sometimes when others did not. None more harrowing, or crazy than the time I was in the Thai Royal Air Force.

Yes, you read that right, I was a captain in the Thai Royal Air Force. You might ask yourself, how could this happen? All I have to say for most of you to understand is three little letters:

CIA.

In 1971, in the midst of the Vietnam war, a tremendous amount of supplies was flowing along the infamous Ho Chi Minh Trail. The US rules of engagement prevented US forces from entering Laos to interdict the trail. So some bright person in Washington, DC, came up with the following plan: Give artillery and ammunition to our ally, Thailand, to give to their ally, Laos, to shell the trail. Problem solved, yes? But wait, who would show the Thais or the Laotians how to construct and set up fire bases? The answer, of course, was US military advisors, but wait, they couldn't be in Laos . . . or so said President Nixon in *Stars & Stripes* magazine. So another bright Washington, DC, person surmised that if the US *lent* some of their advisors to Thailand, similar to the Fighting Tigers in China in World War II, the mission could be accomplished without technically there being any US forces in the country.

So, Staff Sgt. John Olin Brown of the US Air Force 819 Red Horse Squadron (combat engineers) became Capt. J. Brown of the Thai Royal Air Force engineers. Everything was going great: bases built, artillery functioning well, trail being blasted day and night, until the morning of December 17, 1971, when the North Vietnamese Army attacked all fire bases simultaneously! Unfortunately I, and my team of volunteers, were still on one of these bases.

What happened next is best described in an article entitled "The CIA and the Secret War in Laos: The Battle for Skyline Ridge, 1971–72": "On the afternoon of December 17, after intense fighting at one forward base, it became apparent that the base would soon fall. Present on this forward base was a small contingency of US combat engineers, on 'loan' to the Thai and Laotian governments. The group evacuated the base in an old C-47 aircraft in an attempt not be captured or killed by the attacking North Vietnamese forces. The C-47 aircraft was severely damaged by small arms fire and was only able to take off and fly a small distance from the base before crashing into the dense forest."

You guessed it, yours truly was on that plane. Couldn't stay with plane since crash was only about ten miles from base, rescuers not coming because, oh yes, we weren't really there. So, thank goodness for Boy Scout and Air Force training, as we evaded capture for two days in the jungle, before finally being rescued. So you see . . . I really have been extremely lucky or karma or fate or whatever you want to call it, to be here.

Back to Civilian Life

Jay retired from the Air Force with the rank of captain. Apparently, he had had enough engineering, and his focus turned to becoming an attorney. He earned his law degree from the LSU Law School, followed by an LLM in taxation from the University of Alabama. He has maintained a private law practice in Baker for the past thirty-nine years.

According to Jay, his retired father, who had been appointed to the first board of directors of the newly established EBR Council on Aging, dragged him to participate with him. Over the next three years, Jay found that he loved and appreciated the older generation, while this work also fulfilled his desire to serve others.

During his time at the Council, seniors would ask, "What's going to happen to my stuff when I die?" Jay began forty years of counseling seniors and writing simple wills, without charge. He has written thousands of wills, and some for three generations of the same families.

In 2011, life came full circle when Jay was elected to the EBR Council on Aging board of directors. He later served as committee chairman of the bylaws rewrite, and vice chairman of the board in 2013–14. Now he says he enjoys being one of those senior citizens.

My Personal Note

Jay is one of our younger seniors. You can find him in his law office, living independently. His humanitarian work takes precedence through Rotary and the community of Baker. Jay is truly living a life of significance and purpose.

Takeaways

Courage is being scared to death, and saddling up anyway.
—John Wayne

No one has ever become poor by giving.
—Anne Frank

There is no exercise better for the heart than reaching down and lifting people up.
—John Andrew Holmes

Part V

Confronting Death

Fear can be your foe or your friend. When you find yourself in the path of a frightening storm—whether figurative or literal—fear can be a paralyzing force spiraling you down into the depths of darkness . . . or a propelling motivator moving you to higher ground. . . . What role does fear have in your life? Immobilizer or energizer . . . foe or friend? What you do in the face of fear identifies its role in your life. Instead of being paralyzed by fear, allow your fear to move you to entrust your life to the Lord. Come to see the Lord as your only place of safety. He promises that He will not only be with you, but that He will also lead you *through* your fear.

Fear not, for I have redeemed you; I have summoned you by name; you are mine. When you pass through *the waters, I will be with you; and when you pass* through *the rivers, they will not sweep over you. When you walk* through *the fire, you will not be burned; the flames will not set you ablaze.*
     —Isaiah 43:1

Excerpt from "Fear: No Longer Afraid"
Hope in the Night with June Hunt, Hope for the Heart ministry

Section 1

Professionals Weigh In

Harold Kushner writes, "I believe that it is not dying that people are afraid of. . . . Something more unsettling and more tragic than dying frightens us. We're afraid of never having lived. Of coming to the end of our days with the sense that we were never really alive That we never figured out what life was for."

I believe that to truly live we must get in touch with the spiritual part of our nature and develop a sense of our life's purpose. My faith is the essence of my being, as inseparable as the air I breathe. This joy defies age. . . .

To quote *Dr. Fulford's Touch of Life*, his book published in 1996 at age 81, "To feel genuine satisfaction at your life's end, you must try to leave something behind that has been truly beneficial for the genuine welfare of mankind. . . . So much of the world's joy and happiness derives not from how much money we accumulate, but from how much we give to the world for the benefit of others."

Living in the Shadow of Death
by Janice McDermott, M.Ed., LCSW

"Everyone is destined to experience both the exhilaration of life and the fear of mortality. We all face the same terror, the wound of mortality, the worm at the core of existence" (Yalom 2008).

With windows raised, fans swirling, and the outside temperature promising to fall from 80 to 72 degrees in the middle of night, I fall asleep listening to happy night creatures. I'm wearing an eye mask to block the little red light shining from the ceiling fire alarm. I am the epiphany of the princess from the "Princess and the Pea" story. Even my skin senses the hint of dawn and awakens me with the urgency of an anticipated forest fire. I embrace the morning light's vibrant energy. However, the next morning, I addressed it as though it were an enemy. I closed all my windows, blinds, and drapes in an attempt to keep the light from increasing the room's temperature to the forecasted high of 90-plus degrees. This started me thinking about our mental relationship with both light and dark.

Nine times out of ten, we associate positive aspects with light and negative ones with darkness—good for one and evil for the other. We disrespect the dark by whistling in its face and assigning it negative emotions such as fear and hate. However, Love lives in both dark and light. Nature grants them equal respect; shouldn't we? "God commanded the light to shine out of darkness" (2 Cor 4:6, KJ). Think about that . . . there was God and Darkness before Light. Therefore, we need to love our shadow.

Love joins; fear separates. Fear is associated with darkness and comes from uncertainty. The poet William Congreve (1670–1729) reminds us that "when we are absolutely certain, whether of our worth or worthlessness, we are almost impervious to fear." In fact, we begin this process of embracing our darkness with a decision to surrender to our fear of the unknown, even death. Our first step in letting go of fear is simply to surrender, to listen and discover without judging. We open our minds to allow all points of view to be valued and to permit new understandings to emerge. With this simple decision, we also arrive at the doorway of enlightenment.

Enlightenment is our willingness to embrace our internal darkness, our unexplored terrains of the subconscious, for new insights and knowledge. The much-sought-after silent inner dark space of meditation becomes the rich soil from which sprouts inspiration and creativity. I invite you to play a game with yourself by shifting your perception to embrace your internal sense of darkness with the same positive description and sensations as you assign to your lightness—become enlightened.

Concerned with the attainment of tranquility, the ancient Greek philosopher Epicurus (341 BCE–270 BCE) believed that the root cause of misery was the frightening vision of inevitable death. Unlike plants and animals, humans are gifted with self-awareness, and therefore we know we will die even though we seldom admit it. We need to bring the idea of death, shrouded in all its darkness and fear, into the light.

"Death anxiety is an existential fact of life, the ultimate climax common to everyone yet seldom shared with others" (Yalom 1980). Irvin D. Yalom believed that confronting death allows us to reenter life in a richer, more compassionate manner. I have to agree. He also believed that interequanimity stems from knowing that nothing disturbs us but our interpretations of things. Change the meaning you assign to anything, including your assigned meaning relative to death, and you can arrive at a comfortable, peaceful coexistence with your thoughts and your perceptions. No one has to agree with or affirm your perception for it to be valid for you.

This process reminds me of a formal wedding, with Dark being the groom dressed in all black standing beside Light, the bride in her exquisite traditional white gown. Together, they make a marriage apart, they're simply an advertisement for a hoped-for event. When we grow with new insights toward transformation, we become enlightened; our dark has married our light. We are comfortable engulfed by darkness and flooded by light.

Of course, we can never completely subdue our fear of death, no matter what methods we use, and that's a good thing because it helps us protect our life. Epicurus emphasized that death concerns are not conscious to most individuals but can be inferred by disguised manifestations that offer a counterfeit version of immortality, such as excessive religiosity, an all-consuming accumulation of wealth, and blind grasping for power and honors. The following are other examples of ways we cope with our knowledge of our inevitable death:

- Generalized unrest or a psychological symptom that seems to have nothing to do with death (anxiety about nothing is anxiety about death);
- Projecting our life dream into the future through our children and grandchildren;
- Compulsive rituals or belief in an ultimate rescuer;
- Living dangerously or heroically without regard for self or others' safety;
- Merging with a loved one, a cause, community (ex.: Gold star parents), or a divine being;
- Music, poems, games, or prayers exchanged among children (i.e., pretend funerals; songs such as "The Hearse," where worms crawl in, worms crawl out; dramatic readings like "The Doll's Funeral"; made-up games such as stepping on a crack in the sidewalk breaks your mama's back; prayers such as "Now I Lay Me Down to Sleep");
- Supernatural beliefs in entities such as vampires and the devil with horns and pitchfork.

Awareness of Death

We first become aware of death between the ages of 3 and 6. I specifically remember the death of a neighbor when I was four years old. The quiet morning was overcast and damp with the suggestion of winter soon to arrive. I awoke early, climbed onto the sofa, and stood looking out the double window. Across the postage-stamp yard was another row of yellow, tiled government buildings, housing for military families. On this particular morning, a figure of a man in navy blue coveralls lay sprawled upside down across four concrete steps, his head on the ground and feet on the porch. He never moved. I remember asking many questions and my mom finally allowing me to sit outside on our steps. I was wearing a pink sweater and holding my doll wrapped in a white blanket. It was a long time before the police came, even longer before the ambulance took the man away. My behind got cold sitting on the concrete steps, exactly like the steps where the man was lying. I wondered if he was cold; I asked if we could take him a blanket. My mother said, "No, he is dead." I understood that she meant that he couldn't feel the cold.

While I waited, I held my doll and imagined she, too, was dead; I made myself cry and recited in my mind the first four lines of a descriptive reading from an old book of my grandmother's that my mother had read to me a few days earlier. Even though the feelings of grief were pretend feelings, I knew they were expected feelings for when someone died. How different would I view death today if my mother had acted as though it was an important transition, a normal occurrence? Following is the descriptive reading she read that day.

"The Doll's Funeral" (1899)
by Will Allen Dromgoole

When my dolly died, when my dolly died,
I sat on the step and I cried, and I cried;
And I couldn't eat any jam and bread,
'Cause it didn't seem right when my doll was dead.
And Bridget was sorry as she could be,
For she patted my head, and "O," said she,
"To think that the pretty has gone and died!"
Then I broke out afresh and I cried and cried.

And all the dollies from all around
Came to see my dolly put under the ground;
There was Lucy Lee and Mary Clack
Brought their dolls over, all dressed in black;
And Emmeline Hope and Sara Lou
Came over and brought their dollies, too.
And all the time I cried and cried,
'Cause it hurt me so when my dolly died.

We dressed her up in a new white gown,
With ribbons and laces all around;
And made her a coffin in a box
Where my brother keeps his spelling blocks;
And we had some prayers, and a funeral, too;
And our hymn was "The Two Little Girls in Blue."
But for me, I only cried and cried,
'Cause it truly hurt when my dolly died.

We dug her a grave in the violet bed,
And planted violets at her head;
And we raised a stone and wrote quite plain,
"Here lies a dear doll who died of pain."
And then my brother, he said, "Amen,"
And we all went back to the house again.
But all the same I cried and cried,
Because 'twas right when my doll had died.

And then we had more jam and bread,
But I didn't eat, 'cause my doll was dead.
But I tied some crape on my dollhouse door
And then I cried and cried some more.
I couldn't be happy, don't you see!
Because the funeral belonged to me.
And then the others went home, and then
I went out and dug up my doll again.

I never played with dolls again after that morning. Dishes for tea and jam became my pass-time toys and to this day comfort me in the living of life. However, in retrospect, I did ask for a Christmas doll when I was twelve. She was in a two-foot-long white box with a lid. I looked inside at her pretty dress, her shoes, and her closed eyes. Slowly, without disturbing the doll, I returned the lid and placed the box in the bottom dresser drawer, never to see her again. She remained there undisturbed until I left for college at seventeen. My younger sisters resurrected her in my absence to a new life. For years, I thought I was saving the doll as a keepsake, but now realize I was burying her in the drawer, giving her a long-awaited funeral along with my childhood.

Fear of death goes underground between 6–12 years old. Then as teens, we become preoccupied with death and defy it through violent video games, horror movies, music about death, and taking daredevil risks. As adults, we push death into the background by focusing on career and family, only to have it show up again between 38–43 years of age as a midlife crisis. The following are examples of life situations that can evoke death anxiety at any age.

- Major milestones—school/college reunions, estate planning, end of therapy;
- Life-threatening illness;
- Loss of a loved one (disappearance, death);
- Irreversible threat to one's basic security—divorce, loss of job, breakup of an intimate relationship;
- Cataclysmic trauma—abuse, rape, fire, robbery, war (usually results in overt death fears disguised as post-traumatic stress disorder);
- Life events that cause a change in one's perception of self—marriage, graduation, children leaving home, retirement, move to nursing home, aging (milestone birthdays—30, 50, 60, 70);
- Major decisions around freedom and mortality—impossibility of future life.

The following chart is an exercise that helps to map your own experience with death. Use a larger sheet of paper if needed to list the death events that occurred under each age category. Include the ones you expect to happen in the period of your life unlived. Note the change in behavior that followed each event; some will be small and others huge. Make a note of each change for pondering in the next few days. What were you thinking?

TIME LINE
Past, Present, and Anticipated Death Events Relative to Your Past and Future Life

0–6 yrs	6–30	30–50	50–70	70–100

Death anxiety is manageable. Deepak Chopra, along with many other personal growth leaders, affirms that our core beliefs underlie everything that happens to us and that the four primary ones have to do with feelings of security, self-worth, wholeness, and love. Abraham Maslow arranged human needs as steps on a ladder with the most basic physical needs—air, water, food, sex— on the bottom. On the next step up from the bottom, he placed our need for security and stability. Both Chopra and Maslow agree that a person with unfulfilled needs low on the ladder cannot climb to the next step. Chronic pain or hunger (physical needs) or disrupted family life (lack of security) creates a barrier to success (self-actualization).

Self-actualizers have a clear sense of what is true and what is phony. They are spontaneous and creative, and for the most part are free of social conventions. At the top-most ladder rung (transcendence), we feel loved and lovable, kind and appreciated, with a lightness of being.

As we climb the ladder, we draw on the internal resources we have acquired. Chopra directs us to turn our needs relative to love, self-worth, feeling secure, and feeling whole into expectations—expectations from our self to our self. To the extent that we do that, we can expect the world to reflect the same back. We are treated as worthy and as lovable as we treat our self. I make my bed when I don't feel like it because I'm worthy of an orderly environment. I take a nap when I'm tired because I love the baby in me. I reassure that baby's separation anxieties by telling her that I will take her with me when I die. I say kind and encouraging words to myself when I awake in the morning and when events fall short of expectations. I remind myself that I'm only alive in this moment, and that in all past moments, I did the best I could with the resources and circumstances at my disposal. I maintain a consistent routine of self-care to create a sense of security. I buy myself flowers, healthy food, and get enough rest. I fill up my heart with all those emotional things that were missing when I was a child, and in doing so I have much to give to others. In return, the world mirrors everyday how I treat myself, and I'm grateful. I encourage you in this moment of life to internally climb this imaginary ladder by first believing that you too are indeed unique, lovable, and worthy of love as evidenced by how you treat yourself. Create in you that wonderful safe place to retreat and be at peace.

The following is Deepak Chopra's technique to find and then gently return to a state of mental calmness that is useful in managing anxiety:

1. Get comfortable. Sit in a position that is comfortable to

you—not so relaxed that you might fall asleep, but relaxed and alert at the same time.

2. Choose an object of attention. This might be your breath, an image, or a mantra—something that allows your mind to relax into the silent stream of awareness.

3. Don't judge. When thoughts arise, as they inevitably will, you don't need to judge them or try to push them away. Instead, gently return your attention to the object of attention—your breath, your image, or your mantra. Continue to do so as often as you need to.

4. Know this is time well spent. When these thoughts intrude, know that your time is not being wasted. Even if it feels like you have been thinking throughout your entire meditation, there were seconds (or microseconds) when your mind slipped into the gap, which means you are still receiving the benefits of your practice.

From this state of calm, we are able to acknowledge our anxiety regarding the inevitability of our own death. Yalom, in his 1980 textbook, *Existential Psychotherapy,* lists four ultimate life concerns—death, isolation, meaning of life, and freedom. All four play a part in death anxiety.

Existential evidence of death anxiety is found in irrational ideas about death (e.g., death can feel cold and dark), memories and fantasies, and sexual orgasm difficulties (fear of letting go, surrendering). Those racked with death anxiety may have

- encountered too much death at an early age;
- failed to experience a center of love, caring, or safety in the home;
- never shared concerns of death—feel isolated;
- rejected religious myths—overly self-aware or a black-and-white thinker.

We experience a taste of death in sexual orgasm, a total letting go, releasing. We experience it in dreams of falling, roads ending, being buried alive, acts of forgetting (lost past), and being alone. We experience a taste of death every time we fall asleep. We are conscious of our body and then we're not. It's impossible to recall the moment we move from awake to asleep, and so it is with death. It is impossible to know the moment we move from life on planet Earth to nonphysical life.

An awakening experience, a message from our deeper self, can make its first appearance in a dream, a profoundly useful catalyst for major life changes. Every nightmare is the release of imprisoned death anxiety. Scrooge's transformative dream is an example of an awakening experience. Scrooge became aware of his mortality and isolation—his existential loneliness—and because of his dream, sought to change it.

Awakening experiences create existential life changes such as the following:

- deeper communication;
- greater willingness to take risk;
- less concern about rejection;
- compassion in self for self.

In my book *Healing Mind: Five Steps to Ultimate Healing, Four Rooms for Thoughts,* I describe a way of organizing our thinking with the intention of awakening to our complete self. Because our conscious and unconscious thinking creates our life story, the power of our thoughts affects us in profound ways—contentment and health, illness and turmoil, peace and calm. The choice is ours. We must choose wisely.

Human Connectedness

The most effective approach to death anxiety is human connectedness. Loneliness lives in existential isolation, the unbridgeable gap between the dying individual and other people because we collude with each other around the dream that we will live forever. We can be lonely because no one visits or because we don't belong. However, the loneliness shrouding death anxiety is the loneliness of not being connected when someone does visit or we do belong to a group. Those approaching death remain silent so as not to depress others, while the living avoid the dying to escape thoughts of their own inevitable death.

When we fail to marry our light and dark, to recognize and embrace the gift in our own death anxiety, we mistakenly mask or mislabel others' death anxiety as being a different problem. In doing so, we fail to give support to those in their moment of crucial need of companionship and presence. "It is the synergy between ideas and intimate connection with other people that is most effective both in diminishing death anxiety and in harnessing the awakening experience to effect personal change. . . . confronting death allows us, not to open some noisome Pandora's box, but to reenter life in a richer, more compassionate manner" (Yalom 2008).

This past year, I had an unexpected cryoablation procedure on my heart. I was scared. There were no complications, no need for supportive care; all seemed uneventful. After all, I live only two miles from the hospital. I felt cautious but trusting enough to stay home alone. There was no pain or discomfort to keep me from falling asleep. Everything went smoothly for two weeks. Then suddenly, in the middle of the night, I awoke with intense chest pain, more pain than I'd ever felt in my life. In a flash, my body went into fear mode. I sat up. My mind quickly ran through the procedure of getting dressed and driving . . . not a good idea . . . in too much pain . . . would take too long. The pain left as quickly as it had arrived; it lasted no more than two minutes. However, it served as an awakening experience. I had had others—when my dad died suddenly at an early age and when I had to live alone in the country for the first time—but this one I consciously knew was about my death.

The next time the pain struck, I stayed calm and looked death in the eye. My mind reached for the higher levels of omnipotent knowing, much in the same way that it does when knowing a wreck is in process and you watch yourself move through time and space to the inevitable crash of your car with another.

This sharp, intense chest pain occurred three more times during my healing period, always awakening me in the wee hours of the morning. I comforted myself with the thought that I would pass from life into death in the blink of an eye . . . that the pain will be over, or I will be dead. Either way there is nothing to fear.

In the months that followed, I presented workshops to social workers on recognizing and addressing the fear of death underlying many issues they would encounter in their practice. Now I'm sharing my insights with you, as part of the process of accepting my own inevitable death. We need to be comfortable talking about dying to be truly present with someone whose death is imminent.

There's no greater service than the power of presence, the here-and-now focus, rather than the now-and-then or the there-and-now. As laypersons, we need to address our own anxiety before visiting or ministering to someone dealing with death. The visit needs to be relationship driven. If necessary, practice with others before you go.

Be an accurate observer. Do your feelings and sensations in the here-and-now provide information about the dying person or about yourself? Don't ask the question "why." Instead, ask the following:

- "What" are you thinking as you imagine or relate this?
- "How" do you know that?
- "When" did you feel, think, learn, etc., this?
- "Where" were you when you discovered/heard/saw/felt this?

Respond with:

- I feel mad, sad, glad, or afraid hearing this or recalling this in my life, too.
- I feel angry that someone did that to you, sad that you are going through this.

- I'm afraid too.
- I'm happy you're sharing this with me.

Focus on his or her unlived life, their regrets, and think of new actions—thoughts that will create less future regret—for instance, telling someone you're sorry or thanking someone.

We must stay present in the process of relating rather than caught up in the individual's story. Remember, we are not the rescuer. Each person's fundamental responsibility is this: if you are responsible for what has gone wrong in your life, then you, and only you, are able to change it. The focus is on the terminally ill person, not on getting our own emotional needs met or sharing our contradicting beliefs or points of view. In some aspect of our mind, we all want to think that our life mattered, that what we leave behind will live long after we are gone, maybe forever; allow the person leaving to believe anything that makes them feel happier. Regardless of your beliefs, join in the fantasy of their idea; create and expand the vision of happiness, whether it's Jesus, golden gates, reincarnated life, or one spirit. This is a time to support, not a time to convert.

Yalom suggests that we recognize the rippling effect of those that came before us. Rippling refers "to leaving behind something from your life experience; some trait; some piece of wisdom, guidance, virtue, comfort that passes on to others, known or unknown. . . . Look for her among her friends" (Yalom 2008).

Let this mind be in you, which was also in Christ Jesus.
    —Philippians 2:5 (KJV)

References

Chopra, Deepak. Tips to Quiet Your Mind. Healerpedia.com. Accessed February 7, 2017.
Congreve, William. BrainyQuote.com. Accessed February 7, 2017.
    https://www.brainyquote.com/quotes/quotes/w/williancon3933

24.html.

Maslow, Abraham. *Motivation and Personality.* 3rd ed. Delia, India: Pearson, 1987.

McDermott, Janice. *Healing Mind: Five Steps to Ultimate Healing, Four Rooms for Thoughts.* Bloomington, IN: Balboa Press, 2015.

Yalom, Irvin D. *Existential Psychotherapy.* New York: Basic Books, 1980.

———. *Staring at the Sun: Overcoming the Terror of Death.* London: Piatkus Books, 2008.

A FEW HOSPICE EXPERIENCES
by Kathryn Grigsby, Retired CEO, Hospice of Baton Rouge

There are things in life that we don't want to know and there are things in life that we need to know sooner rather than later. How to die with grace and dignity is among those things we need to know, and probably sooner rather than later. It is a "taboo" topic that we all need to address with those we love. There are simple ways to ease into a conversation with your loved ones. Start the conversation. If you want guidance, visit www.http://theconversationproject.org/death-and-dying.

When I began working in the hospice world, I had known only one individual who had died at home with hospice. I was fortunate to become a part of the hospice movement in the very early stages of hospice in our community. The hospice I worked with was the only nonprofit hospice in the community for many years.

My own father died in the hospital. Even though his doctors painted an optimistic outcome, instinctively I knew he would not make it through the night. I asked the nurse to call me if he changed significantly. The call came at 1:30 a.m. the next morning to say that his blood pressure was dropping quickly and that if I wanted to see him again, I should get there quickly. I asked her to please tell him I was on my way and to please wait for me. I don't know what prompted me to ask her to tell my father that, but she assured me she would.

When I arrived at the ICU, I walked up to him and held his hand. I told him I was there and it was okay for him to let go. Within minutes, the lines on the multitude of machines that were connected to him went straight. Enough television shows had educated me on the meaning of flat lines. I will be forever grateful that I was with my father and able to give him "permission" to let go. Again, I don't know what prompted me to say those words.

The importance of giving the dying permission to let go is

among the many things I learned in my decades of work in hospice care. Most patients die on their own terms and when they are ready. Often the dying wait for a loved one to arrive. Decades after my father's death, I witnessed my mother die with hospice. She waited for my brother. With encouragement from our hospice chaplain, he gave Mother permission to let go. She died within minutes.

It is one thing when the patient has lived a long, full life. We expect our parents and grandparents to die. We do not expect our children to die before us. It is different when a young person, a child, or an infant dies. It is not the natural order.

As the only nonprofit at one time, we were the only hospice that had a special program for infants and children. We once cared for a beautiful baby boy who was legally deaf and blind. It was a time in my life when I could spend time with the family. Four generations of family surrounded the baby. He lived about six months, being doted on by his family and a group of young friends, mostly college age. When he started going down, the nurse removed the feeding tube to ensure that his passing was peaceful. His mom asked me to hold him while the paternal grandparents came to say good-bye. I was in a back room all by myself with the baby. After the grandparents left, the baby looked straight at me and smiled. He then took a very deep breath. I was afraid he had stopped breathing. Uncertain what to do, I started looking for the mom. She came, and he beamed even more at her. It was like he could see and hear. For about four hours, he was just like a normal baby: he cooed, he smiled appropriately, he responded. The grandmother asked if we should put the feeding tube back in. I told her we would wait until morning and see how he was.

I was leaving the next day for a hospice meeting out west. I explained to the mom that I would not be able to come by in the morning, but to please call me. When we landed in Dallas, she called to say he had simply closed his eyes and stopped breathing. He was peaceful. Two of the young college boys drove to Lafayette to pick up a small coffin. Everyone who had cared for him while he was alive continued to care for him after he died. It was one of the most beautiful experiences I had in hospice.

    Some people are more ready than others to let go. A friend of mine told me about her mother, who had been discharged from hospice care three times because she improved so much each time she was readmitted. Then came her final weeks; however, her most favored son was out of the country. Even though she weighed less than seventy pounds, she was determined to tell him good-bye. She waited and waited and waited. Weeks passed. The nurse hadn't a clue how she was still alive. The night the son came home, he didn't go straight to her room. The chaplain had to encourage him to go talk with her. Finally, he made a quick trip in and out of her room. The daughter went back in and the mother stated clearly, "I am ready now." The daughter explained that it was on God's terms, not hers. Within minutes she closed her eyes and slipped away.

    Hospice care makes a difference for all ages. I remember one day a social work intern asked me if I had a minute. We sat down and she was beaming. She proceeded to tell me that the patient she had just visited had smiled at her and said, "I know I am dying, but I want to assure you, I plan to live every minute until I do." And that is what hospice care is all about: making whatever time is left the best possible for the patient and the family. Good hospices handle pain control beautifully, and they are available afterward to guide loved ones through the grieving process. Some do most of their grieving before the loved ones die. Anticipatory grief is what they experience; others, not so much. One thing is certain: all grief is individual. Avoid telling someone who is grieving, "I understand." Seldom is grief the same. No two wives grieve the same way, nor do husbands. Remember grief is as individual as DNA.

My Observations about Hospice

Each week for almost two years, I visited a former neighbor who lived in the St. James Place Health and Wellness building, for residents, as well as other seniors, needing more nursing care. She had progressed from Independent Living to Assisted Living to Health and Wellness.

During that same period, I visited another resident who had progressed through Continuing Care, as she had. He had palliative hospice care for over two years, which focused on quality of life, providing emotional and spiritual support for the entire family as his organs slowly shut down, leading to his death. He stayed pain-free and upbeat, whereas my friend lived in constant pain, explaining that her doctors said there was no cure. I tried to talk with her on several occasions, telling her hospice was not a death sentence, while she remained silent. I even took my other friend for a visit occasionally. Apparently, a few weeks prior to her death, she did receive hospice visits.

Like doctors trying to cure medical problems, specialists in hospice palliative care face dilemmas as well. I read that one said, "If there is no cure, we can at least offer comfort."

Another, "We are not gods who can cure everything, and it's a mark of honesty to understand when the time has come."

Apparently there is a normal progression toward death in cancer patients, whereas a heart failure patient, which I am, experiences highs and lows and is harder to read. I agree with my cardiologist and internist that quality of life is more important than quantity. I agree on avoiding strokes as long as possible, by choosing blood thinners over procedures, once the heart is permanently out of rhythm.

THE GIFT OF GRIEF
by W. Nicholas Abraham, PhD, LPC

To live in this world you must be able to do three things: to love what is mortal; to hold it against your bones knowing your own life depends on it; and, when the time comes to let it go, let it go.
    —Mary Oliver

My daddy gifted me with his death on February 18, 2014.

A gift that allows both the absence and presence of mind to commingle.

Death is not just a loss of another. It is a loss of mind, of soul, of spirit, of meaning, but it is also a gain of new opportunities and perspectives, strength of character and self-respect. Death allows us to defy all logic and be present to the dust to which we shall all return. When the gift of death strikes the core of our being and we are reeling from the loss of part of our soul, if we are real, we open ourselves to mystery and move from our human time zone into a space where gravity takes over.

Grief is a gift that awakens in us a need for quiet time, reflection, and solitude to sift through memories and come to grips with what has happened to us.

Grief awakens in us a need to outright reject those who out of their own insecurity attempt to sidestep the pain through phrases like "he's in a better place." On the other hand, we are just as profoundly possessed by a powerful force that helps us resist lashing out at those who mean well, but who are unable to understand the emptiness—or who have not the strength to face their own soon to be.

Grief awakens anger and a hurt that cannot be hospitalized, biopsied, cured with antibiotics, or surgically removed. We enter a crazy time of raw rage, when we are at the same time angry with the one who left us and even more so at life itself, for giving us the gift of love and then asking us to let it go. We enter a period of deep distrust and cynicism.

Grief awakens a recovery—a time when we reevaluate the *what* and the *who* that can be relied upon, who are significant to our redemption—those who nourish us, who intoxicate us, who use us, who give to us the essentials of true love, who allow us to expose the ugliness of death without shaming us, who respect our disbelief and apathy—it is a time when in the midst of loss, we can honestly appraise our lives and the future investments of our limited time on this earth.

Grief awakens an acceptance of the limitations of humanity. Through our loss, we come to more fully appreciate how messy life is, how broken and hypocritical we all are, how limited and impure human love is, and how people are at times unavailable when we most need them.

Grief awakens the age-old question *What's it all about?*, and beckons us to live peacefully within the doubt and meaningless existence in order that something larger than our visions, plans, and dreams may provide a new purpose to life.

Grief awakens a season to reset the boundaries of what's acceptable and what's not, whom we'll carry and whom we will not, whom we can share our values with and whom we cannot. It is a time for cleaning out the clutter and washing the windows of life so that we can see more clearly and breathe more easily.

All these awakenings, all these seasons, all of the time zones of grief are entangled like Christmas lights that can only be separated with patience and gentle pacing. And even when we begin to untangle the wires of grief, we find our wires moving in so many more directions, with no certainty of where we will be transported.

Hope is perhaps trusting that while we are untangling it all, we are being transported back into the arms of love—ironically, the very arms that we felt dropped us when we lost our beloved.

But then what else is there? What other arms are there but the arms that unfold before us each day we awaken and ask us to be carried by a power greater than our own needs and wants.

What else is there? Than to return to the arms that both

hold and let go? That both protect and wound? That both seduce and betray.

It may sound cynical to trust love again after watching a loved one slowly fade into the night and do so with the sobering realization that "I am the only one I will never love or leave"; but it is authentic, if nothing else. And it is worth it.

Years ago, when I was in treatment for severe depression and wanted to die, one of the rituals in the group was for the other six men to seek my trust. I was to fall slowly backwards, hoping they would hold and rest me in their locked arms. Once in their arms, they gently rocked me back and forth as if I were an infant in the arms of the world.

It was one of the most powerful experiences of my life. When I was put down, the therapist asked me what I experienced. The memory is vivid. I tearfully said, "It wasn't only the assurance of things unseen. It was also the reality that I couldn't be held forever and that I wanted to rest as long as I could with gratitude." These men loved this broken man back to life through a gesture of simple holding and gentle rocking, and then put me down and asked me to learn to rock myself.

My daddy rocked me to sleep each night when I was a child, and as these men were rocking me in 1993, I recalled how much we all long to be held. How much I love to this very day rocking myself into a quiet zone.

One night recently, when I returned home from a long day of counseling, I rocked and rocked, slowing my flood of emotions—and asked God to quiet my mind that I might also have a time for rest and restoration.

I slowly faded out, much the same way my father fell into eternal rest.

The only difference was that we awakened to a different time zone.

His zone is now eternal rest, eternal peace, eternal love, and eternal light.

Mine is limited.

Therefore, there are but three things I ask of the Lord of

Life through this gift of grief.

    That I continue to love what is mortal, hold that love against my bones believing my life depends on it, and, when the time comes, let it go.

Section 2

Facing Your Own Mortality

The 23rd Psalm is the most read and quoted psalm in the Bible, offering assurance and acceptance in our hours of need:

The Lord is my shepherd; I shall not want.
He maketh me to lie down in green pastures: he leadeth me beside the still waters.
He restoreth my soul: he leadeth me in the paths of righteousness for his name's sake.
Yea, though I walk through the valley of the shadow of death, I will fear no evil: for thou art with me; thy rod and thy staff they comfort me.
Thou preparest a table before me in the presence of mine enemies: thou anointest my head with oil; my cup runneth over.
Surely goodness and mercy shall follow me all the days of my life: and I will dwell in the house of the Lord for ever.

MARGARET OSWALD:
GIRDED FOR LIFE AND DEATH

Recently, I was blessed to talk with a fellow resident, Margaret Oswald, who is a step ahead of me in facing the end of her life. Our conversation resonated with me deeply, as we have the same heart disease. Not knowing Margaret was receiving hospice care, I had invited her to my apartment, as she had previously indicated she would like to be the first person to be interviewed about her wonderful ten-year marriage to Tom Oswald, while both lived at St. James Place. She had long fought advanced heart disease and congestive heart failure, yet her concern was about Tom and how he had lovingly taken care of her on the many days when she was bedridden. Pale and frail, she said she was pain-free. It was obvious Margaret had a deep inner peace, buoyed by her deep faith. She said, without a quiver in her voice, she was tired and ready to leave this life. She wanted to free Tom, her beloved husband, now 96, who had become her constant caregiver. I was quick to remind her that if their roles were reversed, and she agreed, she would care for him. I was content to listen to her and did not pose my questions for their story.

Both Margaret and Tom had long first marriages. Margaret was married to Dallas Fiandt for sixty-three years and had four children: daughters Ann Fiandt Andries and Kate Fiandt Siam, and two sons, Wes and Jeffrey (deceased).

Tom was married to Martha for sixty-two years and they had sons Tom Jr. and Wiley. In their families combined, Margaret and Tom have eight grandchildren and one great-grandchild.

Margaret talked about many seniors waiting so long to move to retirement centers, waiting until health conditions demanded attention. She reminisced about the many social activities St. James Place life enrichment managers facilitate, and in their case, opportunities to meet and fall in love, after years of living alone after the death of their spouses. Such is the love story of Margaret and Tom Oswald.

Tom's Story of Their Romance

Later, after Margaret's death, I asked Tom to write about their courtship and marriage. He summed it up very appropriately, in true male fashion, "We met and our personalities fit like a glove. First date was July 4. The rest is history." All friends and family knew Margaret and Tom had such a wonderful marriage that it indeed fit like a glove!

Margaret Now at Peace

Not unexpectedly, one day as I went to lunch, Margaret's death notice was posted. She had died peacefully in her sleep on November 16, 2016. Through tears, I celebrated how Margaret had set the example of being truly girded to enjoy life to its fullest and, most importantly, to be at peace and girded for death.

For everything there is a season, and a time for every matter under heaven:
a time to be born, and a time to die;
a time to plant, and a time to pluck up what is planted.
    —Ecclesiastes 3:1–2

Margaret Zimmer Fiandt Oswald's Eulogy

The St. James Place Convocation Room was filled with family members and residents, assembled to celebrate the life of Margaret Oswald. The service, obviously planned by Margaret, included her favorite inspiring and uplifting hymns. The minister from St. John's United Methodist Church framed the celebration with Lucille Clifton's poem, "the lesson of the falling leaves."
    I asked Tom's oldest son, Tom Jr., to allow me to include his testimony given during the eulogy, a testimony of being welcomed into the family by Margaret:

"Soon after my dad and Margaret married, Margaret told me that she wanted to be referred to as my stepmother, which delighted me. I had always liked her from the first day that I met her. She and my dad went with me on July 4 to watch the fireworks from the top floor of one of the buildings at LSU. She was quite the good sport—she had a beer and some potato chips as we sat and watched the distant fireworks. She and I had an immediate liking for each other. Later as she met my sons, niece, and nephew, we all drew closer. She was always interested in what my two sons were doing as well as my niece, nephew, and their children. The fact that there was a bond between her and my side of the family is evidenced by the presence of my son from Chicago, my niece from Fort Collins, and my nephew from Los Angeles. They came to be supportive of my dad, but also to show their respects to Margaret and to honor her memory."

"In addition, I would like to thank Margaret's children for accepting us into their family and for being so gracious to my dad. Margaret has been a wonderful partner for my dad these many years. We have enjoyed traveling together—to Chicago and Spain. The two of them have gone on cruises and other trips to Europe and North America. For years they lived a full life and gave to others. They were generous with their time—tutoring children in a low-income public school—and generous with their church and various charities. It can truly be said that Margaret lived a good life and had a positive effect on all who knew her."

Accepting Our Own Mortality

What a gift to have lived life with joy and fullness as Margaret did, and yet to be ready to die. I see many who perhaps have not faced their own mortality. Many who would not enter the secured doors of our Memory sections, nor visit those receiving hospice care in their apartments or in the Health and Wellness building (a nursing center).

Quoting from my book, *He Lays the Stones for Our Steps:*

I believe if we are walking in awareness of God's presence daily, He steps through the door of death with us, to a bright pathway of a new and better life. I have a recognition and respect of others' beliefs. There are nuances of faith and philosophies, but I think this poem may hold truth for all of us:

When you walk to the edge of all the light you have
and take that first step into the darkness of the unknown,
you must believe that one of two things will happen:
> *There will be something solid for you to stand upon,*
> *or, you will be taught how to fly.*
> —Patrick Overton

    A number of friends have commented, with a quick twinkle in their eyes and a faraway look, "I want to be taught to fly!" Could that mean they have already found something to stand on—perhaps their faith and joy in living. . . .

Takeaways

The fear of death follows from the fear of life. A man who lives fully is prepared to die at any time.
> —Mark Twain

For life and death are one, as the river and the sea are one.
> —Kahlil Gibran

Life and death are one thread, the same line viewed from different sides.
> —Lao Tzu

HENRY AND MONICA BRADSHER TAKE TURNS CONFRONTING MORTALITY

Monica Bradsher tells this moving story:

Keeping one's affairs in order, updating the will, simplifying the estate to minimize probate—Henry and I have done those sorts of things for decades. But knowing that one will die some day is an abstract understanding. Wanting to provide for the family and avoid burdening them is not the same as truly confronting mortality. We have experienced that confrontation because each of us nearly died in the last two years.

Henry was first. We were concerned about his gradual loss of weight, but we continued to accept contracts to lecture on cruise ships. In May 2015, the month of his 85th birthday, we were cruising from South Africa back to Florida. Henry was eating great food five times a day and giving great lectures, but he lost four pounds in only a month. Something was wrong.

Our primary care doctor ordered an MRI. It showed that Henry's right kidney looked abnormally small and misshapen. The next stop was the urologist, who found an obstruction between the kidney and the bladder. He didn't think it could be cancer because Henry has never smoked. However, when the urologist removed some cells from the obstruction, the cells proved cancerous. Urothelial carcinoma, or bladder cancer, had moved up the ureter into the kidney and destroyed it. Henry underwent major surgery to remove the right kidney, ureter, and part of the bladder. He was terribly weak and sick after the surgery.

Then we got more bad news: the biopsy showed the cancer had reached the outer wall of the ureter. From there it might have spread. This was Stage 3 cancer. What's more, the most effective chemotherapy for bladder cancer is toxic to kidneys. Since Henry had only one remaining kidney, he could not have that chemo.

Our sons were deeply concerned and wanted Henry to go to a top-tier cancer center, such as MD Anderson in Houston. Henry said no, the same protocol would be used in Baton Rouge. He had no desire to go to Houston for treatment. We didn't know anyone there and would be living in a dreary motel. He didn't say so, but I think he believed he was dying and preferred to stay in our home. I felt caught in the middle and prayed to God to show me the way forward.

Many people were praying for us, and I believe the prayers worked. It was almost as if a bright light shone on the path we needed to follow, step by step, to save Henry's life.

Our son Neal has his own financial investment company in New York City and is known in medical circles for investing in innovative solutions. He had recruited a doctor at Sloan Kettering to serve on the board of directors of a small company. Over lunch, Neal mentioned that his dad had urothelial carcinoma. The doctor revealed his specialty. He was the head of the department of genitourinary cancers. He urged Neal to bring Henry to see Sloan Kettering's top researcher on urothelial carcinoma, Dr. Jonathan Rosenberg.

Just then I received a phone call from a rabbi and his wife whom we had met on the cruise. They were among the many people praying for Henry. Amazingly, they knew Jonathan Rosenberg from a time when they and he had been at Harvard. "Oh Monica," they said, "he is a rock star of cancer research!" Henry was willing to go to New York because our son and his family would welcome us to stay with them there. We flew to New York to see the "rock star."

Dr. Rosenberg's research focuses on the relationship between genes and cancer cells. He added Henry's cancerous tissues and blood samples to his research data. He ordered a PET scan for Henry, and we saw the results in his office. A PET scan measures glucose uptake, showing where sugar is fueling energy. On the computer monitor, we saw a black universe with a glowing circle of fire, like the sun, and six little white stars. The "sun" was Henry's heart, Dr. Rosenberg assured us, using energy as it should. That was normal, but those little white "stars" were enlarged lymph nodes. Cancer in them was growing, using energy, causing Henry's weight loss. Having spread to the lymph system, the cancer was now Stage 4, the last stage before death.

"If you were my father," Dr. Rosenberg said, "I would take you to my colleague Dr. Arjun Balar at New York University, who is starting a clinical trial of a new drug." This drug isn't a chemotherapy that kills some good cells as well as cancer cells. Instead, it's an immunotherapy that stimulates the immune system to fight cancer. We headed to NYU.

Two months passed before Henry was accepted into the clinical trial and received his first infusion of pembrolizumab, a Merck drug with the commercial name Keytruda. Not long after, we read that former president Jimmy Carter had made a miraculous recovery from last-stage melanoma in his brain. His wonder drug was Keytruda, which had been approved by the FDA for melanoma but not yet for other cancers like Henry's.

Henry had no side effects from Keytruda. He felt very tired, but he had experienced fatigue for months. He gained strength gradually and was able to walk farther, to enjoy strolling in Central Park. By December, he had had three infusions. Henry said he thought he was only recovering from the kidney surgery. He wasn't allowing himself to hope for a miracle. I bought us tickets to go home for Christmas. Both sons and their families and my sister and her husband all planned to join us for the holiday. I wondered if it would be a celebration or a last reunion.

Henry had a second PET scan. We went back to Dr. Balar for a fourth infusion and an office visit. The black screen showed the "sun," Henry's heart using energy to beat. But there were no "stars," no sign of cancer in the lymph nodes! Our Christmas was a joyful celebration.

In the year and a half since that time, Henry has continued to see Dr. Balar regularly to get MRI and CT scans. He has not needed any more infusions of Keytruda in the last nine months. Another PET scan has confirmed that there is no sign of cancer recurring. Henry's weight is almost back to normal. The FDA has now approved Keytruda for use in treating bladder cancer. Henry played a small role in history!

People vary somewhat in their reactions to a major confrontation with their mortality. In Henry's case, he has resumed all his favorite activities, mostly volunteer work but also playing tennis with friends. His tennis seems even more important than before, as if he can't get enough of being with the other guys and running around, often getting a kick out of winning a match. He loves his life.

For me, almost losing Henry made me love him all the more after fifty-four years of marriage. But most of all, the experience brought me closer to God. I felt His guidance every step of the way and thank Him every day. I also thank both of our sons and their families for their love and support through the whole ordeal.

My own confrontation with mortality is a less complicated story. The day before Thanksgiving, 2016, more than a year after Henry's cancer diagnosis, I had a shocking experience. Walking across our kitchen, I felt some numbness in one thigh, then in both. Within an hour, Henry had driven me to the ER at Baton Rouge General Hospital. Already completely paralyzed from the waist down, I had to be lifted out of the car into a wheelchair.

An MRI showed a problem in my T12 vertebra. At first the doctors assumed this was a common problem, a slipped disc, a herniated or collapsing disc. But the next morning, Thanksgiving Day, a CT scan revealed a much more difficult problem. My disc was not herniated but calcified. It had become a big white marble pressing more than halfway into my spinal cord. The spinal surgeon on call that day said this situation is rare and the most difficult kind of spinal surgery. Nobody he knew in Baton Rouge had ever done it before, and he could promise only a 50% chance of success. I faced possible death or complete paralysis.

Our son Neal came to the rescue again. He found a surgeon in Miami who had done this rare kind of surgery multiple times and was willing to take me as a patient. The Baton Rouge surgeon was visibly relieved that I was to be flown to Miami for the surgery. However, the Miami surgeon was in Poland giving lectures and would not be able to do my surgery for almost a week.

The week I spent waiting, in Baton Rouge and then in Miami, was one of the most difficult in my life. I was kept on my back, unable to move and hooked up to various life-preserving tubes and instruments. I was most worried about Henry because he was so worried about me! Fortunately, some dear friends and our visiting grandson took turns relieving Henry at keeping me company and watching over my care. I had plenty of time to think, and what came to me most powerfully was how blessed we were that Henry's brush with death and mine were not at the same time.

One of our pastors visited and asked if I was frightened. I answered quite truthfully that I was not. There was absolutely nothing I could do in my situation, nothing but wait and pray. I felt that it was up to God whether I should live or die. To my surprise, I was at total peace about either result. I felt that God had brought me through so many trials and dangers that He would take care of me. It was going to be good however things turned out. This was the "peace that passes understanding," a deep peace that is still with me.

Today, after successful surgery in Miami to remove the calcified disc and many months of therapy to re-learn how to walk, I am getting around with a walker. I can do almost all my favorite activities except playing tennis and walking around University Lake. At some point I may even be able to use a cane by myself without falling down. I will keep trying to improve, but I insist on also living my life, helping Volunteers in Public Schools, going to Bible study, talking with our sons and their families and my sister.

Life is so good, and God is good all the time.

Takeaways

Death is not the greatest loss in life. The greatest loss is what dies inside of us while we live.
—Norman Cousins

Love has no age, no limit; and no death.
—John Galsworthy

Even if you have a terminal illness, you don't have to sit down and mope. Enjoy life and challenge the illness that you have.
    —Nelson Mandela

SHARING AN AFTERNOON OF FAITH WITH MY FRIEND MARIA KONERT

Maria borrowed a phrase to use on her green granite burial marker with gold Art Deco motif: "Ancestors Plant the Trees; Descendants Enjoy the Shade."

Maria is a vibrant 65-year-old, afflicted with chronic obstructive pulmonary disease (COPD) for thirty years, and has worn oxygen 24/7 for fourteen years. Her personality is upbeat and inspiring. She has planted her trees well. . . . Maria's descendants will indeed enjoy her shade, as she has instilled in them love, faith, and a closeness that will live on. Her values are faith, family, friends, fun, and work.

This quote best explains the true meaning of life, the gift Maria has given her children:

> *Good, better, best.*
> *Never let it rest,*
> *'Til your good is better,*
> *And your better is best.*
> —St. Jerome

Maria's Path to Self-Forgiveness

"I never told any family member or anyone else of my abortion, until after I forgave myself. It took me seven years to forgive myself."

We all have a choice to continue carrying our unfinished business to the grave, unless we are fortunate enough and willing to face it head on, as Maria so unexpectedly did at St. Patrick's Cathedral in New York City. She felt moved to share with us what she had never told any of her family or anyone else of her abortion until seven years afterward. She forgave herself for having an abortion. Maria's forgiveness of self is all that matters, and I said, we have no need to know more.

We had an opportunity to share our faith, Maria a Catholic and I a Methodist. We share the same belief that God has given us all grace, which we cannot earn. However, we must have faith, which brings self-forgiveness, to be able to accept and live life to its fullest, under God's grace.

Maria's Ancestors *Planted Their Trees* . . .

Maria was born in St. Paul, Minnesota, to Carlos G. and Doris June Wells Gallusser. She has two sisters, two brothers, four children, and three grandsons. She said, "A good Catholic family in those days had five children."

Her father, of Swiss, German, and Argentinean descent, was in international advertising with Ford Motor Company in Michigan, aka the CIA, and translated catalogs in twenty-nine languages. His unique background included his father and mother's starting the family-owned Bank of Argentina. His father's father (Gallusser), a diplomat, started El Bank of Guatemala.

Maria's mother was a southern belle from Birmingham, Alabama, of Scotch, Irish, and English descent. Fortunately, she hated the cold, as the family lived in Caracas, Venezuela, and Mexico City while their children were young. Their mother set an example for her children of how to live, then gave them wings and set them free, which fits Maria's adventurous spirit.

Maria, a Successful Tree Planter, Exemplified in Her Children

Maria considers her four children her blessings and success in life. All are very loving and thoughtful individuals. Nicole is 40 years old, has a master's degree in education, and lives in Chester Springs, Pennsylvania. Carmen is 37 years old and works with a nationwide prescription assistance program. Joseph is an artist currently residing in Los Angeles. Nicholas lives in New York City and is global art director for Tory Burch.

Maria Becomes a Gemologist

Maria studied with the Gemological Institute of America (GIA). She worked with a jeweler in Baton Rouge, specializing in diamonds, colored stones, organics, and pearls. Despite her diagnosis with COPD, she did not retire until 2009. (My immediate thought: a beautiful Maria, working with God's beautiful stones, bringing beauty to others.)

Moving to St. James Place Assisted Living

After Maria was diagnosed with COPD thirty years ago, she chose to continue life as normally as possible, continuing her work as a gemologist for six years. She said she asked her pulmonologist recently what is the longest time one of his patients had received oxygen 24/7 and he said thirteen years.

 Maria moved to St. James Place in 2015 and sings praises of the attentive care she has received in Assisted Living. She said that she now realizes she should have moved to St. James Place earlier for her own as well as her children's well-being and peace of mind. Her children have in hand the plans Maria wisely made to ease the transition after her death.

 Maria is quick to praise the attendants from Baton Rouge hospice who have assisted her during the past year. She said they are quick to answer every question and fulfill every need.

 I had the pleasure of meeting Maria shortly after she moved to St. James Place, when I held the first Rotarian book fair for residents' children's home libraries. She stopped and helped me sort books.

Spiritual Renewal at Cypress Springs Mercedarian Prayer Center

Maria is a devout Catholic, strong in her faith, who looks forward to her periodic visits to pray with Sister Dulce Maria at the Cypress Springs Prayer Center. She has volunteered with the sick of mind, heart, and health with Sister Dulce. She has also volunteered with Christmas projects in any way possible. "It helped me feel good and to fully forget my weaknesses."

Takeaways

So that in the ages to come, He might show the surpassing riches of His grace in kindness toward us in Christ Jesus.
 —Ephesians 2:7

My God shall supply all your need according to His riches in glory by Christ Jesus.
 —Philippians 4:19

Following Jesus is such a paradox. It requires death and promises life.
 —Daniel Colston

WALKING THROUGH THE SHADOW: MY PERSONAL JOURNAL

Fall 2016

I was hospitalized twice, and heart conversion to normal rhythm was unsuccessful. The first time, I told God I was not afraid to die, yet hoped to share my faith message later that month when I was invited to speak at the St. Joseph Cathedral luncheon. I was weak, but I spoke.

My second hospitalization was for six days and once again was unsuccessful. I told God that if He was ready, I would step through the door with Him. I had hoped to finish a book I was writing.

Later, I solved that concern by making sure staff had all the chapters. I constantly updated contact information—editor, publisher, CPA for payment. I strongly encourage relieving fear and concern. . . . It is possible!

December 5, 2016—Another Path with Deeper Meaning

I am awed each time God opens a new path. I thought I was writing another book because I love to write! He always has a deeper walk, as revealed in the title of my inspirational memoir, *He Lays the Stones for Our Steps*.

You will be with me in spirit, I pray, as you perhaps identify with some of my chronic illnesses. Hopefully, as I walk through the shadow, faith-filled and unafraid, you will have that same faith to embark on a journey we will all take. . . .

I am a cancer survivor and presently have 20/40 eyesight, which means I see at 20 feet what most see at 40 feet, and I use magnification six reading glasses, the highest number available. Your guess is right—macular degeneration.

However, I have greater blessings—a spring in my step and love in my heart, feeling great except that I have a jaded appetite. I was totally unprepared for the reading of my pacemaker. I had assumed the second hospitalization for A-fib conversion was successful, although I know I have advanced heart disease, another inherited condition. The reading showed that over the last 165 days my heart has gone in and out of A-fib, losing efficiency totaling four hours each day. This is congestive heart failure, and I know my path ahead. I have been through this with my mother and others.

On Being Girded for Life and Death

We all have different stories and may not have faced the reality that none of us will live forever. Let's live life in its fullness, just as Margaret Oswald set the example as revealed in her story in this book. Yes, living a faith-filled life, with joy and passion for others, girds us for death. Now I realize why God sent me on His mission to share the lives revealed in this book. We can all gain perspective and identity as we approach death—what I believe is stepping through the door of death with Him. I pray that we never forget that as we walk through the shadow, God is with us.

Cicero reminds us that our lives live on after death: "The life of the dead is placed in the memory of the living."

December 22, 2016—A New Awakening

I awoke last night softly singing one hymn line after another, which paralleled my experience in Gestalt therapy in my 50s. In my memoir I wrote, "I began to wonder when I would know that it was time for me to leave group therapy sessions." Unexpectedly one session, the litany in my brain, *I'm lovable, I'm lovable*, had changed to one line of a hymn after another, in rapid succession. I wrote, "I had arrived at total acceptance of God's love and His gift of deep inner grace." God was reminding me last night that He never leaves our side. In our humanness, we must never forget, even more so, as we approach the shadow. . . .

1980s—Who Am I?

This was a period of my life when I was exploring *Healing the Child Within,* through pastoral Gestalt therapy and later, Group Gestalt. I also took a course in the enneagram, a study of nine interconnecting personality types. I was quick to see my predominant type was Type 3, *the Achiever*, a journey I began when I was 15. Having never lived with electricity, running water, or a telephone, I boarded the Panama Limited train en route to Chicago, where I represented the state of Louisiana in 4-H leadership. My journey as an Achiever had begun. My side-wing personality type is *the Helper.* In those days, I could meet someone and in less than two hours, I knew their personality type. My daughter is a Helper with a side-wing of Achiever, a fortunate relationship as we became business partners.

    After Susan, my only child, graduated in interior design, we opened Fireside Antiques and I moved my office there. I continued designing and building homes, fulfilling my dominant Achiever role. Within four years, Susan left her Achiever role (her son was 14) and fulfilled her dominant role of Helper. Within two weeks of her in vitro pregnancy with quadruplets, spending part of each day in bed, I ended my 27-year career as a designer and home builder, and managed Fireside for seventeen years while Susan raised her children.

Fall 2003—Retiring at 75, I Began My Most Meaningful Years

Susan and Jim moved from our family compound in West Feliciana so that their children could attend school in Baton Rouge. Now that they were older, Susan wanted to resume her management role at Fireside.

    I had fulfilled sixty years as an Achiever in exciting, creative careers. Now I could more fully serve as a Helper. Thus, at age 75, I dedicated the rest of my life to humanitarian work, as my mother did at the same age. She died at age 94, still focusing on service to others.

January 2004—God's Call to Mexico

For four years in Mexico, I became a true humanitarian, joining Rotary and serving as grants writer in Rotary International, as detailed in my memoir. When the high altitude began taking its toll on my heart, I moved back to Baton Rouge.

My cardiologist asked me recently if I thought I would live forever. "No," I said. "Perhaps I did at age 75, but I hope the humanitarian projects I founded will."

January 5, 2017—Could It Be a Heart Attack?

I tried several things and foolishly dragged my feet, though I knew I was in trouble. I had had too many calls to 911. . . . Today the 911 emergency personnel were alarmed by my erratic heartbeat.

En route to the Our Lady of the Lake Hospital emergency room, I was at peace and not afraid to die, wishing only to have reached my daughter and realizing no one had my book chapters in their computer.

Tests and bloodwork revealed I had not had a heart attack. They showed that I had fluid in my lungs, despite continued diuretics and weight loss. Diuretic by IV eliminated the excess fluid.

During these two days, I learned to drink water only when thirsty, and to take only two sips. My advice to everyone: Mend any bridges separating you from family or friends. If you have not accepted God's gift of abundant grace, pray and seek your forgiveness of self. This is the only path to the peace that passeth all understanding.

January 18, 2017—Continuing Weight Loss

Today was a follow-up visit about chronic A-fib, which I will have the rest of my life. I had lost five more pounds. My cardiologist gave careful directions to add additional diuretics to my one daily, depending on weight gain or breathing problems, thus preventing emergency room visits when possible. This regime has worked, once I quit focusing on my weight loss of 20%.

(Please forgive me if I am boring some of you, as you have enough medical visits of your own. I pray that how I am able to *walk through the shadow* might be an inspiration to some who might feel deserted, to *once again feel the love and peace of God*.)

February 4, 2017—A Day Out

Today a friend and I are going to lunch at the Houmas House, so named for the Houmas Indians who once lived in the area. The Burnside Plantation, on which the home sits, was established in the late 1700s and the home was built in 1840. It, like so many plantations that line the banks of the Mississippi River, was positioned for easy access to ship agricultural products. Long before the levees were built, rich silt coming downriver was deposited on adjacent land. The vast fields and plantation home gardens thrived in hot, humid summers.

It is a cool, sunny February day, and I am excited to once again walk through the gardens filled with live oak trees with limbs reaching to the ground for support; the water features and European statuary. . . .

We will see our shadows, undimmed by age and health issues, or past losses. I continue to bask in the joy of living *in the now*. . . .

After lunch at Houmas House, we traveled the historic River Road to Reserve, to interview legendary jazz musician Jimmy Jules.

February 7, 2017—Macular Degeneration

I have been fighting inherited macular degeneration since 2009.

A miracle happened today. I read three of the four lines on

the eye chart. After further testing, I received another eye injection. God was *paving the way* for the finishing of this book. How else can we explain this?

March 21, 2017—A-fib 97 Percent of the Time

Saw my cardiologist for a three-month checkup. The monitoring of my pacemaker revealed I had been in A-fib 97% of the time in the last three months. My weight loss had continued despite emphasis on a healthy diet. On his way out, the doctor made the sign of the cross on his chest.

March 22, 2017—Macular Degeneration

Had injection 26 after being stable three years. I was encouraged as I read three lines once again on the eye chart and received another injection. Increasingly, it is harder to read headlines in our newspaper. I haven't resorted to reading the newspaper online yet. My biggest challenge is that my right hand moves over a key on the computer, trying, I assume, to compensate for total loss of central vision in my left eye. Regardless, I have a book to finish!

June 20, 2017—Accepting Reality, Laughter vs. Fear and Tears

The reading of my pacemaker revealed I have been in A-fib 99.9% of the time. The last three months, my doctor has confirmed that staying busy, rather than reflecting on health, is a positive. As we went out the door, I told him he failed to make the sign of the cross as he did last visit. As we laughed he said, "You don't need it." Laughter, instead of fear and tears—God's gift.

July 4, 2017—Head Start with the Fireworks

Early morning, still dark, the 4th of July red lights were twirling above the ambulance as I thought, *God, we are navigating together.* A recent blog from Nick Abraham, psychologist, had explained that *an optimist navigates through a problem, realizing this too will pass. . . .*

For two days, I had not eaten and was sleeping around the clock. An esophagus-gram showed a suspicious lesion that appeared to be a partial hole burned in the side of my esophagus. I had told the emergency room doctor that I was taking an antibiotic for a stye in my eye. He said it was bad on tissue. Word of caution, we should never take medication and lie down!

I was beginning to feel better, and with fears of blood thinner, I chose not to have an upper GI.

July 19, 2017—A Broken Tooth

Today, a tooth broke off as I used a toothpick. I spent the morning in the dentist's chair for what was assumed would be a root canal. My dentist said the nerve had died and my body had built sufficient calcium to anchor the new tooth, without an expensive root canal.

October 23, 2017—Take Me Home Lord, Take Me Home . . .

I was dreaming . . . I was in outer space, filled with peace and tranquility, looking back down to earth, realizing life's tensions had let me go . . . *Take me home Lord, Take me home Lord* were the words on my lips as I awoke, with deep pain across my entire chest. . . . As I reached for the nitroglycerine, I thought I was dying. Then the concern that I wanted to finish this book, quickly allayed with the realization that staff had all of my chapters . . . peace again. Regretfully, the three nitro tablets taken five minutes apart left me with that all-too-familiar 911 call.

This time the pain was almost a ten. I had not had a heart attack, which the doctor said was a good sign. It had been six years since I had the second 90% blockage removed by a stent. To have a heart catheter, if this pain continues, means coming off blood thinners for five days, with the possibility of having a stroke or heart attack. I agreed with my cardiologist to forgo any procedures, electing quality of life over quantity. I will continue eight years of visiting and singing with Alzheimer's residents, serving humanity through Rotary, perhaps writing another book . . . until *our Lord walks through the hour of death with me.*

      I have found a place of peace and tranquility with Him. I am unafraid. . . .

To adapt a saying from Methodism founder John Wesley:

I will do all the good I can,
By all the means I can,
In all the ways I can,
In all the places I can,
At all the times I can,
To all the people I can,
As long as ever I can.

Another Wesley prayer is my prayer: *God, grant that I may never be useless.*

These links share more of my humanitarian work:

Weekends with Whitney:
https://www.youtube.com/watch?v=rjL9VFjicYQ at 10:29 minutes.

Your Mark on the World, Cheri McDaniel:
yourmarkontheworld.com/tag/cheri-mcdaniel/

Takeaways

Idleness is to the human mind like rust to iron.
    —Ezra Cornell

When faith replaces doubt, when selfless service eliminates selfish striving, the power of God brings to pass His purposes.
—Thomas S. Monson

It is one of the most beautiful compensations of life, that no man can sincerely try to help another without helping himself.
—Ralph Waldo Emerson

LOVING GIFTS FOR OUR FAMILY

There are very important *gifts* we should prepare for our family, thus relieving them of the stress of having to assume what our wishes are.

Living Will

This document is not actually a will; it simply makes clear our wishes concerning medical treatment in the event that we cannot communicate them ourselves. In my own case, I have filed papers giving my primary care physician the authority to make end-of-life decisions for me if I become incapacitated.

Donor Designation

Many years ago, I signed to be an organ donor at my death. A small red heart with the word *Donor* underneath, on a driver's license or identification card, indicates our wishes.

Obituary

My family has a copy I wrote. I encourage you to access the reading list at the back of this book and read the article "How to Write Your Own Obituary." Your family will be grateful!

Funeral Arrangements

Your family will want to know whether you want a church service or other memorial service, and who should preside. If you have favorite hymns, make that known as well. (Mine are "How Great Thou Art" and "In the Garden," which I want led by granddaughter Sarah Roland.)

Disposal of Body

Tell your loved ones if you desire cremation or a traditional burial. My own grave marker is soldered from Gothic fragments from a European church, and I have shown family members where it is to be placed in our family compound—under the circa 1790 live oak, one of ten trees registered with the Life Oak Society, in the names of grand- and great-grandchildren. There are others growing, awaiting the names of future generations.

      Until my death, my grave marker is flanked with plants in my living room, seen by some as symbolic of a church, the Trinity, the wise men. . . .

An Executor

Be sure to designate the person you want to handle your will, or a trust if you own property. The trust eliminates probate proceedings.

Part VI

Centenarians

The centenarians I interviewed exhibited contagious laughter and joy, with no mention of death. That is why I put their stories last in this book, after the "Facing Your Own Mortality" section, as the fear of death is no longer evident.

According to *US News and World Report,* a growing number of Americans are living to age 100. The number has grown almost 66% over the past three decades. Nevertheless, Americans lag behind Europeans in longevity. And the Japanese have the most centenarians—3.43 for every 100,000 people.

105-YEAR-OLD MILLIE SAUCIER WOOD GLADNEY: DOING IT MILLIE'S WAY

The St. James Place Assisted Living parlor was filled on April 7, 2017, with Millie's fellow residents and her son Robert and his wife Maryetta. The Jimmy Jules Jazz Band was led by 80-year-old Jimmy. When the music began, Millie danced out in a brilliant blue dress to her seat of honor. A TV cameraman and *Baton Rouge Advocate* reporter were recording the celebration.

Robert said that each time he comes from his Texas home to visit, she asks, "When is the Lord going to take me?" His pet answer is, "Mama, God has His way of doing things and He doesn't want you telling Him what to do!"

Millie's Move to St. James Place

Maintaining her home to her perfectionistic standards and living alone was the impetus for moving to St. James Place in 2001. Millie selected one of the new garden homes that was part of a significant expansion of the facility at that time. Many fish in the pond behind her garden home took her bait.

Bill Morgan, who lives with his wife Helen in a nearby garden home, shared this story of their rescue and Millie's fishing: "Several years ago, a buddy visited us for the first time, so we toured him around our house. Quickly, we noticed someone in long pants fishing on the other side of the lake, who then fell back-of-the-head into the water at lake's edge. We rushed over. It was a lady, not a man! She was hanging onto her fishing pole with a nice bass intact. A self-sufficient Millie Gladney, then in her late '90s, really didn't want our help getting up the lake bank and into her home. After she put her catch into an iced container, we insisted on calling the St. James Place nurse to make sure Millie was fine. She resisted strongly, but finally gave in, worried that with a report, her son would stop her from fishing. But days later, Millie was back fishing again. What a lady!"

Millie lived independently in her garden home until 2011, when she moved to the Assisted Living area. I recall attending a concert in the Duplantier Auditorium at the other end of the St. James Place campus. Millie had recently moved to Assisted Living at the age of 99, yet was leading us down halls to our apartments, walking with long strides and no walker. Fortunately, she continues with good eyesight, despite impaired hearing.

Much of the following description of Millie's early life is taken from *History of Avoyelles Parish,* by Corinne L. Saucier.

An Easter Birth

In *History of Avoyelles Parish,* Corinne L. Saucier describes Millie's birth:

"In 1912, Easter Sunday fell on April 7. In Marksville, Louisiana, Dr. Merrick E. Saucier and his wife Florence were excited that their second child was to be born. Dr. Saucier left his wife's side to run across the street to buy some cigars to pass out to his friends in celebration of the birth, and in the short time he was gone, Florence gave birth to a baby girl. They named her Mildred (Millie). Maxwell, their first born, a son, was two years old."

"Dr. Saucier had met Florence Hasson of Gueydan while in residence in surgery at the New Orleans Charity Hospital and she in the nursing school. After marriage, it seemed natural for him to return to his hometown to begin his practice as a surgeon. But in that era, the Southern Pacific Railroad completed the stretch from New Orleans to Houston, which resulted in a huge population growth in southwest Louisiana. When Mildred was just past one year of age, the Sauciers made the decision to move to Lafayette, seeing it as an expanding market to ply his trade in surgery."

Dr. Saucier Becomes a Lafayette Rotarian and Mason

According to *History of Avoyelles Parish,* Dr. Saucier established his practice in Lafayette and became president of the local Rotary Club. He founded the Rotary Boys Band and was an active Mason. He was a busy man, appointed to the Louisiana State Board of Education and instrumental in construction of the Lafayette Sanitarium. During the historic 1927 Mississippi flood, thousands of people from surrounding areas came to Lafayette to escape the high water. "Florence inoculated them as they arrived, and Dr. Saucier delivered many babies that came to term provoked by the escape from the flood."

Diagnosis of His Own Pending Death

Dr. Saucier diagnosed his own impending fatal heart attack. It occurred the night his son graduated from SLI, while Millie was at a boarding school in Vicksburg, Mississippi. She was able to make it back to talk to her father before he died. "I have always been proud that you were a little lady. I want you to always be a lady," he said to her. Dr. Saucier was only 48.

Six months later, Florence underwent surgery for a ruptured ovary.

Maxwell's Tragic Early Death

Maxwell had completed his first year at Tulane Medical School when he made plans to drive to Lincoln, Nebraska, with his good friend Johnny Morris from Abbeville. Johnny was set to compete in an AAU track meet in Nebraska, in which he hoped to qualify as a hurdler for the coming Olympic Games. Somewhere in Arkansas, Maxwell began to feel ill. He checked into a Lincoln hospital on a Friday. Johnny had to run heats on Saturday morning. When he went to the hospital to check on Maxwell, he was in a coma. No doctor had seen him over the weekend. Johnny called Florence.

Aviation was in its infancy in Louisiana, but pioneer Jimmy Wedell based his flying speed planes in Patterson. Arrangements were made and Millie drove her mother and Dr. Hamilton to the Patterson airport. As they boarded the small plane, Millie pleaded, "Mama, I want to go." The plane departed with Jimmy, Dr. C. E. Hamilton, Florence, and Millie sitting in her lap.

Arriving at the hospital, they found Maxwell in a comatose state, and Florence was horrified to see the blisters on his feet from the nurses placing hot water bottles on them. He never came out of the coma and no autopsy was performed. Florence was convinced that she lost her son to a ruptured appendix. They returned to Lafayette by train, with Maxwell's casket in the luggage compartment. He had died at 21 years of age.

1930 and 1931, Devastating Years for the Saucier Family

After losing both her husband and her son, Florence fell into a deep depression. Millie, who was attending SLI, switched to LSU at her mother's suggestion. She made friends and also met a law student, C. C. "Red" Wood.

Millie decided to go to business school in New Orleans. Just before graduation, she received a letter from Red Wood: "If you're not married, I would like to come see you." She wrote back that she was still single and told him to come. Red had also lost his father, and was practicing at a law firm in Shreveport.

A Whirlwind Romance Leads to 1939 Wedding; Birth of Son Robert

A whirlwind romance ensued, and in September 1939, they were married in a grand affair orchestrated by Florence. After the wedding, they made Shreveport their home. Later, Red secured an assignment with the Louisiana attorney general's office in New Orleans.

They lived in an apartment near Audubon Park. In April of 1941, Millie had a difficult pregnancy. Her baby refused to be born. A decision was made to return to Lafayette for the birthing so Florence could assist with the baby. On February 4, 1942, her ten pound, five ounce baby boy was born. "We were planning on naming a boy Maxwell, but when he arrived he didn't look anything like Maxwell, so we named him Robert." Robert was a sickly child and almost died several times in the first few weeks of life. They decided to leave Robert with nurse Florence until he began to thrive.

Uncle Sam Points His Finger at Red Wood

December 7 was Red Wood's birthday. On his 29th, the Japanese attacked Pearl Harbor. A short time later, Germany declared war on the United States. Red thought he was too old, had a child, and would not be drafted. However, as he said, "Uncle Sam pointed his finger at me!" Mildred and Robert moved back to Lafayette for the duration of the war.

Wood took basic training at Camp Fannin, near Tyler, Texas. His unit received orders to cross the Atlantic to Southampton, England, to prepare to join the fight.

Fierce Fighting in France, Belgium; Wood Captured in Germany

They crossed the English Channel in mid-August in a replacement infantry battalion to be assigned to the 30th Infantry Division. They fought through France, Belgium, and Holland. Hitler knew that the Allies would consider Aachen their first target on German soil and ordered it defended at all costs. Wood's undersized company had been placed a little north of Aachen at a roadblock, when Panzer tanks counterattacked and overran their position. Wood and his foxhole buddy sought protection in an abandoned farmhouse cellar. The Germans searched the house, and when they opened the cellar door Wood and his buddy chose to surrender, in hopes of not being killed.

Mildred's Role in the War Effort

In Lafayette, the Red Cross had set up a canning facility behind Lafayette High School to collect foodstuffs, cigarettes, and other items for the troops. Millie would be there often to prepare hams, chickens, cakes, etc. . . . Red had written that he was more starved for information on the war than anything. Millie sent *Time* and *Newsweek* magazines to him as well. Sadly, it all came back marked "Undeliverable." There was a big box just inside Florence's front door that collected returns. *Why did they send it back?*, she wondered. *They should have just given it all to some other soldier if they couldn't give it to Red!*

Telegram from War Department: "We regret to inform you . . ."

In October 1944, a telegram from the War Department arrived with an embossed red star. "We regret to inform you that your husband, Private C. C. Wood, has been reported missing in action." Devastation for Millie! Would he return? Thanksgiving passed, then Christmas. It became 1945. Almost a month after he wrote Millie, on December 11, a postcard arrived from Stalag II-B. The postman came running up the front walk yelling, "He is alive! He is alive!" The message was short and censored: "I have been a prisoner of war since October 9th, and am all right."

    Red Wood did come home. Stalag II-B, in Pomerania, Poland, was liberated by the British 9th Army. He was flown to England, fed and clothed, and in time crossed the Atlantic to the West. Millie got another telegram. He would be on a troop train destined for Camp Shelby in Hattiesburg, Mississippi. Millie waited on the platform. When the train arrived, a strange figure approached her. He had left weighing 180 pounds, with thick red hair and pearly white teeth. Malnutrition had changed Red, now weighing 112 pounds. Millie was able to identify his voice when he spoke.

    Millie had groomed Robert to near perfection. One of his curls would not cooperate, and she placed a clip to hold it in place. He was waiting on the front steps when the car carrying his parents arrived. "Boy, what in the hell is that in your hair?"

    Red was still in the Army, stationed at Fort Lee, Virginia. Millie made an extended visit to Richmond. He was discharged from the Army on November 30, 1945, with a Purple Heart.

Wood Appointed Attorney for the Louisiana Department of

Public Works

Early in 1946, C. C. Wood was named to the position of attorney for the Louisiana Department of Public Works. The Wood family decided to live in Baton Rouge, despite Millie's affection for Lafayette. After all, her former roommate at LSU had been largely responsible for lifting her spirits after the death of her father. Her brother was in Baton Rouge. The other love of Red's life was the LSU Tigers. So Baton Rouge became their home.

Within a year, they bought a house in University Hills. It was an ideal place to raise Robert. Millie, who had always enjoyed having her hands in the dirt, planted colorful azaleas and learned to graft camellias. Wherever Millie lived, she strived to make her home and gardens a showplace. Robert is quick to say his mother was an excellent cook and anyone who never partook of her gumbos and soups had missed out!

In 1961, the Wood family moved to Meadow Lea subdivision just east of Southdowns. Shortly afterwards, C. C. "Red" Wood became attorney for the secretary of state's office. He would remain in that position until September 1979, when he had a stroke, which led to his death.

Millie grew even more independent as the years rolled by. A year after she became a widow, her mother passed away in Lafayette at the age of 96. Robert and his wife Mary Etta were living and working in Houston. She took up china painting as a hobby and joined an investment club called the Sharks, became a member of the Novel Club, and was a regular at the Mary Bird Perkins Cancer Center as a volunteer. She also took trips around the globe to see many of the world's star attractions. Six years passed.

Her Passion for Fishing

There was something else that Millie was attracted to, and that was the sport of fishing. As it happened, a widower lived four houses down the street in Meadow Lea, a retiring banker named Bill

Gladney. Bill had a camp on Belle River, and before you knew it, he and Millie were regularly trekking down there to go fishing. On one occasion, Bill suggested they stay down there so they could fish the next day too. "But Bill," Millie objected, "we can't spend the night together; we're not married."

Wedding Bells for Millie, 72, and Bill, 84

The wedding between 84-year-old Bill and 72-year-old Millie was a grand affair with a large reception at the Baton Rouge Country Club. When Wally Gladney, Bill's youngest son, delivered the newlywed couple to the Baton Rouge airport, in a car decorated for their honeymoon trip, the skycap exclaimed, "Now I have seen everything!"

It wasn't the last trip they took together. They traveled to numerous destinations, some as far away as New Zealand and Australia, as well as to the Caribbean, where Robert and Mary Etta were cruising on their own sailing yacht. An annual event was to the American Bankers Association conventions as Bill was a member of their board of directors.

Bill Gladney died from cancer in September of 1993, with Millie nursing him to the very end. He was often heard saying to her, "I don't mind being henpecked just as long as you are the hen."

Robert and Mary Etta have no children. Millie's lineage will end at her death. *Wow!* What a life!

Takeaways

Fishing is much more than fish. It is the great occasion when we may return to the fine simplicity of our forefathers.
—Herbert Hoover

Our greatest glory is not in never falling, but in rising every time

we fall.
        —Confucius

The very basic core of a man's living spirit is his passion for adventure.
        —Christopher McCandless

"*I REMEMBER* . . .: LIFE STORIES BY MARNIE": MARGARET GRIER BESTE, AGE 102

I first met Margaret Beste in the St. James Place writing group, begun in 1997, which I joined upon my move here in 2008. I always enjoyed Margaret's interesting and beautifully written stories. In the absence of a computer, Margaret relied on her friend and neighbor Philip Pizzolato to type her writings, filling 170 typed pages, in her book titled *I Remember*. . . .

As I was just learning the computer at age 80, necessitated by my new role as Capital City Rotary Club's service chair and grants writer, Marilyn Rosenson volunteered to type for me.

When God inspired me to write and publish my first book, *He Lays the Stones for Our Steps* (sales to help fund Rotary projects), I devoted many hours to writing my memoirs, hired a transcription service, dropped out of the writing group, and lost track of Margaret.

What a delight to renew our friendship! She answered my questions, usually with the aid of her caregiver Eleanor, while she burst into song and laughter, as free as a bird. With her love of music, still line-dancing until age 100, coupled with the companionship and care of her dear Eleanor, she may well make that 113th birthday as she predicted!

"We've both got eleven more years in us!"

During our interview, Margaret kept saying she was not 102 years old. When Eleanor reminded her she had been her companion for eleven years, Margaret laughingly agreed, "We've both got eleven more years in us!" And she may, considering how she lives with music in her heart and on her lips and in her quiet contentment with her companion. . . .

I am drawing on her book of stories, which are not in the sequence of her life but in the order in which she chose to write.

The Early Years

Margaret was born in a suburb of Pittsburgh, Pennsylvania. The household was composed of her parents, James Harper Grier, a preacher, and Jeanie Elizabeth McKee Grier; Margaret's grandmother, Margaret Sophia Templeton McKee; and Margaret's great-grandmother, Mary Elizabeth Biddle Templeton, who was heard to say, "Another woman in the family!" Margaret was an only child.

Many of the chapters in Part I of her book attest to her love of music. She begins her third chapter, "My Father James Harper Grier," with these words: "I first thought of calling him 'My Dad,' for that is what I called him. But he was a man of dignity in a very proper time." James Harper was born in a small Pennsylvania town, the son of a Presbyterian preacher from that area, who later became president of the Pittsburgh Theological Seminary.

"The war to end all wars"

Her fourth chapter begins with "Over There, Over There," a World War I song. (This brings back fond memories of my father, a World War I veteran, who became draft age too late to be sent overseas. I can still *see* the moonlit backyard and barn as I sat on his knee, on the back step of our four-room frame house, singing, "Over there, Over there.")

Margaret was two years old in 1917, when World War I broke out, the war to end all wars. She wrote, "My dad, a minister wanted to do his part, joined a YMCA group of 57 men, all from the Pittsburgh area, who sailed from New York in a convoy of ships. On the long voyage, they published a newsletter, titled *Mid-Ocean Pickle.* The reference was to the Pittsburgh headquarters of the H. J. Heinz Company that advertised '57 varieties.'"

The night before they were to land in France, the *Oronsa* was torpedoed by a German U-boat and sank in twelve minutes, during five of which Margaret's dad slept. When he awoke in the dark, he found his way up the stairs to the open deck, which by that time was level with the sea. He stepped directly into a small lifeboat that was picked up by another ship in the convoy, and landed the next morning on the coast of Ireland, in his pajamas.

Fortunately for Margaret's mother, the first she heard of the incident was a telegram from the YMCA saying that all 57 were saved.

Her Parents' Deaths

In her next two chapters, Margaret talks of her mother's death in 1964, and her father's only nine months later. Margaret felt he died from a broken heart.

She continued her nostalgic journey with family, writing chapters on her grandparents, her mother's cousin, and her own cousin.

Westward Ho!

We begin our journey with Margaret to Monmouth, Illinois, to a liberal arts college affiliated with the Presbyterian church. We can hear her singing the college song, "Onward Monmouth," as well as "Auld Lang Syne," "Nostalgia," and another Monmouth song, "If You Want to Be a Badger Come Along with Me."

She received her master of arts degree from Monmouth.

New York, New York

In the summer of 1937, Margaret returned to Monmouth and became engaged to George Beste. She titled this chapter "Oh Promise Me." She wrote, "My thoughts turned to getting some kind of work to occupy my time and efforts, until he got out of Columbia and got settled somewhere." Margaret went to New York, where she did secretarial work, followed by two years at the Brooklyn Friends School.

In 1939, she took leave from her job and returned to her parents' home to prepare for her wedding.

Baton Rouge

After their marriage, George went to work with Ethyl Corporation in Baton Rouge. When their daughter, Jeanie, was eight months old, President Franklin Roosevelt announced that World War II had begun. Their son Jim was born in 1944.

Margaret wrote ten chapters about her happy life shared with George and their two children.

Adventures Abroad, 1957

These chapters, not surprisingly, are titled "To Go or Not to Go," followed by "Europe 1957." As George was director of administration of research and development at Ethyl, his boss asked how he would like to take a trip to Europe, to set up basic research departments for chemistry professors in various countries to develop marketable products. Ethyl was considering universities in Holland, France, England, Scotland, Ireland, Germany, Austria, Italy, and perhaps Norway and Sweden. He further added that George could take his family with him.

This blew Margaret's mind. She had spent six weeks with her parents in Europe when she was eleven and loved every minute. What would 15-year-old Jeanie and 11-year-old Jim think?

Although some readers have just met Margaret, I am sure you know what happened . . . of course the family went, to the dismay of their teenagers. Her chapters as they traversed Europe for eight months read like a fascinating travelogue. Now you will understand that I asked Jeanie if she had ever considered publishing her mother's book. I hope she does someday.

More Travels

In her later chapter "Play It Again, Sam," she describes how son Jim has joined the Peace Corps after college graduation. George and Margaret cannot resist going to visit him at his first assignment, Morocco. In the summer of 1950, both she and George retire and head to . . . (surely we all guessed right) . . . Europe! There are stories, not necessarily in chronological order, about New Zealand and Australia, the Middle East, Hong Kong,

Thailand. She describes Bangkok as "beautiful, exotic, hot, fascinating, noisy."

Life at St. James Place

In her chapter "One More Gate to Pass," Margaret begins, "It is 1992 when we finally locked the door of our Knollwood Drive home that we had built and loved, and moved to St. James Place. We believed we had passed through our last gate in Baton Rouge. It was fourteen years later when we found one more gate—George was moved to the Health and Wellness building."

Fortunately, St. James Place is a continuing care facility, providing options as needs change. George had experienced numerous stumbles and falls, making the move necessary. She ends that chapter with this line, "In some ways George and I are closer than ever before. I count my blessings."

Margaret's book ends without her writing about George's death in 2010, nor about her move to Highland Court Assisted Living, for residents with some memory issues.

I am sure we will all agree, Margaret Beste has experienced life in its fullness, and has a heart still filled with music and laughter.

And for all of us who think we have seen the world, compared to Margaret, we are just getting started. . . .

Takeaways

The world is a book, and those who do not travel read only one page.
—Saint Augustine

A good traveler has no fixed plans, and is not intent on arriving.
—Lao Tzu

To travel is to take a journey into yourself.
—Danny Kaye

LUMINA "MINA" NEWCHURCH: AN ANGEL IN OUR MIDST

If you call and Mina doesn't answer, please wait for the message: "This is New Angels Haven, Michael. Raphael and Gabriel are busy polishing their halos and cannot greet you at this time. However, if you will leave a short message, Michael, Raphael, or Gabriel will return your call or the Head Angel, Mina Newchurch, will return your call as soon as possible please. Thank you."

I am sure you may be puzzled. Michael, Raphael, and Gabriel, commonly known as the three archangels, are among Head Angel Mina's collection of 4,500 angels.

Mina is becoming quite a celebrity! The Ascension Catholic Alumni Association honored her with a scroll:

> OUR OLDEST LIVING ALUMNA,
> MISS "MINA" NEWCHURCH
> IS 101 YEARS "YOUNG" AND
> AS BEAUTIFUL AS EVER

These excerpts from the *Catholic Commentator*'s article on Mina Newchurch, by Richard Meek, December 9, 2016, tell it all:

> Walk into Lumina Newchurch's apartment and one is immediately mesmerized by thousands of angels, each inviting a visitor to sit for a spell.
>
> The angels are in all shapes and sizes, can be seen on a clock, towels, napkins and even a shower curtain. But spend just a few minutes with Newchurch, affectionately known as "Aunt Mina," and one immediately realizes that perhaps the real angel is the lady sitting in her favorite chair, her prayer book and rosary always by her side.
>
> "She is faithful to her prayers," said Father Paul Yi, chancellor for the Diocese of Baton Rouge, who as a newly ordained priest at St. Aloysius Church in Baton Rouge several years ago was first introduced to Newchurch. "She believes in angels and their wonderful intercessory vocation for all of us." . . .
>
> Newchurch's life is one that could fill a storybook. At the least, it provides a firsthand glimpse into a much simpler time,

long before smart phones and laptop computers.

Born September 21, 1916, in Paincourtville along the shores of Bayou Lafourche, Newchurch did not enjoy the luxury of electricity until she was seven years old. Such modern conveniences as a telephone and television would come much later. After-school activities included hauling coal, helping younger siblings with their homework, or cleaning coal lamps.

Ice came in large blocks, delivered by the "ice man" every other day. Meat also came via a deliveryman on a horse and buggy.
. . .

From the beginning was her devotion to prayer and church, instilled in her by her Catholic parents. But her youthful memories of church likely differ from many. She remembers a time at St. Elizabeth Church in Paincourtville when the priest would preach the homily in French and then English. During the homily the men would go outside for a smoke. When men went to confession, or "Easter duties" as Newchurch said it was called then, women were not allowed into the church because Paincourtville is a small town and "they didn't want the women to say this man did not go to confession and this one did."

She remembers how once a year, on a Sunday, a sale was held when families would buy a pew for a $25 annual fee.

"Nobody else got in your pew," she said. "In a small town something like that never happened."

A Calling to Become a Nun

Newchurch's faith was so deep that at a young age she followed what she believed to be a vocational calling to become a nun and spent three years at a convent operated by the Ursuline Sisters in Missouri, only to be told she would not be accepted for her final vows. Although she was never officially informed of the reason, Newchurch believes it was because of health reasons since she had endured a health scare that included double pneumonia as a young child.

"Daddy wasn't thrilled about me going to the convent," she

said. "When I left (home) he told me, 'I'm not coming to see you unless to get you out.' I called him (when she was not accepted) and said, 'Come get me.'"

"The Lord has led me through many roads," she said, flashing an infectious smile that is as warm as it is genuine. "My whole life has been wonderful. I feel so blessed."

After graduating from Loyola University in New Orleans in 1937 with a bachelor of science degree, Newchurch spent five years teaching in Donaldsonville, Belle Rose, and back in Missouri before landing a job at a defense plant in Lake Charles, where she would spend two years and even help in managing a local CYO. In 1944, she embarked on a 38-year career with Exxon, a move that would bring her closer to home and play a major influence in her life.   Shortly after landing the job, she was able to purchase a black-and-white television for her dad, which she financed for $20 a month.

Eventually, she moved from her downtown apartment to a house in St. Aloysius Church Parish in 1957. For many years, she attended daily Mass at Sacred Heart of Jesus Church in Baton Rouge.

It was by happenstance early in her 38-year career at Exxon when she developed a passion for collecting angels. She recalls sharing coffee with coworkers one night and "everybody asked me what did I collect?"

"I thought in my dumbness that I had to collect something to live in Baton Rouge."

At that point she remembered that a secretary "for one of the big shots at LSU" had been collecting angels for several years, and a "light went on in my brain."

"I went home that night and decided I was going to collect angels," said Newchurch, adding that her mother's middle name was Angelle, which is French for angel. . . .

"The Church is my life"

"I've had marvelous spiritual directors," she said. "I tell you I have been blessed. My whole life has been wonderful. The Church is my life."

Newchurch has served in various ministries at St. Joseph Cathedral, Holy Family Church in Port Allen, Sacred Heart, St. Aloysius, and St. James Place, where she has been living since 2001. She helped coordinate and assist with weekly Catholic services at St. James until 2010. Turning 100, which she celebrated with a birthday party that attracted more than eighty family members, has now slowed Newchurch, who never married. She continues to put out a family bulletin, is involved with two prayer lists, and provides notary services at St. James Place at no charge to residents. . . .

Besides electricity, she said the biggest change she has seen is Vatican II. "I think (Vatican II) has been wonderful," she said. "I think the Mass in English should have been a blessing to everybody."

Newchurch spends much of her day in prayer, including praying the Angel Prayer daily, or putting the final touches on the family bulletin. . . .

Longevity

Newchurch has no answer for her longevity other than to say the Lord "isn't ready for me yet." But however long she lives, she knows her faith will never waver, although she admits to her own struggles. She said the roots of her faith are to surrender to God, but quickly added her new prayer at night is to learn patience.

"Oh yeah man, I have lived," she said. "The poor Lord, he thinks I'm crazy."

Takeaways

Love your neighbor as yourself. There is no other commandment greater . . .
　　　—Mark 12:31

Love does no harm to a neighbor. Therefore love is the fulfillment of the law.
      —Romans 13:10

And now these three remain: faith, hope and love. But the greatest of these is love.
      —1 Corinthians 13:13

ELDINE COLLIGAN'S LOVE OF LIFE

Eldine was only 16, living in Church Point, Louisiana, when she began noticing tall and handsome James Patrick Colligan, five years older. His mother had died when he was two years old. As his father traveled while working for the railroad, James Patrick and his sister Sarah were raised by their paternal grandparents.

James Patrick was working as deliveryman for the Church Point bakery, across the street from Eldine's Aunt Rose Simon's restaurant. Eldine would go after school to the restaurant to help her Aunt Rose.

Like most of us, Eldine said she felt older than her sixteen years. She kept her eye on the bakery, in hopes of seeing James Patrick ("Pat"), who might have a cup of coffee and perhaps talk with her. She graduated from high school in May 1935 at the age of 17 and worked at the Church Point post office, anticipating Pat's stops to pick up mail for the bakery.

Her Younger Years

Eddie Guidry, a building contractor, and his wife Ethel had four girls and two boys. Life was quiet and idyllic in small-town Church Point, settled by the Acadians in the late eighteenth century. Buggies were the main method of transport, earning the town the title "Buggy Capital of the World." Beginning in 1981, yearly buggy festivals have been held as fundraisers.

Guidry's home was raised, as many homes were, prior to the building of the world's longest levees along the Mississippi River after the Great Flood of 1927. The children loved to play under their home and build pretend roads. The girls had dollhouses. Children in the village could walk to school and to the nearby Our Lady of the Sacred Heart Catholic Church. Catholic churches were the centerpiece of many south Louisiana communities, and the church bells still chime the hours of the day.

Eldine's Prospects Grow

About a year and a half after Eldine's high school graduation, Pat asked if she would like to go to the movies with him. (His girlfriend had left to get a college education, rare for most girls in her day.) Eldine asked her father, and after he told her Pat was too old for her, he said not to be late. This was their very first date! When they returned to her home after the movies, she invited him to come in for a while and visit with her family. Pat continued with his courtship. . . .

Marriage and Honeymoon

Eldine and Pat were married at Our Lady of the Sacred Heart Catholic Church in Church Point on November 19, 1939. They borrowed her brother Berton's car for a short honeymoon and drove to Monroe, Louisiana, to visit Pat's parents.
     Pat had started a restaurant in Church Point across from the church, but later sold it and worked for the town of Church Point. Pat's best friend had married a young woman who came to teach school at Church Point, and the two couples enjoyed activities together.

Their Move to Port Sulphur

In 1941, they moved to Port Sulphur, Louisiana, a small Freeport Sulphur Company, a town site below New Orleans, now known as Freeport-McMoRan in Freeport. Pat was personnel supervisor and also served on the board of Delta Bank.
     Their first child, Linda, was born when Eldine was 24. Two other children died at birth.
     After Pat retired from Freeport Sulphur, they moved to Belle Chasse, where Pat worked for Delta Bank in human resources.

Their Move to Baton Rouge

At the age of 76, Pat retired again, and they moved to Baton Rouge at the request of their daughter. Linda is married to Dr. Aaron Roy, an ENT specialist, now retired. They have four children and six grandchildren.

Eldine and Pat made wonderful friends and enjoyed retirement life together until Pat's death in 1991, when Eldine was age 74. They had been married fifty-two years.

Eldine had always been independent and made friends easily. Although she missed Pat terribly, she continued to live in their home.

Moving to St. James Place

After about five years of living alone, Eldine decided it was time to move to St. James Place, near the home of Linda and Aaron. They travel frequently and have peace of mind that Eldine is happy and well cared for in their absence.

Eldine entered St. James Place as a Continuing Care resident, living first in Independent Living for ten years, followed by Assisted Living for three years, where she enjoyed arranging multiple bouquets of flowers weekly and played bingo daily. In late 2016, she moved to the Health and Wellness building, where she receives more nursing care. Attesting to her many friends and exceptional care, she says, "I am 'Living Life Well' and enjoying every minute!"

Eldine's life is good at age 100. She is surrounded with her own paintings of orchids, magnolias, and reminders of the nostalgic bayous and cypress trees of her life. Always pleasant, she reads and basks in the love of her husband's family, remembering Pat's great personality and their deep love for each other.

Takeaways

Marriage is the most natural state of man . . . the state in which you will find solid happiness.
 —Benjamin Franklin

Love Is a Many-Splendored Thing
    —title of a 1955 song and movie

Happy is the man who finds a true friend, and far happier is he who finds that true friend in his wife.
    —Franz Schubert

DR. ED HAWKINS, BORN JULY 19, 1917

What a wonderful opportunity to interview Dr. Hawkins this morning! His mind is bright, his twinkling eyes and friendliness are contagious. We celebrated his 100th birthday on July 19, 2017, in the St. James Place Health and Wellness building, where he moved from Independent Living following several strokes.

Dr. Hawkins's Favorite Town

When I asked his favorite of all remembrances, he said New York City. He wished that all young people would have an opportunity to experience it and hopefully get to live there for a while. Yes, New York has an aliveness, a vibrancy, unlike any other city.

Dr. Hawkins enjoyed walking down Madison Avenue window shopping, when he was not enjoying a musical or a classical music venue, among the many offerings of the city.

I am also a fan of New York, remembering the exhilaration I feel each time I travel there to experience Christmas at Rockefeller Center, plays on Broadway, the Rockettes, and the exciting, never-to-be-forgotten, watching the ball drop in Times Square on New Year Eve!

Early Years and the Military

Edward had three brothers and a sister, and was born in 1917, in Marion, Virginia, where his father was a merchant. He received his medical degrees at the University of Virginia.

He was a member of the US Naval Reserve for five years. He was called to serve as ship's officer/surgeon on a restored minelayer in the invasion of the South Pacific's treacherous seas, during the invasion of Okinawa and Iwo Jima. He said they were fortunate to have few casualties, aided by well-equipped hospital ships and port hospitals.

Dr. Hawkins's Career Path after the War

Edward, like most service members, was left with no money when

World War II ended. He was hired by Exxon Corporation in New York and served as plant physician in New Jersey, followed by a transfer to Exxon's Baton Rouge facility. Later he was transferred back to New York City, where he worked in their world headquarters for two years. During this time, he worked in Iran and, quoting him, "made the Grand European Tour, all on Exxon's dime."

Another of his exciting employment opportunities was in New Jersey, working for the famous Roebling Construction Company. The company's highest-profile project was building the Brooklyn Bridge.

Columbia Medical School

With no place left for Exxon to send him, Edward decided to freshen his medical skills and earned a degree in occupational medicine at Columbia University.

Dr. Hawkins retired at age 67 and bought a home small-town St. Francisville, Louisiana. He enjoyed vegetable gardening until he discovered there was too much shade to grow vegetables.

St. Francisville Library

Dr. Hawkins became a regular volunteer at the first St. Francisville library. Seeing the success of the small town's yearly Audubon Pilgrimage of historic homes, he envisioned the potential of an annual fundraiser for the library. Thus began the annual tour of five personal residences, known as Christmas in the Country. The first year, $3,000 was raised. Several years ago, when our two family country homes and extensive gardens were among the five homes shown, $10,000 was raised.

Moving to St. James Place

When Dr. Hawkins was 92, he moved to St. James Place as an independent resident. He has enjoyed his new home and only recently, I suspect with some resistance, moved from Independent Living to the Health and Wellness building, awaiting his 100th birthday.

Dr. Ed Hawkins's 100th Birthday Celebration

On July 15, 2017, the St. James Place Convocation Room was filled with both on- and off-campus friends greeting an animated and obviously happy Dr. Hawkins. Nancy Rinner, his niece from Chula Vista, California, had planned the festive gathering. Her daughter Rachael, Hawkins's grand-niece from Texas, and another from St. Francisville were in attendance.

Resourceful Ed

I asked the family if they had an amusing story to tell. Rachael recalled the Christmas when Ed came to spend a week with her mother's family. He arrived with a backpack, and when they asked where his clothes were, he replied, "You have a washer and dryer, don't you?" His backpack contained a t-shirt and a pair of pajamas, which was all he needed!

Takeaways

Kindness and a generous spirit go a long way. And a sense of humor. It's like medicine—very healing.
—Max Irons

Try to keep your soul young and quivering right up to old age.
—George Sand

The secret of genius is to carry the spirit of the child into old age, which means never losing your enthusiasm.
—Aldous Huxley

Epilogue

DR. ED HAWKINS AND ELDINE COLLIGAN ELECTED MARDI GRAS KING AND QUEEN

Louisianians love Mardi Gras, and age is no exception! On February 2, 2017, St. James Place Health and Wellness Center held its annual celebration reigned over by a radiant royal couple, Eldine Colligan and Dr. Ed Hawkins, both over 100 years young. And young they were, as lively music played and some danced, all with strings of bright, glittery Mardi Gras beads encircling their necks. Of course, it would not be Mardi Gras without traditional king cake. An understatement—a good time was had by all. . . .

My Observations

Age is a mindset, and we are in control! When I was corresponding with Helen Reisler, she wrote: "I love the title *Snazzy Seniors*, of course the purpose of your book. Many seniors do not realize that they have the option to lead full and meaningful lives. This book should also target a younger audience so young women have the inspiration to prepare themselves for more meaningful and interesting senior years. It's an attitude as well."

I thought Helen's reference to a "younger audience" rather strange, but rushed to another endeavor without processing what her statement fully meant.

God in His inevitable way stays ahead of us as "He lays the stones for our steps." Yesterday I invited a young woman, perhaps in her 30s, to lunch as I had heard she wanted to help feed schoolchildren in Haiti. She had visited the impoverished country over a year ago when her husband, a professional photographer, spent two weeks filming schools for an American-Haitian pastor. She said she often wakes during the night hearing hungry children crying. She had not been aware of Rotary and its over 100-year history of matching funds for humanitarian grants.

Before ending our two-hour visit plotting a course of action, she suddenly leaned back on my deep couch with a faraway look in her eyes and said, "Do you know what I am most afraid of? It's growing old." I immediately grasped what Helen meant about a "younger audience." I responded that despite my creative and exciting careers, my most meaningful years have been from 75 to my present age, 89. I project it may be years before she fully processes what I told her. Maybe, after reading *Snazzy Seniors,* she may begin to lose her fear and realize that while she is feeding hungry Haitian children, she is laying her foundation for fulfilling senior years. . . .

Some girls and young women dream of dressing up as queen of the Mardi Gras. Dreams live on as seniors are living longer, as evidenced by our 100-year young-at-heart queen and king!

RECOMMENDED READING

Brandon, Emily. "What People Who Live to 100 Have in Common," *US News and World Report,* January 7, 2013. https://money.usnews.com/money/retirement/articles/2013/01/07/what-people-who-live-to-100-have-in-common.

Eisenberg, Richard. "The Next Housing Crisis: Aging Americans' Homes." *Forbes,* September 22, 2014. https://www.forbes.com/sites/nextavenue/2014/09/02/the-next-housing-crisis-aging-americans-homes/#1ef66ab62edc.

"How Can I Learn Acceptance of an Alzheimer's Diagnosis?" *Baton Rouge Advocate,* February 26, 2017. http://www.theadvocate.com/baton_rouge/entertainment_life/health_fitness/article_79f94962-e4a5-11e6-acee-4fab374e9d31.html

"How to Write Your Own Obituary." Obituary Guide.com. http://www.obituaryguide.com/writeyourown.php.

"Laughter Is the Best Medicine." Helpguide.org. https://www.helpguide.org/articles/mental-health/laughter-is-the-best-medicine.htm.

Mather, Mark, Linda A. Jacobsen, and Kelvin M. Pollard. "Aging in the United States," *Population Bulletin* 70, no. 2 (2015). http://www.prb.org/pdf16/aging-us-population-bulletin.pdf.

Millard, Charles E. F. "Everybody in the Risk Pool." *Bloomberg View*, March 16, 2016. https://www.bloomberg.com/view/articles/2016-03-16/the-case-for-hybrid-corporate-pensions

Morris, George. "Charlie's Place a 'Country Club' for Dementia Patients, a Respite for Caregivers." *Baton Rouge Advocate,* October 25, 2017.
http://www.theadvocate.com/baton_rouge/entertainment_life/article_89ace36e-ad13-11e7-b878-7fca644348cf.html

"Nurses with a Mission: Send Older ER Patients Home with Help." *New York Times,* February 2, 2018.

Stevenson, Sarah. "Dangers of Seniors Living Alone." *Senior Living Blog,* May 4, 2017.
https://www.aplaceformom.com/blog/2013-4-1-dangers-ofseniors-living-alone/.

"Ten Early Signs and Symptoms of Alzheimer's." alz.org.
https://www.alz.org/alzheimers_disease_10_signs_of_alzheimers.asp

Also by Cheri McDaniel

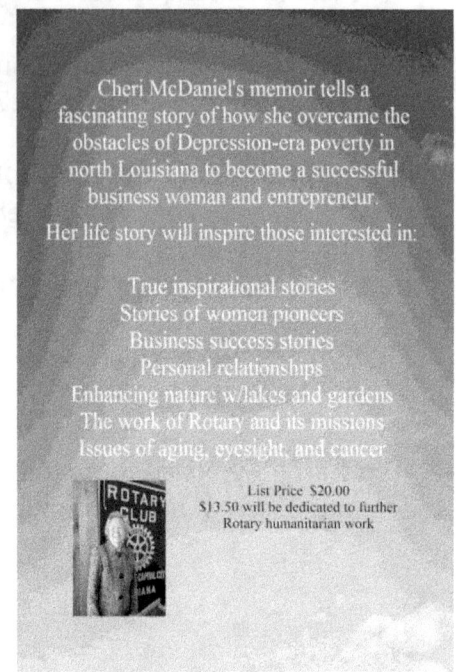

Available through helaysthestones.com

www.ingramcontent.com/pod-product-compliance
Lightning Source LLC
Chambersburg PA
CBHW071554080526
44588CB00010B/910